YOUR FILM ACTING CAREER

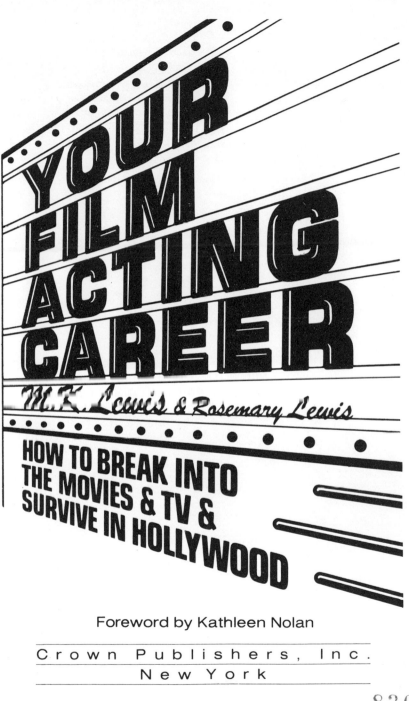

YOUR FILM ACTING CAREER

M. K. Lewis & Rosemary Lewis

HOW TO BREAK INTO THE MOVIES & TV & SURVIVE IN HOLLYWOOD

Foreword by Kathleen Nolan

Crown Publishers, Inc.
New York

Published by Crown Publishers, Inc.,
One Park Avenue, New York, New York 10016 and simultaneously in Canada by General Publishing Company Limited

Manufactured in the United States of America

Library of Congress Cataloging in Publication Data

Lewis, M. K.
Your film acting career.

Includes index.
1. Moving-picture acting—Vocational guidance.
2. Acting for television—Vocational guidance.
I. Lewis, Rosemary.   II. Title.

PN1995.9.P75L48 1983   791.43′028′02373   82-18187

ISBN: 0-517-549115 cloth
0-517-549123 paper

10   9   8   7   6   5   4   3   2   1

First Edition

To Marguerite and Jozef
for the talent and background,
and
To Mama Ru and Papa Ru
for their loving support.

CONTENTS

Foreword by Kathleen Nolan   ix
Preface   xi
Acknowledgments   xiii
Authors' Note   xv

I PREPARING TO GO AND GOING   1

1. Making the Decision   3
2. Preparing to Go   12
3. Arrival in L.A.   16

II A BASIC BUDGET AND SUPPLIES   35

4. A Basic Budget   37
5. Résumé Shots   39
6. Resumes   54
7. The Unions   61
8. Other Items on the Budget   70
9. Attitudes: Need—The Career Killer   79

III THEATRICAL AGENTS   87

10. What They Are and Do   89
11. Seeking a Theatrical Agent   92
12. Choosing a Theatrical Agent   99
13. Dealing With/Motivating an Agent   105
14. Changing Agents   110

IV SEEKING WORK   115

15. The Buyers of Talent   117
16. The General Interview/Look-See   123
17. The (Almost) Cold Reading   134
18. Office Scenes   144

V WORKING   147

19. Making a Deal   149
20. On the Set   152

VI COMMERCIALS   163

21. Commercials: The Wonderful World
of Happy   165
22. Commercial Agents   168
23. Composites   172
24. From Audition to Payoff   176

VII OTHER KINDS OF WORK   187

25. Stocking Stuffers   189
26. Theatre   199
27. Acting Classes   208

VIII MERRILY YOU ROLL ALONG   213

28. Publicizing Yourself   215
29. Your Management Team   220
30. General Financial   225
31. Miscellaneous   229
32. Assessing Your Career   234
33. Conclusion   238

IX APPENDIX A   241

Getting What's Coming to You (and Keeping It)

1. Agency Contracts   243
2. Films and TV   248
3. Commercials   261
4. "Typical" Tax Deductions of the Professional
Actor   267
5. Pension and Welfare   270

X APPENDIX B   272

Lists   272
Index   297

FOREWORD

For me, the choice to become an actress was clear almost at birth. I never longed to be a doctor, fire fighter, scientist, or politician. I like being an actress. Acting is a joyous adventure.

Over the years I have eagerly read or reviewed countless books on the technique of acting, most being exclusively geared to the stage actor. Some of them have been excellent, for example, Uta Hagen's *Respect for Acting*, Stanislavski's *An Actor Prepares*, etc. Sanford Meisner, to me without question tne master teacher, has a book ready for publication this year.

Any serious actor should have more than a passing knowledge of the technique and craft expressed by these formidable artists/teachers. In my opinion, one should also possess a sound background in theatre and film history from the earliest times to the present. The Greek theatre, German playwrights, Scandinavian filmmakers should be studied, and certainly much emphasis should be placed on our cousins in the English-speaking world. However, an actor's research should not ignore American theatre, film, and television. We tend to belittle our own cultural contributions, when, in fact, they have been enormous—in all fields.

It is most useful to be familiar with the approach other actors take to their work. The recently published *Actors on Acting* is excellent.

We have also experienced a proliferation of "star turn" books in recent years, written with or without the actor's permission. If one cares to wade through the sex lives, illnesses, traumas, and disappointments over which these actors have triumphed, one might receive some small measure of information about how it all came together for them—but I seriously doubt it. *Being a voyeur does not prepare one for a career.*

I have had the privilege of addressing university students in recent years and have been astonished by their lack of information about the artist's role in the United States—no practical application to add to Strindberg and Brecht. The mere mention of unions, agents, or how to survive outside the ivory towers seems to be considered pedestrian and out of place. In most universities, the film department is separated from the theatre department. Television, cable, and satellite television are only touched upon in the communications departments. A curious exercise in "territorial rights" seems to block the student from the interchange that is essential for making decisions that affect life choices in the arts.

We come to New York or Hollywood ill-prepared to survive the shock of the commercial world.

M. K. and Rosemary Lewis's book deals exclusively with the film capital—Hollywood. It was not written by renowned stars or academicians. It was written by two people who have worked the system and, in an intelligent and entertaining fashion, have chronicled that experience. As a professional actress and longtime advocate of the actor's role in American society, I welcome their contribution.

Wherever and however our creative lives begin, we must have a foundation of preparation—total preparation. To "wing it" is more an expression of how we got by than how we prevailed.

Is the "joyous adventure" for you? The chapters that follow are a map with clues. Only you have the answers within you.

If you decide the answer is yes . . . relish the journey.

Welcome!

KATHLEEN NOLAN

KATHLEEN NOLAN has appeared in every form of entertainment—showboats, tent shows, repertory companies, Broadway, film, and television. She came to national prominence as Kate on the long-running TV series "The Real McCoys." After sixteen years' service on the board of directors of the Screen Actors Guild, she was elected president of SAG in 1975 and served two terms—the only woman president in its fifty-year history. Currently, she is a presidential appointee to the Corporation for Public Broadcasting and a panelist for the National Endowment for the Arts.

PREFACE

It's enough to make you want to stand in the middle of the patio of Mann's Chinese Theatre, shouting . . .

"How do you crack this town?!?"

Each year, hundreds of actors point themselves in the general direction of Hollywood and Vine—they've decided to become pros. Thousands more all over the country are thinking about it. Their relative shapes, sizes, talents, educations, and egos are as varied as their chances, but almost all have one thing in common: they have no idea how to start (or establish) a career.

Maybe you're among them.

Even if you've been to college, you're probably as lost as the sixteen-year-old starlet with stars in her eyes. You can graduate with a Ph.D. in Drama (having written a dissertation on the costumes Minnie Maddern Fiske wore in *Our American Cousin*) and still not know what a *Daily Variety* looks like or be able to recognize an agent if he fell on you.

"The universities are pumping out well-trained repertory theatre actors that the world never needed in the first place," says John O. Mahoney, a drama critic for the *Los Angeles Times*.

Unfortunately, this lack of knowledge can often lead to your paying phony "agents" to take you on; sending out résumé shots that look like something out of a high-school yearbook; attending so-called "acting classes" that do you no practical good, and sometimes great psychological harm. And on and on.

Ultimately, your pocket—not to mention your mind—can be picked to the point that you either jump on a bus or off a building, shouting all the way down . . .

"How do you crack this town?!?"

Even if you're an "old pro," experienced New Yorker who has migrated to L.A., it's possible to be totally frustrated. Suddenly, when you weren't looking, *somebody changed the rules.* All bets are off. What you've been doing for years to get ahead not only doesn't work anymore, sometimes it's literally hurting you. And as you walk away from that stern-faced guard at the Burbank Studios, that *creep* who wouldn't even let you onto the lot to drop off a picture, for crying out loud, you might just be tempted to cry out loud . . .

"How do you crack this town?!?"

In an effort to help, about six years ago we began to teach a course called The Hollywood Actor's Survival Seminar. It was originally taught at Sherwood Oaks College (for four years), with a more or less annual sojourn to New Orleans under the sponsorship of that city's Artists Information Bureau. Currently, we're teaching

xi

it at our studio (in association with Pamela Campus's Casting and Workshop) at Television Center Studios.

Over those years, besides drawing on our own experiences, we've engaged in hundreds of hours of interviews with producers, directors, agents, casting directors, personal managers, publicists, and the like—even a cinematographer or two—so that our students could have the opportunity to hear the opinions of the most important people of all—those in a position to do the hiring.

At the end of every session, some student would almost inevitably say, "You know, you ought to write a book."

Well, here it is. We can't promise it'll help you "crack this town"—but we do believe it can at least help you make it bend a little.

ACKNOWLEDGMENTS

Hollywood is a selfish city?
This book could not have been written without the generosity of more than 150 members of the Hollywood community. Many graciously took the time to speak at one of our seminars (a few more than once); to grant us interviews at their offices or over the phone; to appear as guest speakers at other seminars or classes we attended. And they all had one thing in common . . .
. . . They all donated their time.

Grateful thanks to: Maxine Arnold, Simon Ayer, Kevin Baar, Vikki Bandlow, Fran Bascom, Angela Bath, Miriam Baum, Mel Becker, Jim Bennett, Barbara Best, Noel Black, Merritt Blake, Buddy Bregman, Michael Campus, Pamela Campus, Reuben Cannon, Bonnie Carstensen, Don Ciminelli, Jerry Cohn, Diana Daves, Sally Dennison, Debbie Devine, Karen DiCenzo, Angie Dickinson, Bernie Distler, Michael Dixon, Bill Eaton, John Edwards, Jane Feinberg, Mike Fenton, John Fisher, Larry Fonceca, Jerry Franks, Bud Friedman, Melinda Gartzman, J. Carter Gibson, Edmund Gilburt, Susan Glickman, Susan Goldstein, Lois Graner, Jim Green, Marci Helzig, Nancy Hereford, Norman Herrman, Bob Hester, Sharon Himes, Bobby Hoffman, Judith Holstra, Tawn Holstra, Richard Irving, Myrna Isenberg, Tracey Jacobs, Cathryn Jaymes, Marsha Jeffer, Kathy Juden, William Kayden, Johanna Kelly, Gary Klopus, Eileen Knight, Harvey Laidman, Elna Lawrence, Terry Lichtman, Marci Liroff, Bob Lloyd, Morgan Lofting, Pegge Logefeil, Judy Lowry, Philip Mandelker, A. Morgan Maree, Sandy Martin, Renee McGill, Mickie McGowan, John Mekrut, Arlin Miller, Don Nagle, Gary Nelson, Patti O'Brien, Fran O'Bryan, Cliff O'Connell, Al Onorato, Penny Perry, Don Pitts, John Randolph, Barbara Remsen, Michael Rhodes, Jack Rose, Doris Ross, Brady Rubin, Ira Rubin, Doris Sabbagh, John Sanchez, Sylvia Schneble, Mort Schwartz, Ralph Senensky, Jerry Shea, Barry Shear, Walter Shenson, Bill Shephard, Tony Shepherd, Marilyn Sherman, Sandra Siegal, Deborah Sills, Kathy Smith, Mary Spencer, Lea Stalmaster, Ron Stephenson, Danny Stewart, Viola Kates Stimpson, Mac St. Johns, Susan Sukman, Arne Sultan, Dale Tarter, Judy Taylor, Bob Towers, Howard Trustman, Doug Turner, Renee Valenti, Colee Viedelle, E. Duke Vincent, Howard Wexler, Bob Wollin.
Thanks also to: Joseph Garber, George Ives and David Westberg of Actors Equity Association; Frank Messineo and Rose Morris of the American Federation of Television and Radio Artists; Dennis Moss, California Executive Director of the American Guild of Musical Artists; Georg Duuglas, Special Assistant to the President of the American Guild of Variety Artists; Sean Bainbridge, Susan Conners,

Kim Fellner, Roxanne Fitzgerald and Lucy Pegues of the Screen Actors Guild; Roy Wallack, President, Screen Extras Guild; Bill Edwards of *Daily Variety*; Ruth Robinson of the *Hollywood Reporter*; Sylvie Drake, John C. Mahoney of the *Los Angeles Times*; Harry Orzello, and Executive Director David Ralphe, of the Los Angeles Theatre Alliance; Arthur Bartow of Theatre Communications Group.

With a special tip of the hat to: Ellie Abrahamson, Kat Krone, and Mark Locher of the Screen Actors Guild; Mel Blank and David Perren of the firm of Barkin, Blank, Perren and Elam.

Thanks too to Larry Gordon and Walter Hill for taking a shot on a newcomer; Becki Davis, for starting it all; the New Orleans Public Library and the New Orleans Department of Recreation, for helping it to continue; Gary Shusett of Sherwood Oaks College, for making room on the schedule; and workshop colleague Pamela Campus, not only for the many hours of interviews but also for not yelling when the camera was left on all night.

And, finally, thanks to Jack Rose, Jack Teeter, Linda Kendrick, and Chris Redgate, for their enthusiasm; to Brandt Aymar for his kind assistance; to Cindy Randall and Diana Carpenter for lifesaving efforts; to James Hamilton for sticking his neck out a little; and to Joe for the inspiration of July 1, 1978.

AUTHORS' NOTE

Throughout the book, we've chosen to use the "universal 'he' "; we find the use of "she" or "s/he" calls too much attention to the writing. (Would somebody please come up with a solution to this problem? "Heshe"? "Sherm"? "Shey"? "Zortplatt"?)

For the record, we'd like to make it clear that many casting directors and agents are women, and their numbers are increasing in related fields such as writing and producing.

We've also opted to include prices. For every year beyond 1983, add a 10 percent "inflation factor" and you'll be in the ball park.

Finally, the titles and job descriptions of the people we've quoted throughout are as of when we interviewed them and subject, if not to a 10 percent inflation factor, at least to change.

I
PREPARING TO GO AND GOING

1   Making the Decision
2   Preparing to Go
3   Arrival in L.A.

1 MAKING THE DECISION

*Before I take on a client, I look for three
things: talent, guts, and imagination.*

Barbara Best, Publicist

Welcome to the job-getting business . . .

. . . That's the *real* business there's no business like.

And if you're in the midst of packing, certain that Hollywood had better
batten down its hatches just because you're the best damn actor this side of
John Barrymore, we'd like to shake your hand, pat you on the back—and
tell you to stop right there.

There's a fundamental flaw in your thinking. You're confusing being a
good actor with being a *working* actor.

Working actors know they're good, but they also have come to grips with
one very essential fact: if you're thinking of becoming a professional actor,
above all understand that you're really thinking of becoming *a door-to-door
salesman—of yourself.*

An actor's true vocation is selling and job getting: his avocation is acting.
Most would-be actors either fail to understand this or they've never been
told it. They spend all their time honing their craft and little or no time on
the business of acting. They sit by unrelentingly silent phones, idealistically
waiting for someone to "pick up on" their talent. Occasionally this happens,
but more often than not they begin to feel like Edgar Allan Poe's famous
"Purloined Letter"—there they are, sitting out for all to see, and nobody
knows they're there.

Eventually they quit, believing they were failures as actors. They weren't.
They were just poor job getters.

So, if you're thinking about becoming a professional actor, put aside
your talent for the moment and examine your basic personality. Can you
sell? And—equally important—can you live with the idea of being a salesman? Do you have the emotional makeup of a go-getter?

If you can't answer yes to that, we'd honestly recommend you remain a
nonpro. You'll probably be a happier man or woman if you don't act for
money.

Now don't misunderstand: we're not saying that being an actor is one
long toothache. There are many rewards to the profession, not the least of

3

which is simply being a member of a very exciting, highly creative community.

But that community, to say the least, is overcrowded. There are 55,000 members of the Screen Actors Guild (SAG) as this book goes to press, 70 to 80 percent of whom earn less than $2,500 a year. That doesn't include the other acting and related unions, and it doesn't include you (probably) and the thousands of others who are trying to get into them.

And even being the greatest talent *and* the greatest job getter won't guarantee success. Consider the following rather depressing little story:

Years ago, we attended a seminar for beginning actors. The guest speaker looked over the sea of eager faces, sighed, and said, "Of all the people in this room, I would say that seventy-five percent will have quit by next year; twenty percent more will have given up by the following year; and in five years, two—maybe three—of all of you will still be pursuing a career in acting."

Regardless of whether or not he was right, the point is that this is a business for people with very special personalities—survivors.

It's like being in a lifeboat with 55,000 other people—a boat that can accommodate only 100 (that's about how many roles are available in any given week in Los Angeles). Somehow, you're going to have to figure out a way to stay in the boat. You're going to have to think of ways to make money to keep yourself afloat and ways to pull yourself out of the crowd so that people will sit up and take notice of you.

That means this is no business for the meek. And it's not a business you should get into if your pride can't stand more than the average quota of bruising. After all, in terms of type, there always will be at least twenty-five other people who can easily do the same roles you can do. God gave you the right to think of yourself as special—you are. Now you've got to convince everybody else.

You're going to have to be smarter, quicker, and far more of a hustler than your fellow actor. (That doesn't mean you'll need to sleep with anybody; let's get that out of the way right now. You're out to make friends—not lovers.) And part of making friends will involve not only being able to act but being able to talk a good game too. In show business, the people who talk the best, work the most.

In short, either you are going to have to develop a darn good business sense and a strong sense of "street smarts" or you are going to have to understand that in five years or so you may wind up part of that angry, frustrated crowd that continually streams toward the exit doors.

Here are some other questions you should ask yourself before you finish your packing.

CAN YOU HANDLE STRESS?

Since nobody pays you for your chief occupation—seeking work—the financial stress of being an actor should be obvious. Don't get us wrong— there's no need to starve—that's a lot of artsy-craftsy baloney that could even be harmful to your career (see "Attitudes," Chapter 9). But you will have to give up certain things—the hog just ain't that high.

Besides not being an awful lot of fun to live with, financial stress can also hurt. Picture your reaction when, ten years after going to Los Angeles, you return home to see a classmate who became an accountant, living in a beautiful four-bedroom house—and you've still got a non-air-conditioned flat in Van Nuys. So if it's money you're after, go into banking.

Far more than financial stress, however, is the *emotional* stress of being an actor. . . .

First, there's the stress of constantly having to make decisions. Everything from the little decisions like what résumé shot to use, or whether to call that producer today, or wait until next week, to the big decisions such as whether or not to fire that agent who has become a friend but who doesn't seem to be getting the job done anymore; whether or not to get married, to get pregnant, and so on. And these decisions don't get easier as you go through your career—they get harder. For example, a beginner doesn't have to decide whether or not to take "three lines and a spit" on a major TV show. A working pro does.

So if you can't handle the stress of making decisions all the time, become a professional bureaucrat, not a professional actor.

Then there is the stress of often being treated like a beggar. A bum. A social pariah. Secretaries will hang up on you. Your own relatives, when you're not doing well, will constantly be on your back to quit and, when you're doing well, will talk about "the obscene amounts of money you're making." Even your fellow actors will look down their noses at you if they're working (currently) and you're not. We've seen established stars—who should know better—treat bit players as if the criterion for being a human being is having more than ten lines to say in a movie.

And sooner or later, someone who is very close to you, someone you really care about, will walk up to you and say, "Why don't you stop fooling around and get yourself a *real* job?"

If you don't have the personality to shrug off all this and much, much more, then this profession will drive you crazy, drive you into deep depression, or drive you out. And never forget, *the stress never ends.*

During interviews with industry people, one question we almost always posed was, "If you had to give an actor a single piece of advice, what would it be?" Said one casting director: "Get a good shrink."

ARE YOU MORE IDEALISTIC THAN PRACTICAL?

There is nothing "idealistic" about doing a deodorant commercial, but it sure beats heck out of waiting tables. In other words, the more idealistic you are, the tougher you'll find this profession to be. No, you don't have to be cynical, and you don't have to join the sharks who are already in the water.

You will, however, have to develop a healthy practical streak. For example, don't always expect to be performing Shakespeare. To paraphrase the old saying, you're going to have to kiss a lot of frog roles before the prince part comes along.

And once again, there's that ugly word: BUSINESS. Idealism has nothing to do with writing a good "covering letter," choosing an agent, reading and understanding a contract, filing your income taxes, battling it out with a producer for an extra fifty bucks a day in order to get your quoted salary up, or sweating out a demand for better billing.

CAN YOU STAND HAVING YOUR LIFE CONSTANTLY UPROOTED?

One day you'll be broke; the next, possibly, a millionaire. One day you'll be sitting in your apartment, brooding and ignoring your spouse; the next, you're in Oswego wishing he were there. Your agent never calls, and you decide to quit; inevitably, the phone rings with an offer for a week's work in New York. You're given a two-page monologue to learn in five minutes on the set; you do and you're brilliant; and then the film comes out and the monologue has been cut down to one line. . . .

There's one phrase you'd better drop from your vocabulary if you want to be an actor: "slow and steady."

ARE YOU THINKING ABOUT "BIG BUCKS"? HOW ABOUT GLAMOUR?

Boy, are you in for a surprise.

There's nothing glamorous about looking for an agent; getting up at 5:30 A.M. to stand in a cold, driving rain for twelve hours, alone (because the "stars" won't talk to you), waiting to say your one line; or parking cars in order to pay the rent. If you're thinking about the glamorous lives all those stars live, you're forgetting one thing—they weren't born stars. Every person in this industry has had to go through periods of being treated as if he were a piece of meat. If all you've got is a desire for glamour, we promise you it won't be enough to sustain you through the rough years (at least five— maybe a lifetime).

As to "big bucks," we might point out that, recently, a major star appeared on a talk show and frankly stated she couldn't afford not to work. The audible groans of disbelief ran through the studio audience. But she was probably telling the truth.

We won't deny that a person can make a lot of money as an actor—*if he or she is very, very lucky*. But the big fallacy is that the instant a person apears on a television show or in a movie, he is "wallowing in the dough."

Well, current SAG scale is $298 a day, $1,038 a week. If that sounds like a lot of money to you, you might bear in mind that you may work *one day* out of an *entire year*. And if you do become a "star," you'll probably then have to pay:

- 10 percent to your agent
- About 15 percent (and possibly up to 50 percent) to your personal manager
- 5 percent to your publicist
- 5 percent to your business manager
- And if you're lucky, only 20 percent to the good ole IRS.

That's at least 50 percent of your gross income. And that income is not guaranteed. You may do well one year and not work for the next three. All those people will have gotten their money already, and your house payment will still be due.

Does the star's statement sound a little more plausible now?

ARE THE PEOPLE YOU'RE EMOTIONALLY INVOLVED WITH ALSO ABLE TO HANDLE THIS PROFESSION?

We're not talking about Mom and Dad; unfortunately, they'll probably never understand. But, simply stated, those others who live with and see you every day are going to have to be *very* understanding. After all, you're asking them to go through it with you. If they're not as tough as they need to be—if they're not a positive psychological influence—sooner or later you're going to have a very serious problem on your hands.

"If I didn't have a super wife, I don't know where I'd be right now because she carried me," says one actor about his starting time in the industry. "Talk about guilt complexes. There I was in a one-bedroom apartment in North Hollywood with no air conditioning and a nine-month-old baby, while my wife is in Beverly Hills working. And I *know* she'd *much* rather be with the baby." Any actors who've been in this profession are nodding their heads in recognition.

ARE YOU GOOD AT GETTING WORK IN THE TOWN IN WHICH YOU LIVE? DO YOU KNOW THE PRODUCTION HOUSES, AGENTS, ETC., IN YOUR TOWN?

If you can't answer yes, better get going. Finding and dealing with the people who can hire you to act is a lot easier in a small city than in New York or L.A. There's less competition (albeit less work), and if you can't at least get an appointment with someone who sees, say, ten actors a week, how are you going to get to talk to someone who is deluged with one hundred actors a day?

ARE YOU A MAN?

Seventy-five percent of all roles go to men. Shocking, but true.

ARE YOU YOUNG? ESPECIALLY, ARE YOU A YOUNG WOMAN?

Nobody expects an eighteen-year-old to have a résumé as long as his arm. But if you're over thirty and still don't have professional credits, better think it over. This is especially true if you're female. The "older" women (by Hollywood standards, any woman over thirty) you'll be competing with for an *extremely* small number of roles will already be well established; while the larger, juicier parts, will almost always go to "name" actresses, not to other unknowns. Quote from an over-thirty actress: "Since there are so few roles, I can't look at acting as a profession anymore. I have to think of it as a hobby."

ARE YOU NON-ETHNIC-LOOKING?

Remember that this is a book about surviving as an actor in *Hollywood*. If you're "ethnic looking" (including, but not limited to black, Latin, Italian, etc.), you may do better in New York. If you disagree with that, watch television and then go to a Broadway show or at least watch the Tony Awards. Notice anything?

Also note that *60 percent of all the money earned by actors comes directly from commercials.* In commercials, there is an expression: "White Bread." This means a blandly good-looking person who represents the stereotypical midwestern American. That's what most commercial makers are looking for (see "Commercials," Chapter 21) because, simply stated, the advertiser wants people to remember his *product* not the actor. Thus, the more "special" you are, the more limited your opportunities to get a decent piece of that 60 percent pie.

DO YOU HAVE A CAPACITY FOR CONFIDENCE? DO YOU LOOK CONFIDENT EVEN WHEN YOU'RE QUAKING IN YOUR BOOTS?

The actor who doesn't work is scared and shows it. The actor who works is scared but doesn't show it.

DO YOU HAVE AN EASYGOING, BREEZY PERSONALITY, OR ARE YOU CONSTANTLY UPTIGHT, SCARED, UNHAPPY, NON-SELF-RELIANT?

Most of the time what you'll be selling won't be your talent—it'll be your personality. It doesn't matter if that's not fair; that's show biz.

Also remember the remarks about stress. If you can't handle stress, there are two professions you shouldn't get into: tightrope walking and acting.

ARE YOU THOUGHT OF AS "LUCKY"? DO YOU REFUSE TO QUIT, EVEN WHEN YOUR OPPONENT HAS HOTELS ON BOARDWALK AND ALL THE RAILROADS?

"I know you're talented, but are you lucky?" says theatrical agent Jim Gibson. Yes, there *is* such a thing as pure dumb luck. But, more often, there is *smart* luck—luck created by work, guts, and (forgive the cliché) a refusal to quit. "Don't go around saying 'I never have any luck,'" says theatrical agent Mary Spencer, "because luck is when *preparation* and *opportunity* meet."

And, finally, as to your talent . . .

WHEN YOU DO COMMUNITY THEATRE, DO YOU FEEL YOU'RE NOT ONLY BETTER THAN YOUR FELLOW ACTORS, BUT YOU KNOW MORE?

Remember that you'll be competing with people who have film and Broadway credits, who've been around awhile. At least learn the basics—

and the best way to do that is to do play after play. True, you could go to L.A. specifically to study acting, but even so, the more training you get before you arrive the better.

WHEN YOU TRY OUT FOR LOCAL THEATRE, ARE YOU ALMOST ALWAYS CAST? WHEN YOU'RE REVIEWED, DO THE CRITICS ALMOST ALWAYS RAVE?

It's one thing for *you* to think you're good. . . .

That's basically it. If you can answer these questions to your satisfaction, and you want to go ahead, we'd say, what the heck, give it a shot and stick with it until your gut says "no more, please!" There's nothing worse than sitting over a cup of coffee at age sixty-five wishing you had tried.

Maximilian Schell, speaking at a seminar, was asked if he had any regrets. His answer: "I've never regretted anything I've done. It's always the things that I haven't done that I regret the most." Does that sound as if we're encouraging you to be an actor? We hope not. John C. Mahoney, drama critic for the *Los Angeles Times,* said it best when we asked, "What advice would you give to actors?" He replied:

"Get out of the business. It's the only honest loving thing you can say to an actor because ten percent of your profession will ever work or make a living. If you're interested in the stage, one to three percent of the population gives the slightest damn what it is you do. It's an alien activity. . . .

"The effort you put in is largely wasted, except in whatever it gives you. Half the effort would pay off in used-car sales, marketing, public relations. . . . If you start thinking, 'Wow, is it worth it?' you've already answered your own question. Of course it's not worth it! . . . If you stick with it, it's because it satisfies you, with none of the customary rewards, because you feel you have something to give.

"It is proper that everyone think you are crazy. There's no reason why you should demand that anyone ever understand your commitment or your dedication. And your mother and everyone else is right—you wouldn't have to work that hard, and you could be rich, if you were in any other business. . . .

"I'm very fond of actors, but they are *real* stupid to do what they do. There is no good reason to do it unless you approach it like a monk. . . . You may always be happy doing it, but you should only have a good job besides. . . . The cruelest thing in the world is to encourage an actor. If you can, *in any way,* discourage an actor, you should."

We'd also like to say that we fully recognize that you could take everything in this book, throw it out—in fact, do *everything* all wrong—and *still* wind up signing autographs on Oscar night. "The one thing I've found, the longer I'm in the business," says actor John Edwards, "is that there's no general way it happens. Everybody comes through different doors. Which means you have to keep at it in this business, because eventually something weird will happen your way."

This book can give you the business knowledge you need, and a few tricks of the trade to help that "something weird" to come your way perhaps a little faster. But we can't change your basic personality. We can't make you into the sort of person who can turn this knowledge to his or her advantage. That's your job. In other words, *we'll* supply the knowledge; *you* supply the talent, guts, and imagination.

2 PREPARING TO GO

Be sure you can afford to be an actor.

Vikki Bandlow, Theatrical Agent

First of all, try to make your plans at least a year in advance. Many of the things we'll talk about in this chapter will require that amount of time, and it's just better for you from a psychological point of view.

We assume, too, that you've gotten as much training and experience as possible before setting your "year from now" date. "You'd better be well on your way before you come to Hollywood," says Georg Duuglas, special assistant to the president of AGVA.

GET A CAR

And the more fuel-efficient, the better. You can't pursue an acting career in Los Angeles without one—the distances are simply too great. If you can't/don't drive or can't afford a car, you'd do better in New York.

SAVE MONEY

To do it right, you'll need about $2,000 for business expenses, $3,000 for personal expenses. These figures are based on the first group of items listed in the budget in Chapter 4, and your personal expenses for the first three months (see "Arrival in L.A.," Chapter 3).

Give up the luxuries, and save, save, save. Besides, learning to do without will be terrific training.

GET INTO THE "RIGHT" UNION

Each year thousands of aspiring actors go to Los Angeles or New York. Most of them don't even know what the unions are. They soon find out.

Hollywood agents tell them, "Sorry, I can't help you if you're not SAG." In New York, some burly dude blocks the entrance to an audition, saying, "Sorry, Equity people only."

Finally, they come to the realization that SAG is not a physical condition and Equity isn't life insurance—they're *unions*. And actors who aren't members of these unions will starve to death. So they go out and seek ways to join these unions, only to hear, "You can't join until you've got a job," and conversely, "I can't hire you unless you're union." Eventually, this gets old—

so old that many would-be actors simply quit. And that's a shame. Because, as you'll see, with a little information and ingenuity there are ways to get into them. Yes, all in all, it's probably best, if you can, to join the unions before you leave. But don't despair if you don't. For various reasons you may find it *easier* to get into the unions in L.A. than your native, say, Cleveland.

Whatever, before you join any union, and certainly before you buy that plane ticket, we'd advise reading our chapter on the unions (Chapter 7); it could completely alter your plans for an entire year—or more.

GET FIT

If, by losing a little weight, you would be a beautiful leading lady or a handsome leading man, then, by God, lose it. If you don't, you'll constantly hear that you're "hard to place" (cast) because your face says one thing and your body says another. If you're a character type, your weight may have less bearing on your career, and you can continue to pig out at the dinner table.

If you don't like something else about your appearance, fix it or learn to live with it. You don't want to be going out on interviews feeling bad about yourself—interviews are tough enough without that added little bonus.

You commercial types especially—get your teeth to look at least decent. Broken teeth don't sell toothpaste.

And, finally, get yourself at least one good suit/dress and one good casual outfit. You don't need a wardrobe that would make Gucci go into jealous convulsions—just look clean and neat.

GET RID OF ACCENTS

No, it's not a crime to have an accent—it's just limiting.

If there aren't any dialect coaches where you live (or even if there are), keep a cassette tape recorder by the TV and record the announcers who don't have an accent, then work to sound like them. If you can't manage this by yourself, then run, don't walk, to the nearest dialect coach the minute you arrive in L.A.

GET A JOB SKILL

Don't expect Hollywood to fall into a swoon over your pending arrival. In fact, it's a fairly safe bet that from the time you get your SAG card, it will be at least a year before you get your first paying acting job.

Typing, waiting tables, selling, and the like are all things you can do without the job getting hopelessly in the way of your career. You'll probably find you need to work full-time at first and part-time later, with an occasional foray back into full-time during those really fallow periods.

Awful though the choice is, it is probably better to take a day job at first and do theatre at night than to take a night job and leave yourself "free" for those film and TV auditions. Unfortunately, auditions won't be blowing your way in bunches unless you're lucky enough to get hot fast in commercials. Possible, but don't bet the rent on it.

Getting a job within the industry is a good way to make contacts, but it also makes it tough to establish a proper image as an actor rather than a secretary or go'fer. On balance, we'd opt for keeping paychecks and contacts separate. You'll avoid the unfair, but real, stigma of appearing to be an actor who "can't make a living at it."

ESTABLISH CREDIT

Before you leave—especially before you quit your present full-time job—try to obtain one or two of the major credit cards (American Express, etc.) There are few things more frustrating than trying to establish credit in a new city. Having a major credit card will help tremendously.

You should know that some major banks in California require that one of their depositors recommend you before you open an account. If you don't know anyone in Los Angeles, it wouldn't be a bad idea to go to your current bank and have them transfer some of your money to the California bank of your choice a few weeks before you leave.

TRAVEL LIGHT

. . . Unless you're positive you're going to stay, and until you know exactly where you're going to live. Why add hassles?

WHAT ABOUT PICTURES (RÉSUMÉ SHOTS)?

If you don't live in New York or L.A., local photographers probably won't know exactly what the industry is looking for. Wait until you get where you're going.

SHOULD YOU CHANGE YOUR NAME?

Not if you're thinking of becoming "Rock Granite" or "Jasmine Julip." Those days, thank heaven, are over.

However, no matter what your name ("true" or invented), before you do anything check with the *national* offices of SAG, AFTRA, and Equity to be certain no one else has first dibs on it—*even if it's your real name*. If your name is "Bob Jones," and any of the unions already have a Bob Jones, when you join you'll *have* to alter it (anything from adding a middle initial, to Robert Jones, to a complete change).

Actually, even if your name is "Iznik Prlrdj," that's acceptable in today's Hollywood, albeit still something of a handicap. Only you can decide if you're willing to drive people crazy trying to pronounce it, and it won't be as "commercial" as Bill Smith.

Also, if you're a borderline ethnic type with an ethnic name, a more nondescript monicker could eliminate your "ethnicity" and increase opportunities.

Understand, we're not "recommending" doing anything—that's just too personal a decision. However, whatever you do, do it now—before you have résumés and résumé shots printed up and certainly before you get a few roles under your belt. Changing then will be a big headache for you and your agent.

Once you've done all this, you're ready to go. Take a deep breath (it'll probably be the last pure air you'll get for a long time), kiss your mother good-bye, and point yourself in a generally westerly direction. . . .

3 ARRIVAL IN L.A.

*Actors have to be analysts. For example,
when an actor comes for an audition, he
should be sure to give himself plenty of
'get set' time. Then, when he first enters
the room, he should first make a point to
size up the situation.*

Lea Stalmaster, Vice-President Talent
and Casting, CBS

Even the most seasoned traveler will tell you that moving to another city can be shattering.

Many actors foolishly deny this sense of displacement and confusion—they immediately start to pursue a career. They start running on legs that are at best rubbery—and they make mistakes that may take months, even years, to repair.

Don't do that. The only gun you're under is the one you hold on yourself. You're supposed to be starting a career that is going to last a lifetime.

Take six months or so to get a "lay of the land" and to get yourself settled. Give your life some "get set" time too.

TAKE A MINI-VACATION

California is a beautiful state that should be seen and appreciated at least a little before you start doing all those chores. If you possibly can, see a few of the sights on a short vacation.

L.A.—BASICALLY

"What city, please?" That's the first thing you'll hear when you dial Information. And they're not kidding. Seventy miles wide, Los Angeles is a conglomeration of communities—some with, some without, municipal governments distinct from that of the city of Los Angeles. You can cross the street and literally be in another city—Santa Monica, say, or Beverly Hills. Occasionally this matters—Santa Monica, for example, has its own (cheaper) bus line; Beverly Hills, however, doesn't—but for the most part you're right if you say it all looks like Los Angeles to you.

You'll find it very confusing at first. Later, you'll find these divisions helpful, as the "city" name will immediately pinpoint the location of a friend or job in what is otherwise a huge, sprawling, faceless metropolitan area.

If you're a stroller, then your definition of hell is Los Angeles; if you're a born driver, it's heaven. The city is built around the car, and except in rare spots such as Westwood or the beach areas, you'll find no milling crowds. Unfortunately, you'll find no true Manhattan-style hangouts for actors. The city is fluid, restless. Anything more than ten years old—anything—is either a landmark or a tradition.

The people? As a group, they're friendly, positive, laid back, yet, paradoxically, career-oriented. You're judged not by your family tree but by how well you cut down trees and (especially) by how much money you make doing it.

Appropriately, the architecture is a crazy patchwork quilt of every style importable and imaginable—from English Tudor to Spanish Hacienda to Modern Disneyland—cheek by jowl, connected by a palm tree.

The weather is almost always sunny and mild, except for a few rainy weeks in winter and foggy ones in spring; the ocean is often too cold to swim in. The city's legendary smog has been institutionalized—via the Air Quality Management District (AQMD), which "manages" what is quaintly called the Air Quality Index. The index is at its lowest in spring and at its highest in late summer–early fall. (You want it low. During the worst months you may feel you're coming down with the flu. You're not. The air has merely become unmanageable.)

Food? Anything you want, from fast food to Vietnamese, and the quality, to put it charitably, varies. (Thin counts more anyhow.)

Entertainment? If you want to see it, it's here: everything from female mud wrestling to the Los Angeles Philharmonic. And there's no movie you can name that won't be playing at some theatre in town within the year.

The same goes for just about any item on the face of this earth. If you want to buy it, there's a store somewhere that's eager to sell it to you. And you don't need to go downtown to get it. There is a downtown L.A., but unless you work there, want to see the sights, or have a specific reason to go, you'll almost never find yourself there. In fact, if you were to work and live in the same area of town, you'd almost never have to leave it except to visit friends, do special shopping, or go to a particular restaurant. Each little area really gives itself far more allegiance than it does L.A. in general. A resident of Santa Monica, say, feels only a vague sense of camaraderie with someone who lives in Glendale. During an interview, John C. Mahoney, drama critic for the Los Angeles Times, aptly summed up Los Angeles: "This town is an enormous smorgasbord. You can walk around and create your own city—like a sandwich."

In short, there's really only one thing all Angelinos have in common.

They've had a love affair with it since anyone can remember. It's a status symbol, and according to psychologists, an "extension" of its occupants. They travel in it, eat in it, use it as a baby-sitter, make love in it, and even worship in it—the car.

So in any discussion of what it's like to live in L.A., one has to begin with the topic of . . .

TRANSPORTATION

• *Driving:* One blessing of all this car-itis is that you'll find the city's freeways and streets generally in excellent condition and well marked, often with special lanes for turning left and blue street signs giving block-ahead notice of the next major avenue.

Even so, it's easy to get lost, so pick up street and freeway maps at a gas station, auto club (Automobile Club of Southern California AAA), or bookstore. We like the *Los Angeles County Popular Street Atlas* by Thomas Bros. Maps; and the *Los Angeles Times* publishes a similar, glove-compartment-size version.

You're probably familiar with the famous California right-turn-on-red traffic regulation. For more on the subject, and for information on car registration, pick up free copies of the *California Driver's Handbook* and the *Registration Handbook* at the nearest office of the State of California Department of Motor Vehicles (DMV). California is very tough on the subject of stopping for pedestrians, which makes sense but has produced a breed of supercomplacent pedestrians: while they are supposed to confine themselves to crosswalks and corners, they often don't. Worse, residents have become so used to cars stopping for them, they will step out into the streets without looking. Be on your guard, and if you see someone at the curb, be prepared to hit your brakes.

Since it so rarely rains in L.A., a lot of oil builds up on roads. Combined with water, the mixture can make for very dangerous and slippery streets. Be extra careful when the rain is just a drizzle and the oil doesn't have a chance to run off into the gutters.

Finally, we'll say again that your car is your lifeblood. You'll have to be certain to keep it in good working condition, and since you'll be using it all the time, it will cost you. In fact, everything to do with automobiles costs more in L.A.—from insurance to registration, from gas to maintenance. You have a year from arrival or until your home state registration runs out before you have to shell out any dough, but then it's gangbusters: you must get a Certificate of Compliance (Smog Certification) from an Official Motor Vehicle Pollution Control Device and Inspection Station, which means bringing your car up to snuff if it isn't already, and pay a $23 registration fee; a one-time $10 service fee; a vehicle license fee, based on 2 percent of the market value as determined by the DMV; a use tax computed at 6.5 percent of the purchase price if you've owned your car fewer than ninety days; and a weight fee if you have a pickup or van. Oy!

• *Buses:* If you hit the Big Orange by plane, not car, you don't have to blow your inheritance on cab fare. There are several ways to get to and from Los Angeles International Airport (LAX) by bus. (Dial A-I-R-P-O-R-T for details.)

You can catch a shuttle bus from the airport to Ninety-eighth Street and Vicksburg Avenue, then transfer to a city bus. Or you can take one of several express bus services, such as Airport Services or Flyaway, which will whisk you to various sections of the city for fares ranging from about $3 to $8, one way. (Incidentally, you can buy fifteen days' parking for $1 at the Flyaway terminal in Van Nuys.) There are also several van services, some of which will ferry you door-to-door, others to hotels or other established locations. These cost more than buses but less than cabs, and you must make reservations in advance.

Los Angeles's primary bus system is called the Rapid Transit District (RTD). As of this morning, the fare is 50 cents, transfers are 10 cents. (Full-time students and teens under eighteen can get monthly passes for $4.) You can also mail a self-addressed, stamped envelope to the RTD, and they'll send you schedules of any and all bus lines you request, including a complete route map for your area—free. (Bus schedules are often found on the buses themselves.) Since weather, traffic, etc., will affect schedules, it's best to take the bus *prior* to the last bus that would have gotten you to your destination on time. On many bus lines, you may have to wait twenty minutes to an hour for the next bus.

Above all, remember that riding the bus across this vast city is almost always a time-consuming affair. Don't think you can pursue a career as an actor effectively by riding buses. You need a car.

• *Cabs:*   Unless you're a millionaire, forget it.

TEMPORARY HOUSING

Since L.A. is dotted with motels in all areas, our research, confirmed by people with SAG and Equity, didn't exactly surprise. Unlike the good ole days of Hollywood, apparently there are no places today specifically designed for the housing of actors.

The cheapest lodging we could find was, naturally, the Hollywood YMCA (see "Lists" section in Appendix B for address). They'll rent you a small room for a *maximum of four weeks* at $14.75 per day (two rooms $22 per day). You'll have to be able to prove you're from out of town, and there are no kitchen facilities. Also, showers are "communal." You will, however, be able to use all "Y" facilities. They rent to both men and women.

However, for a few dollars more, you can, if you shop around a little, find a motel room that would provide you with a little more privacy (at least in the shower); perhaps a kitchen, and almost always, a TV set. For example, with a small amount of research, we found a motel in the 7100 block of Sunset Boulevard (Hollywood) that would rent you a room for $120 a week. (The room at the "Y" would be $103.25. For $17 more, you would have total privacy and not have to deal with any additional "rules."

We also checked some rates in some of the *best* areas of town and found a room for $22 per night, $140 per week. The point is, if you check around, you can find something decent without losing an arm or leg and without having to live in a slum.

Above all, don't stay at any of these places longer than you have to. Remember that you can find a darn nice apartment in just about any location in town for what you'll pay for any temporary place after four weeks.

FINDING/RENTING AN APARTMENT

First, the basics. Types of apartments:

1. *Efficiency:* One small room, bath, and kitchen.

2. *Single:* One large room, bath, and kitchen (equivalent to a studio apartment in other parts of the country).

3. *One bedroom:* Two rooms, bath, and kitchen.

The standard rental agreement is first and last month's rent in advance; a refundable security deposit of $100 or more; often, a nonrefundable cleaning fee of $50 or more. You may sign no lease (rent on a month-to-month basis), a six-month lease, or a one-year lease, then either renew the lease or (more likely) rent month to month thereafter. At most places, you'll pay for gas and/or electricity; they'll pay for water. Unless you use air conditioning, your electric bill should average $25 to $35 per month, your gas bill, $10 to $15.

Interestingly, whether an apartment is furnished or unfurnished makes little difference in its rental (if anything, maybe $25–$50 a month). You'll find a greater selection if you stick to unfurnished, however, and these almost always include stove and refrigerator.

If you don't mind driving, you can live anywhere you want. However, since most of the studios and casting offices are in the San Fernando Valley (called simply "the Valley") or in the Hollywood area, we recommend the following locations *on the basis of proximity:*

NOTE: The rental figures quoted below are "ball park" *minimums,* going up all the time.

- *Hollywood:* Inexpensive, but many seedy areas. Efficiencies and singles, $275/month; one bedroom, $350.

- *West Hollywood:* Nicer, more expensive, best for centralness of location. Efficiencies and singles, $350; one bedroom, $450.

- *The Valley:* Includes Studio City, North Hollywood, Universal City, Sherman Oaks, Van Nuys, Burbank, Glendale, and others. All these areas can be very hot and smoggy; in summer you'll probably need an air conditioner, which could triple your electric bill if you're not careful. Rents vary wildly, but on the average, efficiencies and singles go for $300 a month, one bedrooms for $375.

If these don't suit you, there are other areas that may be of interest.

- If you don't mind driving and have some money to spend: anything west of West Hollywood (Beverly Hills, Culver City, Westwood, West Los Angeles, Brentwood). As you move west the apartments and neighborhoods get nicer, cooler, and more expensive (in the $400–$750 range, depending on the apartment and the area). Best chances for bargains are Culver City and West Los Angeles.

- If you don't mind driving and want to live at the beach: Santa Monica, Pacific Palisades, Malibu, Venice, Marina del Rey. Rents vary but lean to the higher side ($400 and up). Santa Monica, though, currently has strong rent control.

- If you like the mountains: Hollywood Hills, Montrose, Glendale, La Crescenta, Flintridge, etc. The farther out you get from L.A. proper, the lower the rents will be (figure $300 and up).

Figure out where you'd like to live, then buy a neighborhood newspaper. These can be more helpful than the citywide *Los Angeles Times* or *Herald Examiner.* Find out when these papers first hit the stands and get them immediately; if you wait, most of the good apartments will be gone.

Contact any of the myriad of real estate agencies listed in the telephone directory for that area. Renting from a real estate company rather than an individual owner has its pluses and minuses; if you have the luxury of enough time to ask around about an individual company's tenant treatment, do.

There are many "apartment finders" services. You pay them a flat fee ($40 and up) and they give you a listing of what they have available. Do this only if you're having a hard time finding a place; you often do better on your own.

One of the very best ways to search for an apartment is simply to go into the area of your choice and drive around. Many places hang out signs without advertising in any other way.

When you do find a place, it might be wiser to identify yourself by your other job identity: secretary, office manager, whatever—even writer if all else fails—rather than your true ambition, actor. After all, writers are respectable; they smoke pipes. Actors conduct Black Masses on the bellies of virgins.

Some other tips:

- You should expect a parking place to come with the apartment.

- Look for a washer-dryer on the premises. Most places have them. (The "corner" laundry may be a mile away.)

- One way to avoid air conditioning is to take a ground-floor apartment. Heat rises.

- To get around the expense of rent, you might consider apartment managing. The deals you can cut are varied: anything from reduced rent, to none, to none plus a small salary. Sometimes handyman duties are required, sometimes not. The smaller the complex, of course, the smaller the hassle quotient. Do-it-yourself skills will come in handy. Also, watch for ads seeking house-sitters.

- The time-honored method of avoiding full rent, of course, is getting a roommate. Only you can decide if the advantages (lower rent; someone to talk to) outweigh the possible disadvantages (an unexpected checkout just before the first of the month; someone who won't shut up). Roommate-finding services, listed in your telephone directory, which charge a nonrefundable fee (about $60), might help. On the application, they'll ask things like what rent you want to pay; what area you want to live in; whether you smoke or will live with someone who does; whether you have or will live with pets; your general lifestyle, etc.

If you don't want to add that fee to your expenses, check bulletin boards at the unions and schools—a great source—and scan the newspaper classifieds (or take out an ad yourself).

• Examine the manager/owner (whoever lives on the premises) as carefully as you do your roommate. There are many Dragon Ladies (of both sexes) out there. Too many house rules? Kill the deal. You're not renting a cell in Folsom Prison, and you'll have enough professional pressure to deal with anyway.

• In recent years, Los Angeles has become quite tenants-rights conscious. In many areas—but not all—there is rent control. It is an ongoing battle, however, and the rules are changing all the time. If you have any questions regarding renting or dealing with your landlord, call the Fair Housing Council in your area (in Hollywood/Wilshire, 464-1141; on the Westside, 475-9671; in the Valley, 781-6943). For referrals on discrimination problems, call H-O-U-S-I-N-G.

TEMPORARY EMPLOYMENT

If you need to get a job right away, temporary work might be the solution. Finding these jobs is relatively easy, especially if you can type. Besides the many "no fee" temporary agencies listed in the phone book, you can check the classifieds in the trade papers. While many of the job openings listed are sales jobs, there are a variety of opportunities, many of them film industry—related. Don't forget the bulletin boards of the unions, either; jobs are often advertised there, many of which say that the employer understands the problem with auditions, etc., and will make allowances for it. (The "catch," of course, often involves low pay or undesirable work—but you never know.)

FULL-TIME EMPLOYMENT

Unless you've got independent income, you'll need to find a full-time day job at first. Remember, it will be probably a year before you get that first paying acting job, and a night job will prevent you from doing theatre and taking most of the classes you will want to take. If you can't do theatre, you will have blocked off one of the best ways to get an agent.

Don't take a job that will have you in and out of town a lot, or will demand a lot of overtime. If you're not doing something to help your career, if all you're doing is punching a time clock, why are you in Hollywood?

Stay with that job, once you get it, until the number of acting assignments and auditions you are getting begins to create havoc. For example, the first time you get an acting job, tell your employer your Aunt Bertie died and you've got to go to her funeral. Keep a tally. When Aunt Bertie has died several times over, it's time to think about quitting your full-time job.

Never pass on an audition for film or TV work because you've got to work. That will quickly lose an agent for you.

Always tell your agent where to reach you if you work, but never tell a casting director, director, or producer that you do anything but act full-time. We once heard a casting director say that actors who work at regular jobs "aren't professional." May all the elastic in that person's underwear crumble at the prom. Most actors have to work from time to time, and anyone who looks down on an actor for this is suffering from a terrible (but unfortunately not uncommon) case of the smugs.

FOOD

Naturally, until you get settled, you'll be frequenting restaurants. Unless you stick to the myriad of fast-food places around town (and even if you do), you'll find eating gets to be a fairly expensive little pastime. So get yourself a place with a kitchen as soon as you can. In the meantime, one tip—make your main meal lunch. You can get a good meal at even some of the most expensive places in town for far less than you'd expect. For example, lunch at a moderately priced restaurant might run you in the neighborhood of $3–$6—but that same meal at the dinner hour would set you back $5–$10. Always check the menu for "Luncheon Specials," and be sure to fill up on breads, etc., as lunches tend to be a little more sparse than dinner.

When you're doing your grocery shopping, avoid the smaller grocery stores, as they tend to be more expensive. Comparison-shop the supermarkets; the savings can be substantial.

Unfortunately, there are no real food-and-drink actors' hangouts in the New York sense. Closest to the mark are spots such as Duke's at the Tropicana Motel; Theodore's, also on Santa Monica Boulevard; DuPars near CBS Studio Center; Lucy's El Adobe near Paramount; the Smokehouse near the Burbank Studios; and most other restaurants near the major studios, especially in the Valley. (Unless you've already made a killing in modeling, save Ma Maison for later.) At any rate, if these restaurants don't actively foster camaraderie, at least you'll get an earful of shoptalk.

And just because you're in Hollywood now, go have a drink at the still-legendary Polo Lounge of the Beverly Hills Hotel, where big-money movie deals are cut over Scotch and sodas. Consider the splurge a preview of coming attractions.

FURNITURE/FURNISHINGS

Under "Bargains" in the "Lists" section (Appendix B), you'll find the names of some books that can help here.

We'll just add that you might make a point of visiting the Goodwill store nearest you (or thrift stores near universities). You can pick up some good deals on what-does-it-matter-nobody-notices-anyway items like can openers, bowls, and mattresses that have been repaired and recovered.

There is a newspaper called *The Recycler,* available at most newsstands, which lists just about every item imaginable that people want to sell or swap. You can get some great buys—especially if you can dicker. Same with garage sales and swap meets, often advertised at nearby supermarkets. The hitch is you'll probably have to pay cash in most cases.

Finally, if you don't want to bother furnishing an unfurnished apartment, you can always rent some or all of what you'll need from any furniture-rental store listed in the telephone directory.

GETTING A PHONE

In Los Angeles, Ma Bell has two daughters: Pacific Telephone and General Telephone. The one you deal with will depend on the area in which you live.

With either company, you'll need a deposit (anywhere from $70 to $100, depending on whether you have decent credit; you can avoid this if you've had a phone in your name in your hometown) and an installment fee. Your basic monthly rate will be somewhere between $8 and $15, depending on what little extras you get (additional phones, push-button phones, long cords, etc.)

Cheap, you say. And you're right. Then bam! You get your phone bill: the list of "toll calls" would choke a horse, and your bill is $30 and up. This is because your basic service only extends a certain distance from where you live, and because L.A. is so big, you are always going to be making toll calls *within the city.*

Let a few months go by, and watch what areas most of your toll calls go to. Then call back the phone company and ask about:

- *Optional Residence Telephone Service (ORTS):* For a flat monthly rate, you "rent" anywhere from one to four areas of the city, into which you can make an unlimited number of calls.

  The cost of renting any area will depend on the distance the area is from you. Tell them what area or areas you're interested in. They'll quote you a flat rate for each. If any flat rates are lower than what you've been forking out, you might order this service.

  If you notice that you don't call *particular* areas continually, but do have a lot of toll calls *all around* the city:

- *If you're a General Telephone subscriber:* You can order a different kind of ORTS service in which, for a flat fee of $3.95, you can call anywhere in L.A. within a radius of 40 miles at no additional charge up to one hour's worth of calling. After that, it'll cost you 6 cents per minute.

- *If you're a Pacific Telephone subscriber:* This type of ORTS Service is different still: you pay a flat monthly fee of $4.75. For this, you get a 50 percent discount on all toll calls you make within the map they'll send you (also a 40-mile radius). No time limit. In addition, they'll give you a $3 credit toward your final bill on these calls.

Other services: Both companies offer:

- *"Call Forwarding":* If you are out a lot and would like to get your calls the minute they come in, this service might be for you, provided you almost always know where you're going to be and that place has a phone. When you leave the house, you "program" your home phone with the number at which you can be reached. When someone calls you at home, their call will automatically be transferred to the phone you're near.

- *"Call Waiting":* If you don't want your agent to get a busy signal if he calls while you're on the phone, you can order this service and, in essence, add an "additional line" on the same phone number, enabling you to take two phone calls at the same time.

Both companies offer additional services (not vital to an actor) such as "speed calling" (you dial one number, the phone does the rest). Also, Pacific offers three-way calling, which permits you to have a three-way conversation.

Anyway, whether you order all or one of these services, Pacific will charge you a $9 installation fee; GTE will charge $19 installation. The services themselves range from $2.65 to $8 per month, depending on the service(s) you order and the company you're dealing with.

It's not a good idea to use these services in place of an answering machine or answering service; but they're fine as supplements.

CUT-RATE LONG-DISTANCE CALLS

If you make a lot of long-distance calls, having a service such as MCI, Sprint, etc., can be a real money-saver. The only requirement is a push-button, not a dial, phone. There's no installation of any equipment. Generally, the cost is about $6 per month, and you save from 30 to 50 percent on long-distance calls. You'll find these services listed in the Yellow Pages.

CLOTHING

Want to dress in quality clothes on the cheap without visiting your friendly neighborhood fence? All over L.A., there are a myriad of clothing discount stores that enable you to dress yourself from head to foot without paying an arm or a leg.

You'll find them in the garment district in downtown L.A. (in the neighborhood of South Los Angeles and Ninth streets), all over the Valley, even—gasp—Beverly Hills (the 200 block of South Beverly Drive), and a number of other neighborhoods.

To actors, one of the most interesting has got to be The Re-Take Room in Studio City. This little store sells slightly used clothing from movie and television shows—some of them worn by the stars. With care, you can pick up some incredible bargains, including designer labels, and have everyone wondering how you can afford to dress so well. For addresses, other bargain ideas, see "Bargains" in the "Lists" section (Appendix B).

ESTABLISHING CREDIT

Whether or not you brought those little plastic cards out with you, you should make a point of establishing credit within the city.

Go to the bank of your choice and open both a savings and a checking account. Let's say you have $2,000. Put $1,000 in your checking account and $1,000 in your savings account.

Then go to the loan officer. Tell him that you want to make a $1,000 loan, using your savings account as security on the loan. (This means you are guaranteeing that the loan will be paid back by using your savings account as collateral. If you default on the loan, the bank simply grabs the money in your savings account.)

Don't tell him you're an actor if you can honestly tell him you're anything else. As a group, actors have terrible credit ratings. Also, don't tell him you're taking out the loan to establish credit. On the advice of a bank officer, we recommend you tell him you want to buy something—a car, etc. Seems banks aren't too crazy about lending money "merely" to establish credit. Hey, don't ask us why.

SIZING UP THE SITUATION

Once you've got an apartment, job, and telephone, you're at least basically settled. But this isn't yet the time to start pursuing your career: now, it's time to get that "lay of the land." It's best to do this at a leisurely, get-yourself-together pace; at least, say, three months. Somehow you'll know when it's time to really get started; you'll feel that "itch" return.

Below, a list of places to visit and size up during this period. The addresses are listed in "Lists" section.

- *The unions:* That is, SAG, AFTRA, Equity. Fascinating places. You'll see nothing but fellow actors bustling in and out, and you'll get a feeling that, by God, you're not alone after all. Check out the bulletin board. You'll find all sorts of interesting information, from photographers advertising their rates to apartments for sublet, cars for sale, a free seminar or two. Talk to the receptionists; tell them you're new in town. Who knows what goodies they might be able to tell you about?

- *Los Angeles Theatre Alliance (LATA):* Put this one on your "must" list. The LATA is an association of not-for-profit theatres, with memberships open to actors and theatregoers as well. If you join the organization, you'll get: a discount card for tickets to plays, a newsletter, a magazine subscription, and invitations to LATA-sponsored events. You will get a "Comptix" telephone number, which you can call to find out what theatres are offering freebies because they need preview audiences, etc.

  These services will pay for membership ($25) as a "performing artist" (a membership category open to members of any performing union). As such, you are eligible for a "skull session." They'll sit down with you, go over your background, knowledge, and general attitude toward theatre, and match you up with the best places for you. Considering the numbers of theatres in L.A., Executive Director David Ralphe is dead right when he says, "By doing this we save someone about six months" of research. You can also get information about acting schools and coaches from LATA. Call (213) 167 6690.

- *Larry Edmunds Bookstore and Samuel French Inc:* Plays, texts on acting and film abound. We've yet to see an actor able to walk out of one of these places without buying something. And, sooner or later, you're going to need to know where to go to get a copy of that play you are going to audition for.

- *The American Film Institute:* Basically, this is a school for filmmakers. However, it is also the home of the SAG Conservatory Program, which we'll talk about later. The institute has its own library, with some fascinating books and film scripts. Don't be surprised to see a fellow actor or two, script in hand, working on an audition for a student film. That goes on all the time. More on this later, too.

- *Those live TV shows:* We're talking here about situation comedies, such as "Three's Company," that tape before a live audience. These are excellent research sources for an actor—someday you'll probably be doing one—and what the heck, they're free. Call the stations on which these shows appear, and find out how you can get tickets. You'll probably have to stand in line an hour or two before the show, even with tickets. Once in, avoid watching the taping on the TV sets

Studio Map Key
(Map not drawn to scale.)

1. American Film Institute, 2021 N. Western Ave., Los Angeles 90027, 856-7600
2. ABC Television Network, 2040 Ave. of the Stars, Los Angeles 90067, 557-7777
3. ABC Television Center, 4151 Prospect Ave., Los Angeles 90027, 557-7777 (same as above)
4. The Burbank Studios, 4000 Warner Blvd., Burbank 91522, 954-6000 (includes Warner Bros., same address/phone, and Columbia Pictures/TV, 300 Colgems Sq., Burbank 91505, same phone)
5. CBS Studio Center, 4024 Radford Ave., Studio City 91604, 760-5000
6. CBS Television Network, 7800 Beverly Blvd., Los Angeles 90036, 852-2345
7. NBC Television Network, 3000 W. Alameda Ave., Burbank 91523, 840-4444
8. Golden West (KTLA-TV, Channel 5), 5800 Sunset Blvd., Los Angeles 90028, 460-5999
9. Hollywood General Studios, 1040 N. Las Palmas Ave., Los Angeles 90038, 469-9011
10. Hollywood National Studios, 6605 Eleanor Ave., Los Angeles 90038, 467-6272
11. Laird International Studios, 9336 W. Washington Blvd., Culver City 90230, 836-5537
12. Metromedia Television (KTTV-TV, Channel 11), 5746 Sunset Blvd., Los Angeles 90028, 462-7111
13. MGM Studios, 10202 W. Washington Bl., Culver City 90230, 558-5000
14. Walt Disney Prods., 500 S. Buena Vista St., Burbank 91521, 840-1000
15. Paramount Studios, 5451 Marathon St., Los Angeles 90038, 468-5000
16. Producers Studio/Raleigh Studios, 650 N. Bronson St., Los Angeles 90004, 466-3111
17. Sunset/Gower Studios, 1438 N. Gower St., Los Angeles 90028, 467-1001
18. Television Center Studios, 846 N. Cahuenga Blvd., Los Angeles 90038, 462-5111
19. 20th Century–Fox Film Corp., 10201 W. Pico Blvd., Los Angeles 90035, 277-2211 (Mailing address: P.O. Box 900, Beverly Hills 90213)
20. Universal Studios, 100 Universal City Plaza, Universal City 91608, 985-4321
21. Warner Hollywood Studios, 1041 N. Formosa Ave., Los Angeles 90046, 650-2500

all around you. Try to watch the actors on the set itself and what they are doing live (as opposed to how they look on TV). That alone is a great free class in acting for television.

- *USC, UCLA:* These two major colleges are on opposite sides of town, but both have fine film schools that are worth visiting. UCLA is a beautiful, sprawling campus adjoining an area called Westwood Village—probably the only true walking area in L.A. It's relatively safe, clean, and filled with college types. Along with Hollywood, it also has the biggest conglomeration of first-run movie theatres in town. One thing—avoid the area during the weekend unless you like a madhouse full of wall-to-wall people.

- *The studios:* At least drive past every studio in town (see map). You'll be going there eventually for auditions, and you should know where they are. Unless you can meet someone who can get you a pass, you probably won't be allowed onto the studio grounds (called the lots), but take a manila envelope with you and wave knowingly at the guard. Who knows, maybe he'll be busy, think you're delivering something, and let you pass. If he does, by God, you're on a lot. (The less daring will prefer a studio tour, offered by such studios as Universal, NBC, and CBS.) However you get in, don't go bursting into anyone's office—these people are busy and they all have long memories.

- *Theatres, plays:* Sooner or later you're going to want or need to do a play. The best time to learn about the various theatres is now, before you're under the gun. After your visit to LATA, you'll have plenty of prospects. See play after play. If you're worried about dents in your wallet, find out when previews are held; they're usually a lot cheaper. Ask yourself if you would have been proud to have been in that production (of course, you already know that no single production is necessarily definitive of the general level of work at that theatre). Ask the actor taking box office how easily the theatre attracts reviewers and industry people. Read the program. Check out the general atmosphere of the place—friendly? Professional? No theatre has the right to be snobbish—none.

  If you go to enough theatres, see enough plays at those theatres and read enough reviews, you'll get a fairly good idea of the ones at which you'd eventually like to work.

- *Acting classes:* No, don't take a class yet—but you might look around and see what's being offered. Especially be on the lookout for classes you can audit. And, of course, attend all the free seminars you can.

- *The trades:* While we'll go into these in more detail later, you should at least get to know what they look like now. The trades are those newspapers and magazines that concern themselves solely with the industry. There are four biggies: the *Hollywood Reporter,* the *Daily Variety, Drama-Logue,* and *Entertainment Monthly.* All of them are available at most newsstands and by subscription.

- *Get to know the city:* Really get to know it. Get out and around; learn the major streets and subdivisions. Set a schedule. Sitting home doing nothing is the actor's greatest trap; don't fall into it. . . . Getting out and about every day you can is a good habit to learn now, at the very important beginning.

II
A BASIC BUDGET AND SUPPLIES

4   A Basic Budget
5   Résumé Shots
6   Résumés
7   The Unions
8   Other Items on the Budget
9   Attitudes: Need—The Career Killer

4 A BASIC BUDGET

*I used to always summarize by saying,
"Persevere." But "perseverance" isn't in my
summary anymore. After all, you have to
know what you're persevering at, and
you've got to have the right materials. So, in
summary: Picture, Résumé, Equity Waiver,
Cassette, Agent, Producer, and Casting Director.*

Buddy Bregman, Vice-President, Creative
Affairs, Columbia Pictures Television

While it's refreshing to know where you're going, it's even better to know where to start. Don't laugh; many would-be actors spend months—in extreme cases, years—just trying to figure that out.

On the next page, you'll find a first year's budget. Toss in your personal expenses (housing, clothing, etc.); add it all together, and you'll have a pretty good idea not only of where to start but of what you're going to have to do and earn at least for the next year.

Which brings up an important point that bears repeating. Unless you're fantastically lucky, it'll probably be a year from the date you get your SAG card until you earn your first money as an actor. Don't quit that job and declare that you are "now an actor." Keep (or get) that job; acquire the items you'll need; learn some basics about the business; and save your money.

The next four chapters will go into detail about the items on the budget.

- ## FIRST-YEAR BUDGET AND SET-UP: THE MUSTS

Telephone ($30/month; installation [see "Arrival in L.A."]	$ 385
Résumé headshot session	85
Headshot printing costs (one theatrical, one commercial)	125
Résumés (typing, printing 300)	50
Union initiation* (assumes two unions)	800
Union dues †	100

* This amount assumes you join two unions, using one as your "parent." In actual fact, it can vary from $700–900 (see "The Unions," Chapter 7). Ultimately you'll have to join three—SAG, AFTRA, and AEA ($1,100–1,150, depending on parent).

† See above.

See Note on next page.

Postage (500 @ $20 per hundred)	100
Envelopes (good-looking manila, some regular)	50
Academy Players Directory listing (one year)	45
Answering device	150
TOTAL	**$1,890**

● **FIRST-YEAR BUDGET: OTHER ITEMS**
  (NOT NECESSARILY IN ORDER)

Composite session	$ 150
Composite printing	110
Good stationery	50
Thank-you notes	10
Card file and notebook	10
Blank labels	15
Label sets	35
SAG agency list	0
Geo. Casting/Breakdown Service Guide	32
Producers Guide	5
Studio Blu-Book	25
L.A. Actors/Drama-Logue Guide	5
Trade subscription (one only)	75
Drama-Logue newsstand purchases	50
Entertainment Monthly newsstand purchases	36
Postcards	100
Good typewriter	250
Desk	?
Calendar/datebook	5
Videocassette (including stock, air check, editing)	150
Theatre/classes/workshops/seminars	?
TOTAL	**$1,113 +**
	$1,890 +
	$1,113 +
GRAND TOTAL	**$3,003 +**

NOTE: Many of the above figures are ball-park sums rounded off to the nearest dollar. You can raise or lower them to some extent. Add 10-percent "inflation factor" for *every* year after 1983. The importance of theatres, classes, etc., and how much you spend on them can only be judged by you.

5 RÉSUMÉ SHOTS

*Q: When an actor comes into your office
and he doesn't look like his résumé shot,
what's your reaction?*

A: I get furious.

Interview with Judith Holstra, Casting
Director

We have a friend who is a roofing contractor. One day we got to talking about how he hires roofers, and this is what he said: "Any guy can come into the office and talk a good game about all the wonderful work he's done, but me, *I look at his tools.*"

Your agent (and yourself) has two tools with which to sell you: your résumé and your résumé shots. If either of these is bad, you've tied one hand behind his (your) back.

Casting directors, agents, producers, and directors are deluged with photographs of actors, day in and day out. Some of these are good, some fair. Many are atrocious. Actors submit shots of themselves taken with a Polaroid-type camera; shots of themselves half-naked; shots of themselves standing at a distance waving languidly at the camera . . . and they will be the first to complain that "ya just can't beat da system."

Unfortunately, the process of obtaining good pictures is like assembling a toy train on Christmas Eve—it's a pain in the neck. It's involved, time-consuming, and filled with all sorts of wonderful little aggravations and things to remember.

Take the time. Plow through it, step by step. Others will. Don't settle for pictures that are mediocre. Eventually, you'll have pictures that you are proud to display—ones that will pay you back in satisfaction and, more important, in income.

RÉSUMÉ SHOTS: THE CARDINAL RULE

The days of the "Joan Crawford glamour picture" are long gone. Today, casting directors, etc., are turned off by photos of painted goddesses and costumed gods. Today what they want to see is *you*—not how you'd *like* to look, but how you honestly *do* look, scars, moles, warts, and all.

No matter what else we say—whether we talk about looking "perky" or "smoldering"—always remember that we mean strictly *within the bounds of looking like yourself.*

We can't emphasize this more strongly. Pictures that don't look like you, in today's market, are worthless. Never forget that.

Now, when starting out, you will need:

- At least one good commercial headshot.

- At least one good theatrical headshot.

Before we explain the differences between these two types of pictures, let's glance at . . .

HEADSHOTS IN GENERAL (WHETHER "COMMERCIAL" OR "THEATRICAL")

A headshot (sometimes called an "eight-by-ten") is a single black-and-white close-up of the actor's face and hair. (Color pictures are a waste of money.) It's eight inches wide by ten inches long, and there is nothing on the back of the photo.

A headshot, once again, must show what the actor honestly looks like in ordinary street garb (leave the sequined evening gowns and Roman togas in mothballs). Women should apply their makeup slightly heavier than usual for the camera, but the end result should be a standard daytime look. And bear in mind theatrical casting director Jerry Franks's comment: "Beefcake or cheesecake photos are very offensive."

A headshot shows the actor facing the camera, looking directly at the viewer. No gazing up into the clouds and no profile shots (you can get away with a bit of profile—a three-quarters view—but still should be looking straight out).

A headshot is *not* the same kind of photo a model would use to get work. There is no tricky lighting or "mists" around the face, and the photographer does not airbrush out scars and wrinkles.

A headshot shows virtually no background(s). You are not selling tree trunks.

A headshot, if it's good, captures the special quality of the individual actor. Goldie Hawn bubbles. Robert DeNiro smolders. As theatrical agent John Mekrut put it, "The overriding consideration is that the picture has to communicate to whoever is looking at it: this is somebody you want to meet."

THE COMMERCIAL HEADSHOT

. . . Is submitted to all those involved with the making of commercials (agents, casting directors, production houses, etc.).

Now, if I'm a commercial casting director and you send me a *commercial* headshot, this is what I should see: you, looking straight out of a musical comedy, showing me lots of teeth (I need to know you've got good ones) and gobs of happiness in a "Gosh, it's great to be alive" manner. (No smolder here, please.)

In short, your commercial headshot(s) must always show you looking happy, warm, and perky—*very* happy, *very* warm, and *very* perky. Happy, warm, perky people sell soap. And happy, warm, perky pictures sell people to the people who want happy, warm, perky people to sell soap.

THE THEATRICAL HEADSHOT

. . . Is submitted to all those involved with films, television, and stage productions (agents, casting directors, producers, directors).

Your *theatrical* headshot should sell your special quality as an actor, whether that includes warmth and happiness or not. If you are a brooding Jimmy Dean type or a burly, villainous sort, project that. Don't lard it on to the extent that you scare people into thinking they might be auditioning Jack the Ripper, but enough so that your photo suggests how you might be used. Ask yourself:

- *How am I normally cast?* Do I play a lot of cold, calculating women? A lot of weak little men? Villains? Moody young heroes?

- *What have my friends told me about my acting personality?* Do they talk about my warmth? My wit? My sensuality?

- *Is there a known star I am often compared to?* Comparisons to Burt Reynolds suggest a casual, rugged look; comparisons to Vincent Price suggest a suit and tie. (Understand, we're not talking about imitating anybody. The industry already has a Burt Reynolds; it doesn't, however, have you.)

- *What roles on television/movies/stage/commercials could I have done without having to stretch as an actor?*

The answers to those questions will tell you what qualities you want your theatrical headshot(s) to show, and they'll also tell you what "type" you are. Understand this—Hollywood isn't a rep company, it's a business of types. The days of your playing Granny (if you're twenty) are gone. Sorry.

One other note. You should have at least *two* theatrical headshots: one for dramas and the other for comedies. Your commercial headshot can do double duty for the comedy.

A NOTE ABOUT COMPOSITES

A composite is a group of pictures of the actor, divided up this way: one photograph on the front, and anywhere from three to six—usually four—photos on the back. In Hollywood, composites are almost entirely limited to commercials.

In any case, save your money. A good commercial headshot will get you an interview with a commercial agent, and once you have signed with that agent—or even have gotten one or two jobs—you can then work out your composite with your agent's help.

If you don't heed this advice and have a commercial composite made up first, we guarantee there will be something about the composite the agent won't like (photo, layout, etc.) and you'll only have to have a new one made up. That's why composites are listed farther down on the budget.

PRACTICING

It's one thing to know what you want to project in your pictures and another thing to project it—especially if you haven't worked in front of a camera.

Buy a friend a beer and convince him/her to take an afternoon to do a mock résumé session with any camera capable of taking close-ups. Have your friend shoot you in different poses, costumes, attitudes, etc., and keep shooting until you get tired or your friend begins to grunt. . . .

What you get back from the drugstore should tell you quite a bit about how to show yourself off to best advantage. You can't expect the photographer to pull out "hidden charms"—that's your job. No photographer can get silk photos out of a sow's ear of a subject.

FINDING A PHOTOGRAPHER

Here's a typical question that, surprisingly, pops up over and over. Our answer follows.

Q: I've got a friend with a camera. Can't I just let him take my résumé shots?

A: We've got a friend with a scalpel. Can he take out your appendix?

In other words, when we talk about a photographer, we mean a pro who knows what the industry is looking for. Fortunately, finding one is fairly easy—they spend a good deal of time and energy trying to find you.

First, ask your fellow actors. They generally know who's good.

Next, check the trades (see "Trades," Chapter 8). Photographers galore advertise in them.

Then check the bulletin boards of the unions, acting schools, and other places where actors congregate.

Print shops specializing in résumé shots often have photographers' calling cards, customers you can quiz if you like their pictures, and employees who may have a lead or two.

And to get you started, we list a few of the city's many good photographers in our "Lists" section.

If you do the above, you'll quickly have a list of potential photographers to call.

CONTACTING THE PHOTOGRAPHER

Every field has its own jargon, and photography is no exception. Here's some "lingo" you'll need to understand before you call:

- *Headshot session:* It lasts about an hour or two, during which the photographer will take in the neighborhood of seventy (and some-times more) pictures of your glorious mug.

- *Exposures; shots:* These are simply other words for "picture" (i.e., 72 exposures = 72 pictures).

- *Negatives:* Few photographers will give their clients the actual negatives of the pictures they take, as this is the only way they can protect their copyright on their work. Rather, they will give you:

- *Proofs; proof sheets:* The photographer will make little copies of each photo he takes (about the size of those you get in a video arcade machine) on sheets of photographic paper, about 16 to a sheet. These are your proofs. From these, you'll choose the ones you want blown up into:

- *Print(s):* These are eight-by-ten blowups of the picture(s) you've chosen from your proof sheets. The photographer includes one to four of these in the cost of your headshot session. Beyond that, he charges a small fee (currently about $5) for each additional print he makes.

Now that you know some of the jargon, here are the questions you should ask a prospective photographer. . . .

- How much for a headshot session, and what the cost includes (i.e., how many exposures; how many "free" prints; how much for each extra print).

- How many costume changes are you permitted? (You won't need more than about four, but be sure you both understand what each of you means by this. One photographer might consider the removal of a tie to be a "costume change." Another might only think of this in terms of a complete change of wardrobe.)

- How long will it be, after the session, before you get your proofs? (Probably somewhere between a few days and two weeks.)

- How long will you have to wait for your prints after you return the proofs to the photographer? (Same as above.)

- Does he keep the negatives? (A *few* will let you have them.)

- How does he work? You want a photographer who snaps away as he talks to you, coaxes you, and strokes your ego. If he constantly "poses" you, that's how you'll look—posed.

- What happens if you don't like your proofs? We know; it's a sticky question. It's also one of the most important to ask—*before the session*. Most photographers simply schedule another session at no additional charge. Some will give you half or all your money back—*if you make this arrangement before shooting*. We wish more photographers would refund. We find it hard to believe that you'll get a good second session from a man whose work, in essence, you haven't liked. In any case, know what the story is before the first click of the shutter.

FIRST MEETING WITH THE PHOTOGRAPHER

When you meet with the photographer (and *never* schedule a session without seeing samples of the photographer's work), remember that the samples he shows you are, at least in his mind, examples of the best of his work. If you can find only a few that are good, you've got some more phone calls to make.

First, ask yourself: Are the pictures clear and bright, or "muddy"? Are the contrasts between light and dark clear and crisp?

Next, check the backgrounds. Are the subjects placed in front of brick

DRAMATIC LIGHT, BUT WHO IS IT??

FIND THE ACTOR...

OH, COME ON!

THE CLEAR WINNER

walls, traffic, etc.? These are too "busy" (distracting) and the photographer should know that.

Do the actors jump off the page? Do they excite you? Is there animation in their faces? If it's a commercial headshot, does the actor have life and warmth or is he just a person smiling? If it's a theatrical headshot, does the actor look interesting?

Do the actors look stiff and posed? Do you keep seeing the same poses popping up over and over again? (We know casting directors who can tell who took the pictures from the poses the actors are in.) It's hard to seem special on an assembly line.

Has the photographer called attention to his technique by using tricky lighting, shadows, etc.? Don't let him upstage you.

Again, and above all, *what is going on in the eyes* of the actors? "The first thing I notice in a picture is the eyes. The eyes sell it," advises theatrical agent Sandra Siegal.

By the way, you will use this same criterion when you choose your own photos from the proof sheets.

If you're satisfied, set up the session. (If it's an outdoor session using "available light" instead of indoor "studio lighting," avoid high noon—shadows cast by the sun will be too harsh.)

PRESESSION PLANNING

Since you've got to look like your pictures, you've got to decide now how you want to look for as long as you use the shots that are about to be taken (probably a year or so). Your hair's color, length, and curliness may vary only slightly. Your makeup should photograph natural, not all-out paint box. And mustaches and beards cannot be grown/cut off without new photos.

Next, raid the closet. Pick out clothing that best suits the moods you want to project. Lighter clothing is best for your commercial headshot; for your theatrical headshot, perhaps you might want to go darker. But avoid absolutes like white or black, and avoid plaids, stripes, and prints—anything that will distract from your face. You might also pick out a dressy outfit (suit, dress) and an informal one—provided, again, that these don't conflict with your type. And don't be shy about bringing a load of clothes to the session and asking the photographer for his advice.

Finally, go over in your mind what you're going to try to present to the camera. A good photo session, like a good play, is a combination of the actors' ideas and those of the director/photographer. Résumé photographer Dale Tarter advises, "It's as important for you to be prepared when you come to see a photographer as it is going on a movie set. *Do your homework.* I love it when an actor knows what he wants."

THE SESSION

The essential thing to remember is do what you planned to do. Don't let yourself be pushed around into poses that are wrong for you. Outside of that . . .

- *If you're nervous, tell the photographer.* A good one will do all he can to calm and reinforce you. (We know one photographer who routinely pretends to shoot a nervous actor for about fifteen shots. Then, with the actor over his jitters, he really goes to work. Works like a charm.)

- *Don't squint.* Occasionally, between shots, squint as hard as you can. Then relax your face, especially your eyes and cheeks. Feel the difference?

- *Every so often, lick your lips.* Moist lips photograph better.

- *"Think" it—don't "show" it.* A good rule for all acting on film. By the way, one way to avoid glassy eyes is to look down to the ground and set your mood; then, when the photographer is ready, suddenly look up at the camera. If he shoots you just as you look up, nine times out of ten you'll get a lively, animated expression.

- *Take off your glasses and contacts.* Do the session "blind." Glasses block the eyes, and contacts reflect light. You might, however, use glasses for a specialty shot.

And, above all, as legitimate/theatrical agent Larry Fonseca put it, "Look at the camera—that's where your money is. Look at that camera and say 'Buy me.' Think about something. Feel sexy. Feel mean. Do whatever you want, but *think about something.*"

EXAMINING THE PROOFS

If this were a perfect world, we'd all be millionaires, we'd never dial a wrong number, and every shot on a proof sheet would be fantastic. Since it isn't, prepare to do some serious staring when your proofs are ready.

First, use a magnifying glass, ideally one with its own light.

Second, use the same criteria mentioned earlier under "Finding a Photographer" (see page 42).

Third, get additional opinions. "Actors should never pick their own pictures," says résumé photographer John Sanchez. "They just don't know what they look like." Just be sure the people you ask know the industry. (Mommy will probably choose a lovely photo that is a disaster as a résumé shot.) Certainly, if you have an agent, you should show your choices to him/her. Eventually, you'll get your choices narrowed down a bit.

Don't, however, narrow your choices to any one shot because *no picture ever looks the same blown up as it did on the proof sheet.* Maybe it's gremlins. Or all those chemicals. In any case, have as many pictures blown up into prints as common sense and your pocketbook will allow. (Remember, the photographer throws in the first few.)

GETTING AND CHECKING YOUR PRINTS

The first thing you'll notice are the prints with the glaring defects. You'll discover a shadow on your face that "wasn't there" on the proof sheet, now very apparent in eight-by-ten size. On another print, those eyes that "jumped off the proof sheet" now look like Dracula at feeding time.

With those prints out of the way, you should examine the seemingly good ones using, again, the criteria under "First Meeting with the Photographer" (see page 44) and add:

- Are there any spots or scratches on the print?
- Is the focus blurry or fuzzy, or sharp and crisp?
- Is the photo too light or dark?

With a little darkroom magic, some of these things can be corrected, but if the photographer says they can't be, forget the picture. You can't look good if you're blurred.

Using all of the above, and once again, the opinions of others in the industry, you should be able to boil down your choices. Remember, you want at least one good commercial headshot and one good theatrical headshot.

Now it's time to say "bye" to the photographer and move on to the printer.

PREPRINTER DECISIONS

Before contacting the printer, it's best to decide on how you want your pictures to look, as most printers specialize in one thing or another. You'll want to know:

1. The finish you want.
2. Whether or not to have a border.
3. The location of your name.
4. The appearance of your name.

1. *The finish:* Since what you decide here might affect numbers 2 and 3, you'll want to pick your finish first. There are three in wide use: "glossy," "matte," and "gloss-tone."

- *Glossy:* Your pictures will look shiny. It's the most-used and, generally, the least-expensive finish.

- *Matte:* (Pronounced "mat.") Your pictures will have a cloth-like look and feel. This, by the way, is the preferred finish when you have your composite made up (see "Composites," Chapter 23).

- *Gloss-tone:* Sort of a toned-down version of "glossy." Open any magazine and look at the photographs—that's what "gloss-tone" looks like.

As far as the industry is concerned, your choice of finish is strictly a matter of taste. However, matte and gloss-tone finishes don't reproduce as well in newspapers as glossy, and gloss-tone tends to scratch more easily.

2. *Border(s)* or *"bleeds".* You know, of course, what borders are—the white spaces between the photo and the edge of the paper it's printed on. "Bleeding" a photo, then, is printing it so that it fills up (bleeds off) the paper, leaving no border. A "four-sided bleed" means your photo has no border at all. A popular variation, the "three-sided bleed," has a border on only one side, usually the bottom, into which your name is printed. Except for the border containing your name, keep all borders narrow, no larger than three-eighths of an inch. You don't want white space stealing the show.

3. *Name location:* Résumés can get lost, so you'll want your name on your pictures. Skip other information such as your agency, which might change, leaving you with a lot of useless photos. (Note: this is not true for composites; see Chapter 23.)

Your name can be in the border or on the photo itself. There are a variety of ways the printer can do the latter, as follows:

4. *Name appearance:* When he puts your name on the photo, the printer uses one of three methods: "knockout," "overprint" (or "overlay"), and "reverse."

- *Knockout:* You tell the printer where on the picture you want your name. He'll put a small block of white there, with your name printed in black letters within the block.

- *Overprint or overlay:* You tell the printer where you want your name. It appears directly on the photo in black letters. There is no white space around your name.

- *Reverse:* The opposite of overprint: your name appears in white letters.

Naturally, your choice of whether to go with an overprint or a reverse will depend on whether the spot where you place your name is dark or light. Having an overprint (name in black) on a dark background could make your name disappear.

One other thing that should be considered: the typeface you choose for your name. Since printers stock their own typefaces, you'll have to choose from what your printer has available. However, you might at least think in ball-park terms about whether you want script, block letters, etc., and how the typeface matches the image you want to project. And remember: don't make your name too prominent. The photo's the thing here.

IF YOU PIN US DOWN

In every class, some student will inevitably ask what we like. We'll answer that question with the understanding that we are dealing with an opinion based, primarily, on aesthetics. We like:

- A gloss-tone finish (we just like the look).
- A four-way bleed (we think it calls more attention to the subject).
- A reverse or overprint (a knockout tends to call too much attention to the name).

CHOOSING A PRINTER

Once you've ascertained that a printer can do the things you want, you'll want to know his cost(s). These will fall into the following categories:

- *Negative cost:* You'll bring the print the photographer gave you to the printer. The printer will then take a picture of that picture and make his copies from the new negative. (You'll get this negative back, by the way, for future use.) The printer will charge you a small fee for doing this. (Naturally, the way to avoid this is to have the original negative from the photographer—nice work if you can get it.)

- *Lot cost:* The number of copies made, i.e., two hundred, three hundred, etc. As with anything else, your cost per copy is less with a larger order.

- *Name imprinting/negative:* As mentioned, you'll choose the type used for your name from the printers' stock. He'll then, in his secret dungeon, spell out your name in that type and take a picture of it. He'll use the negative to make copies. (You'll get this negative back, too, for future use.)

- *Extras:* Anything else you want done, such as cropping, bleeds, overprints, lightening or darkening a picture, etc., may or may not cost extra.

Once you've called a few printers and compared their prices, you can make your choice—except for one thing:

A NOTE ABOUT "LINES"

This isn't a text on photography, so we'll simply say that *the more lines a printer uses in his process, the better your photos will be.* If you're choosing between two printers, both of whom can do the things you want and are fairly close in price, go with the one who uses more lines. Your copies will just plain look better.

AT THE PRINTER

Once again, you bring the photographer's print (or negative, if you've talked him out of it). You tell the printer:

- What finish you want.
- Whether copies are to be bordered or "bled," and how many sides to bleed.
- Where you want your name and how he is to do this.
- What kind of typeface you want.
- Any other "extras" you want done.
- How many copies you want. (If you have an agent, order about three hundred copies. If you don't, order about two hundred—a future agent may like you but not your pictures.)

You will then, we hope, have the good sense to sacrifice a few days' time getting your prints in order to have the printer make:

TEST PRINTS

These are sample copies, done to your specifications, to show what *all* the copies will look like. Some printers include these in your basic costs. If not, pay the small extra amount to have it done. One bad sample copy is a lot better than three hundred bad prints.

The printer will ask for either a deposit or full payment in advance and tell you how long it'll be before you can see your test print (a few days to two weeks). Don't bet your money that the test print (or the finished ones) will be ready when he says it will be—call first.

CHECKING THE TEST PRINT(S)

Hang in there, you're almost done. Check your test print(s) as carefully as you've checked everything else. Use all the criteria we've mentioned before, and add the following:

- Is your name spelled right? Is it straight or crooked?
- Is the printing of your name clear or out of focus?
- Are the letters even or do they pop up and down?
- Are the borders even on all sides?
- Are they "dirty" with white specks or scratches?
- Did the printer do everything you asked for (lightening, additional cropping, etc.)?

If you find anything wrong, point it out to the printer and have another test print done. If you supplied the printer with the negative—as opposed to the photographer's print—and something came out bad, ask the printer about it. If he says the problem is with the negative and can't be fixed, choose another picture.

CHECKING THE COPIES

Don't grab them and run. After all, this is the last step. Pull a copy out from the center of the stack and examine it, using all the criteria mentioned in this chapter. Unless something very strange occurred, you should find that your copies exactly match the test print.

If you're satisfied with your copies, go home, take out one of your pictures, pour a drink, and toast yourself. You're now way ahead of a lot of aspiring actors—you've got good résumé shots!

UPDATING YOUR PICTURES

We've already mentioned that, at least every three years or whenever anything about you changes, you've got to have new pictures done. As commercial agent Kathy Smith says, "Whenever you change your hair, say from long to short, think of it as a two-hundred-dollar haircut." We'd just like to add not to forget weight gain or loss, and getting older.

That last one is a toughie, but it has to be faced. Sooner or later, we all stop looking like ingenues—unless you're Roddy McDowell, who, as "Laugh-In" once pointed out, is under forty by contract.

6 RÉSUMÉS

I can tell a phony résumé at a glance.

Mary Spencer, Theatrical Agent

Some actors treat résumés as a formalized list of little white lies. Others think anything goes. Others think *everything* goes. And still others regard résumés as one big joke and can't understand why the industry treats *them* as jokers.

Well, your résumé is more than just a list of what you've done. It's your trademark. It's a statement about you and how professionally you view yourself. And it starts with . . .

APPEARANCE

This is often the most neglected area of résumés, and just as important as what's on it. Some suggestions:

- *Don't use cheap paper:* The cheaper the paper looks, the cheaper you will look. A good paper is 20- or 25-weight rag bond. The printer can show you what this looks like. Normally, this kind of paper will cost you about 2 to 3 cents more than ordinary bond paper. Not exactly a major investment.

- *Type it on a good typewriter:* . . . Or have it professionally done by someone who knows what the industry is looking for. (An acting résumé is different from the usual business résumé.) It may cost you upward of $25 to have it composed and typed, but it's worth it if you can't do it yourself. Never present to anyone a résumé with something handwritten on it.

- *Have it offset-printed:* This simply means that the printer takes a photograph of the résumé and prints the copies from that. This looks far better than a photocopy and, again, the cost is minimal. Only remember that, when you have something printed offset, you must bring it in "camera-ready," that is, looking exactly the way you want it printed, with nothing more to be done to it. You can have the printer typeset the résumé, but don't. It's too expensive, and while it looks beautiful, it also looks a little too permanent—as if the actor didn't intend to add any more credits.

- *You might use a muted color:* It's just a little more eye-catching. Our favorite is an egg white.

- *Have the résumé cut to fit the photo:* The standard way of submitting a résumé and résumé shot is to staple the résumé to the back of the picture. (No paper clips, glue, spit, bubble gum or tar.) Since the average piece of stationery measures eight and a half by eleven, larger than your eight-by-ten photo, you'll need to cut it down to size (or ask the printer to—*before* he prints the résumé). Allow space on all sides while typing your résumé so that it can be trimmed. This kind of attention to detail pays public-relations dividends. To quote a casting director: "Nothing drives me crazier than résumés that are slightly larger than the photograph. Filing them is a real pain in the neck."

- *Your name:* The first thing anyone should notice is the actor's name. If that sounds obvious, you'd be surprised at the number of résumés on which we'd had to hunt for that lil' item. How large should your name be? Large enough so that it is the most prominent feature of the résumé, without looking like you've got an oversized ego. (See sample.)

  There are three ways you can go about putting your name on your résumé:

  Have the printer do it. This way is easiest for you, but also most expensive.

  Take one of your résumé shots, cut your name from the border or knockout, and glue it onto the résumé.

  Go to an art supplies or stationery store and buy rub-on (dry transfer) lettering. It is inexpensive and will give you a professional look you can do yourself if you can draw a straight line with a ruler.

  One other thing. If your agent gives you a sheet of paper that is blank save for his logo at the top, and asks you to print your résumé on it, decline unless your agent insists. Your résumé should primarily sell you—not your agent.

CONTENT

First, let's go over a few items that should *not* be on your résumé.

- *Your age or age range:* You don't want your résumé saying you're twenty, only to have someone tell you, "Oh, no, this part calls for a twenty-two-year-old." (There are some bureaucrats even in this creative industry.) Don't limit yourself—and, yes, even an age range limits you to the numbers you put on the résumé.

- *Your Social Security number, home address, or measurements:* Résumés can fall into anyone's hands. When a producer hires you, he can ask you or your agent for this information. Discretion will help keep any creepy crawlers out there from trying to enter your woodwork.

- *Emphasis on your singing and dancing:* We know this sounds strange. However, there are people in Hollywood who believe singers and dancers can't act. Dumb? Sure. But the attitude exists. We aren't saying you need to drop all those musical comedies from your résumé; nor are we saying you can't put singing or dancing, perhaps, under "Special Skills." Just don't make your experience here a prominent part of your résumé. Make up a separate résumé for nightclub, concert, or dance work.

- *Your college- and/or community-theatre credits:* We realize that's probably all you have if you're just starting out in the business. The point is there's no need to go out of your way to indicate that your credits are community theatre. For example, put Cambridge Theatre—*not* Cambridge Community Theatre. Then, slowly, as you build up your credits, you might drop those little-theatre credits altogether.

- *Anything cutesy or autobiographical:* For example, "I was born . . ." A résumé is a list of your credits and, possibly, some skills. It is not your life story or a forum to prove you can write comedy.

Now let's talk about what *should* be on the résumé—and where to put it. On the following page is a typical professional résumé in a good, functional format. Your agent may ask for modifications, of course. Little in this industry is writ on stone.

The little black dots on the résumé, by the way, are an easy graphic touch you can add by hitting the lower-case "o" on your typewriter and then filling it in with black ink.

- *Your name:* Again, you immediately note that this is the most prominent thing on Steven Stunning's résumé.

- *The agency name, etc.:* This should include the name of the agency;

Steven Stunning

Messages: (213) 333-STAR

REVOLVING DOOR AGENCY
Agent: Slam Gently
#1 Superstar Path
Colossus, CA 99999
(213) 123-BOMB

- *HT:* 11'12"   *EYES:* Red   *UNIONS:* SAG
  WT: 22   *HAIR:* Blue   AFTRA
                                                              AEA

- *TELEVISION:*

LEW GRUNT	Simian Prods.	Co-Star
NOVA	Celestial Prods.	Guest Star
FOUR'S A CORPORATION	Prod Prods.	
AS THE STOMACH TURNS	Rolaids, Inc.	
I LOVE LOOSELY	Marilyn Chambers Prods.	

- *FEATURES:*

IT CAME FROM OUTER DA SINK	Hal Roach Prods.	
THE CREATURE FROM THE BLACK LATRINE	Rotorooter, Inc.	
A FAREWELL TO ARMS	De Milo Prods.	
AIRPORT 701 B.C.	Tiresome Ltd.	

- *STAGE:*

100 CLOWNS	Theatre of Reduced Expectations	Clown #99
THE BIG SHOW	Performing Theatre for the Performing Arts	Benito
PERFORMANCE	Performing Theatre for the Performing Performers	A Performer
LOOK BACK IN ANGER	Theatre for the Angry	Pissy

- *COMMERCIALS:* On request

- *SPECIAL SKILLS:* [seriously, you may or may not want to include this]
  Fluent in pig Latin, sleeping, Golden Thumbnail in tiddlywinks

the name of the actual agent who handles you; their address (including zip code); and their phone number (including area code).

If you don't have an agent, you might move your phone number over to this spot.

- *Your phone number:* Put your service if you have one. If you don't, put your home phone number, again under the word "Messages."

- *Your vital statistics (often called Stats or Vitals):* These are limited to: your height, weight, hair color, and eye color.

- *Your unions:* Use the standard abbreviations.

- *Your television credits:* These are listed first. Note that the name of the show is in capital letters. Then, reading left to right, the production company followed by any special billing you may have had. (Your agent may want you to substitute or add the character name and a one- or two-word description of the character.) If you don't have any TV credits, you put the next category first.

- *Your motion-picture credits, listed under "Features":* In this case, the actor obviously had no special billing. The format is the same as television credits. If, at this point, you still haven't any feature credits to put on the résumé but have done commercials, industrial films, student films, etc.—anything that puts your face on film—you would put these credits under the heading: "Commercials/Industrials," and you would list them first. Remember that the industry is interested in what you have done "on film" (includes tape). Mr. Stunning has those credits, so he doesn't list commercials, etc., on his résumé. Instead, he uses the standard heading "Commercials: on request."

- *Your theatre credits, listed under "Stage":* Reading left to right: the name of the play in capital letters, the name of the theatre (you can add the city if you like—a good idea if they're New York credits), and the name of the character. "Sometimes where you did it is more important than what you played," says director Noel Black.

If you have no TV, motion picture, or commercials/industrials credits, your stage credits will, of course, be the only credits on the résumé and thus will be a longer list (about ten of your best credits).

Whatever credits you list, be sure everything is spelled correctly. If not, you'll look awfully dumb.

- *Commercials:* List these only if you have to (see above). Otherwise, use the standard "on request."

- *Any skills or talents you may have, listed under "Special Skills":* While we're not all that crazy about listing these, as it tends to look a little eager or desperate, we'll also admit we've heard of cases where this has gotten an actor an audition because the producer just happened to need a person who could, say, ride a horse, speak a foreign language, shoot pool, play a musical instrument, and the like. But don't bluff—if you can't really do it, don't list it.

- *Training:* Mr. Stunning doesn't need this, as he's got film credits. But if all you have are stage credits, you might list your training—especially if it deals with the industry (for example, a film-technique class); if the class was in New York or a foreign country, which tends to impress; or if the instructor is a famous one (Stella Adler [the late], Lee Strasberg, etc.).

- *Education:* By this, we mean your college credits—B.A., M.F.A., etc. Unless these come from well-known and respected schools for dramatic training (such as Yale, UCLA, USC, Northwestern, Juilliard, NYU), they're—well—nice. Please forgive us if we're sounding blasé about four years or more of your life. It's just that a drama degree by itself doesn't mean much in this industry. Again, note that Mr. Stunning didn't mention his because he doesn't need to—he's got credits.

SHOULD YOU PAD A RÉSUMÉ?

It's not a good idea, but if you're determined, use common sense. For example . . .

- *New York credits:* Some of the best theatre today is being done outside the Big Apple, but people in Los Angeles often are disproportionately impressed with New York credits. Fighting fire with fire, you could take a Dallas community-theatre credit (say, *The Glass Menagerie*) and move it to a New York off-off Broadway theatre. However, two cautions:

    1. Remember, these must be off-off Broadway. Saying you played the lead in *Hello, Dolly* isn't exactly the smartest thing—especially if you also don't belong to Equity.

2. If you're going to list any New York credits, at least be familiar with that city and, of course, the off-off Broadway theatres. You'll look pretty dumb if you list New York credits and then tell the interviewer what a lovely strolling area Forty-second Street is.

- *Motion-picture credits:* You *might* get away with this if you list an out-of-town or obscure independent such as *The Bloody Hand with the Greasy Hook That Picked Apart Poughkeepsie,* Sharp Productions, Atlanta. But rest assured that as soon as you do, you'll meet somebody familiar with that picture (if it exists) or who knows all about potboilers or Atlanta production and spots it as a phony. We're not kidding.

- *Television credits:* Forget it.

- *Commercials/industrials:* Here's your best bet for a little padding if you must pad. Every city has commercials, and many cities have industrial film houses. Just be sure you know what you're talking about.

- *Stage credits:* Of course, if you leave them in Podunk, you can pad to your heart's content—provided you are at least familiar with the plays. But if you feel the need to do this, why do you think you're ready to do battle in professional acting?

Having said all this, however, remember that if you're eighteen years old, nobody expects you to have a résumé as long as your arm.

That's it—except for one quote that we really like. It's from a résumé-typing service. We discovered it on a sign hanging in the window: WHEN THEY ASK TO SEE IT, IT BETTER BE GOOD.

7 THE UNIONS

Okay, I can't get into the Guild without a job, and I can't get a job without the Guild. They're not going to screw my head up. I'm going to beat them at this.

An Actress

Some actors may have been born with silver spoons in their mouths, but no actor was ever born with a union card in his hand. When you begin to think that the "system" has made it impossible for you to join the unions, remember that. In fact, it may be a lot easier to get into them than you think. Stay tuned.

Your main concern as an actor will be getting into AFTRA, SAG, and Equity.

THE AMERICAN FEDERATION OF TELEVISION AND RADIO ARTISTS (AFTRA)

Its jurisdiction is over actors involved in *taped* television shows and commercials, and over all other performers involved in television or radio (announcers, disk jockeys, and so on; Johnny Carson and Dan Rather have to be members of AFTRA).

THE SCREEN ACTORS GUILD

Only actors appearing in motion pictures—whether for use in theatres or on television—and filmed commercials.

THE ACTORS EQUITY ASSOCIATION (AEA), CALLED "EQUITY"

Actors and stage managers in live theatre.

However, before we talk about getting into any of these . . .

A CAUTION ABOUT JOINING ANY UNION

If you feel you need more experience, and/or want to do more community theatre, you'll want to avoid becoming union. Once you join *any* of these unions, you may no longer do any non-union theatre. All stage work must then be Equity. All three unions have reciprocal agreements on this,

61

which means that even if you are only AFTRA, you may not do any non-paid, nonunion *theatre* work. (There is an exception to this, called Equity Waiver theatre, which you'll learn more about in Chapters 11 and 26.)

If you are union and ignore this rule, you will be subject to a stiff fine the first time and can be brought up on charges, even tossed out of the union(s) if you continue to ignore it—which, in effect, means the end of your career as a professional actor.

Of course, you can do your community-theatre work under a phony name, and it's true that you stand a much better chance of getting away with it if you live in a small town away from New York or Los Angeles. It's also true that the unions will, on occasion, grant exceptions. But you will be playing with fire unnecessarily—if for no other reason than that union pressure may force you to drop out of a show on opening night, which isn't exactly fair to the others involved.

It boils down to this: the unions consider you a pro if you're a member. If you're not ready to think of yourself as they would, if you're not ready to compete with the pros, then, for now, avoid the unions and continue to work and get experience at the best place for that—community theatre.

THE SIMPLE WAY INTO AFTRA

AFTRA initiation: $600 (may vary depending upon the city in which you join; these are L.A. figures).

AFTRA dues: $32.50 semiannually. (A minimum—as your salary increases, your dues increase. This is true of all unions.)

Believe it or not, anyone can join AFTRA at any time. They've got an "open-door" policy. All you need do is obtain an application form from your nearest branch (see "Lists" section), fill it out, and plunk down the initiation fee and dues in cash (or certified check). It's that simple—for now. As we go to press, there is a strong movement toward merger with SAG, which most union people we've talked to think will be approved eventually by both union memberships. If and when that happens, AFTRA will most likely have to adopt at least some of the SAG rules regarding entry, thereby making it harder for the new guy on the block.

THE *TWO* WAYS TO GET INTO EQUITY

Equity initiation: $500.

Equity dues: $26 semiannually, plus 2 percent of your working salary.

The fast way in

A producer hires you as an actor or stage manager to appear in or work on an Equity stage production. You bring your contract, along with your initiation fee and dues, to your nearest Equity branch, and you may join.

Notice we said this was the "fast" way, not the "easy" way. Whenever a producer holds auditions for a union stage production, he must see only Equity people first, followed by an "open call" to all other actors. If you're not in Equity, your chances of getting the first part are slim. (Frankly, many of these "open calls" are a joke.) Still, go. Who knows? (If you want to find a side door, you've got to hang around the house.)

If you can associate yourself with an Equity theatre in any capacity, they may eventually be willing to hire you as a stage manager (or even an actor) for one of their productions. Bam! You're in.

The slow way in: the Equity Membership Candidacy Program

You will need to write Equity and obtain a list of theatres that participate in this program. Once accepted, you'll fill out an affidavit saying you have not worked as a professional under *any* union. In addition, you send Equity $50 (this will be credited to your initiation fee later).

You will then work at that theatre as an actor, but you will be paid less than other actors who are already Equity. Keep a record of all the weeks you put in and report this information to Equity. Once you've completed fifty weeks of work, you are eligible to join the union.

Note that your fifty weeks need not be consecutive and need not be at the same theatre. You can do this at any number of participating theatres over any length of time.

Note also that you may not join this program if you are a member of SAG or a working member of AFTRA. Unfortunately (for nonmembers), that's it. Equity is the toughest performer's union to get into.

THE MANY WAYS INTO SAG

SAG initiation: $600.
SAG dues: $37.50 semiannually.

Contrary to myth, there are many "side door" entrances to the Screen Actors Guild, some of which even experienced old-timers may not know about. Again, stay tuned.

The two fast ways into SAG

- A producer holds auditions and decides to cast you in his union film, television show, or commercial, even though you're not a member of the union. This is called being "Taft-Hartleyed." Either he or the casting director must fill out a one-page "Taft-Hartley Report," which he sends to SAG. Included in the report are his reasons for hiring *you* instead of a Guild member. If the role calls for a midget who can speak Arabic, the producer will have no problem—but if all he needs is "a blond," he might. If the Guild decides the producer's reasons aren't good enough, he's subject to pay "liquidated damages" (basically, a fine)—but *the Guild cannot stop him from hiring you.*

  Obviously, this route depends on how badly the producer wants you in his show. If he doesn't mind the hassle and expense, he'll do it. Most often, this occurs in commercials, low-budget films, and network pilots. Occasionally, feature-film producers will do it, sometimes even the makers of episodic television shows.

- In the making of a film or television show, there are often instances when a line needs to be thrown in, just to make the scene work better. That's an "unscripted line"—a line that didn't appear in the original script. Often, these are not said by the principal actors. ("Hang him!" shouts one of the townspeople.)

  Here's what a producer had to say: "I like to tell this to aspiring actors and actresses. If you know a producer or director of a movie, ask him to give you an unscripted line. It can't be in the original script because then SAG will ask why the producer didn't [originally audition and] hire a SAG actor to do it. . . . The producer will tell you to be on the set the day he needs someone to yell out a line. He can hire you, *on the spot,* to do that line, and you automatically have the right to join the Guild."

  Be sure to keep the "Day Player" contract he signs with you on the set. Take it and your initiation fee and dues down to SAG, and join. If you don't know a producer or director, you might "luck into" an "unscripted line" when doing extra work (see below).

The many slow ways to join SAG ("Parenting")

The union you do your first job under becomes your "parent" union. If you've been a member of *any* of the unions mentioned below for a minimum of *one year* and can prove you did union work under that union's jurisdiction, you may join SAG. (We'll also tell you a little about each of these unions per se. One or more might be just the ticket for your talents.)

- *Entrance into SAG from AFTRA:* Since you now know that you can join AFTRA anytime you want, the problem here is waiting that year and getting that one AFTRA job. Your best shots are AFTRA commercials, soap operas, radio work, and those "real life" shows as "Real People," in which some audience members are actors hired to tell a joke, say "Stay tuned," and so on. But any AFTRA show is a possibility. Whatever, be sure the show is *signatory* with AFTRA (just ask). If the contract isn't with an AFTRA signatory, SAG may not honor it. If you do get an AFTRA job, wait a year from the date you joined AFTRA and bring that contract down to SAG along with your SAG initiation and dues. You're in.

- *Entrance into SAG from Equity:* You've probably already got a contract from the show that originally got you into Equity in the first place. Now, you've just got to wait that year. If, however, you got in via the "Candidacy Program," you'll have to get that first Equity job. At least, being a member of Equity means you'll have first dibs on auditions, and sooner or later you should get something. Wait the year, bring your Equity contract down with you as proof, along with your SAG initiation fee and dues, and you're in.

- *Entrance into SAG from SEG:* Yep, it's possible to get into SAG via the Screen Extras Guild (SEG), which has jurisdiction over "atmosphere people"—television, films, and commercials.

  First, register with any or all of the *union* casting agencies that handle extra work. Currently, there are six (see "Lists" section). Whether they'll want you to bring or mail a résumé shot and résumé depends on the agency. Some say to call first, but it's very difficult to get through. We'd advise going down and telling them you've gotten nothing but busy signals, which will probably be true. Their methods of registering and/or interviewing you also varies, as does the chances of them accepting your application. "According to need" was the phrase most often quoted as the criteria on whether you're accepted or not. Two hints: the more special skills you can list on your résumé (provided you can *do* them) and the larger your wardrobe, the better. At the very least, if you go to one of these agencies, dress to the nines.

  If they permit you to register (there's no charge), you'll need to call them every day, at least every half hour or so. Of course, it's one thing to register with these places, another to get work, or even thought of. A little pleasantness and a lot of persistent calling will help.

And, if you can, get to know anyone associated with a production, especially the assistant director. He's the one in charge of extras on the set, and it's his job to inform the casting agencies what extras are needed. A "recommendation" from him certainly will at least grease the wheels.

"You'll see wives, girl friends, fathers of everyone from the cameraman to the makeup artist being extras," says one extra. "There's a lot of politics involved. An electrician says, 'Hey, how about my brother?' to the assistant director, and bingo."

If you get a job, assuming it's union (nonunion extra work generally pays about $35 a day, hardly worth it, and useless as far as getting into the unions is concerned), you'll get $79.50 for an eight-hour day for features and television. Commercials pay $195.14 per day with no residuals.

If you're asked to do something like roller-skate, ride a bike, play football, etc., that's called a "Special Ability," and you'll get an additional $10. If you're playing, say, a bartender, in a film or TV show, and the star asks you to pour him a drink, that's a "Silent Bit," and you'll be paid $133.50 per day. And if you're the one who gets to shout "Hang him!," you'll be upgraded, as mentioned, into SAG *on the spot.*

Unless that happens, save your pay stub(s). (Extras don't get contracts.) You then ask the casting agency from whom you got your check—all union extras are paid through these agencies—to recommend you to SEG. If they do, getting in is virtually automatic. You'll then go down to SEG, pay your initiation fee ($400) and semiannual dues ($36), and you're in.

Now, put those pay stubs into an iron vault: one year from the date you join SEG, you're eligible to join SAG, but you will then need those pay stubs as proof you worked. Bring them, your SAG initiation fee, and your SAG dues down to SAG, and you're in.

- *Entrance into SAG from the American Guild of Variety Artists (AGVA):* This union has jurisdiction over singers, magicians, clowns, stand-up comics, etc.—anyone who performs in nightclubs, halls, circuses, and the like—but not when they perform on television or in films.

Getting into AGVA and getting work are, in a sense, the same thing: if you can get anyone to hire you as a singer, dancer, stand-up comic, etc., *anyone*—from a nightclub owner to the president of your local Moose or Elks Lodge to your next-door neighbor who hires you, say, to sing at his party—and he's willing to sign an AGVA contract and abide by all the rules contained in that contract (including paying you a minimum salary of $75 for the first "set," $37.50 for the second, etc.), call, write or go down to your nearest AGVA office (see "Lists" section in Appendix B).

They'll give or send you a contract, which you and your employer will fill out and sign. While what you are paid will vary with the length of employment, how many sets you do, and the type of establishment you're working for, etc., here's a "for instance" of what will happen next:

Say you're hired to perform two sets, by yourself, at a private party. Your employer will send two copies of the contract along with a certified check in the amount of $112.50 to AGVA headquarters, 184 Fifth Avenue, New York, NY 10010. This check will serve as a "bond." It is refundable within thirty days to your employer if he notifies them that you performed and were paid as contracted (a canceled check or pay stub can be used as proof). In addition, your employer will have to send a check in the amount of $3, along with another copy of the contract to the AGVA Welfare Trust Fund, 250 West Fifty-seventh Street, New York, NY 10019. This check isn't refundable, it goes to help pay for the pension and welfare benefits offered by AGVA to its members. You, in turn, will send or bring a copy of that contract along with your initiation fee of $300 and your semiannual dues of $21.

That's how you get into AGVA. Save that contract, wait a year, bring it to SAG along with your SAG initiation and dues, and you're eligible to join SAG.

• *Entrance into SAG from the American Guild of Musical Artists (AGMA):* Not to be confused with the American Federation of Musicians, AGMA has jurisdiction over "classical" singers and dancers, soloists and choral (Luciano Pavarotti, for example, is AGMA), and soloist instrumentalists who perform *live* in concert halls, theatres, etc. Getting into AGMA is virtually the same as getting into AGVA in that you'll have to get a job first.

Hypothetically, you could form your own group, hold concerts, rent halls, sell tickets, etc., and ask AGMA to represent you. Otherwise, look for work at the Los Angeles Master Chorale, San Diego Opera Company, Joffrey Ballet, etc. (If you're willing to go north, try the San Francisco Ballet, the San Francisco Opera Company, the San Francisco Chorale, or the Oakland Chorale.)

However you get that first job (are you/did you sing in an AGMA chorale group in Altoona?), you can then go to, or write, your nearest AGMA office. You'll need $100 initiation plus dues, which will vary depending on your income under AGMA's jurisdiction. The AGMA rep will then ship your application off to New York, and in four to six weeks you'll be in AGMA. Then your AGMA rep will negotiate your contracts with any hiring companies. There's no percentage or extra charge for this. The provisions of those contracts usually will vary depending on, among other things, the type of company (dance, chorale, etc.) and its fiscal background. "Whereas other unions have standard contracts," says California Executive Director Dennis Moss, "AGMA will try to negotiate 'custom contracts' for each employer-employee."

Once again, save your AGMA contract(s), wait a year from the day you joined AGMA, bring the contract(s) down to SAG along with your SAG initiation and dues, and you're in SAG.

DISCOUNTS AND ICE CUBES

You'll have to pay full dues and initiation fees *only* to the first union you join and work under (again, called your "parent" union). All others will give you "discounts."

First, all future unions will cut your dues in half, provided you have worked under your parent union's jurisdiction. Second, you'll also get a "discount" on your initiation fees for all future unions *up to one-half off,* depending on what you had to cough up to join your parent. Three examples:

- You join and work under AFTRA first. You pay AFTRA a $600 initiation fee. One year later, you want to join SAG. Instead of paying the usual $600 initiation fee to SAG, you'll pay $300.

- You join AGMA first. You pay AGMA $100 initiation. One year later you join SAG. It'll cost you $500 initiation. (You can't get a larger discount, because you didn't pay that much to get into AGMA in the first place.)

- You join SAG first. Later, you want to join AGMA. It'll cost you $50 initiation to join AGMA. (Remember, the discount is *up to* one-half off.)

All initiation fees and dues quoted in this chapter are full price. If you're "parenting," cut the dues in half and take your initiation-fee discount accordingly.

And one other thing. It's not too good an idea to tell the people at one union that you're joining only to become eligible to join another union. The atmosphere will get arctic.

ON BEING CHOOSY

Ultimately, you'll need to join all three of the actors' unions and any other that the shoe fits. In Los Angeles, however, it's most important to have your SAG card. In New York, your Equity card is the big prize. Los Angeles is still a film town; New York is a stage town.

Due to the logistics of parenting, however, it's probably best to get your Equity card first, if you get the shot.

As we mentioned, if you've done any Equity work and have been a member of that union for a year, you can join SAG. Unfortunately, the reverse *isn't* true. You can't join Equity "merely" by being a member of SAG—or any other union—even if you wait till your SAG card has whiskers, and irrespective of how much work you do. The only ways to get into Equity are doing Equity work or going through the candidacy program. And the cherry on the hot fudge sundae is, you can't join the candidacy program if you're a member of SAG or a working member of AFTRA.

Ain't we got fun?

8 OTHER ITEMS ON THE BUDGET

When I'm casting, I always check "the
Book." (i.e., the Academy Players Directory)

Arne Sultan, Producer

You can hammer a nail with a rock. You don't have to have all the items below to be an actor. Hammers and the right supplies sure do come in handy, though.

POSTAGE

If you've ever received a piece of junk mail with postage due, you can imagine how a casting director must feel when he or she gets someone's résumé and résumé shot(s) and has to fork out change to the postman or take the time to scribble "Refused" and mail the thing back.

Check to be sure you have the right postage on the envelope—you'll constantly be mailing things out. If you're uncertain, it's better to err in the direction of too much postage.

MANILA ENVELOPES

These are those large brown or gold envelopes with clasps on the backs. You'll be using them to mail your résumé and résumé shot(s). It'll help if they're relatively sturdy. (A piece of cardboard or two in the package adds protection. Of course, it also adds postage.)

ACADEMY PLAYERS DIRECTORY

Often referred to as "the Book" or "the Directory," it's sort of a visual telephone directory of actors: a book of faces with a little information on those faces, which is published every four months. Actors who list in the Directory must be members of at least one union and pay $15 per edition ($45 for a year's worth of three editions). For that small amount of money, they're assured of being in one of the most powerful "opportunity getters" in the business. Your agent, in fact, will probably *demand* that you be listed.

To get in, go to the Academy of Arts and Sciences building, 8949 Wilshire Boulevard. Bring a copy of your theatrical and commercial head-shots. You will then choose the category under which you wish to be listed. These are: Young Leading Man/Lady; Leading Man/Lady; Characters &

Comedians/iennes; and Children. (There is also a small section for Bands, Specialty Acts, Magicians, etc.) If you fall between categories—for example, between a young leading man and a young character actor—it might be to your advantage to list under both categories if you can afford the double cost.

Included with your name and one or two photos, the Directory will also list: the name(s) of your agency or agencies and/or your personal manager; their phone numbers; your own phone number, if you have no agent or manager; and your union(s).

For each edition, the Directory, naturally, has a deadline. While they do send out notices regarding this, don't rely on it (we don't always get a notice). Check to find out when the deadlines are, and if you miss one, bear in mind that your agent's deadline is about a week later than yours. Ask your agent to take your pictures and check to the Directory for you. He'll do it. Some agencies call their clients to remind them about Directory deadlines—get the picture about the importance of this?

The Directory should be notified whenever you have a change of agent, and the publication asks for a change of photographs every two years.

Finally, if you're not convinced about the importance of being "in the Book," go down to the Directory or any agency or casting director's office and pick up an edition. Not only will you see "unknowns," but you'll see pictures of the very top stars. Time and time again, we hear of actors getting auditions directly from their Directory listing. "Next to your agent, it's your best agent," says theatrical agent Vikki Bandlow. "It is the Bible," says producer William Kayden.

There is another directory out, this one purely for commercials. However, in our talks with those involved in commercials, being listed in this directory is nowhere near as crucial, at least not yet. You will want to include a commercial headshot and the name of your commercial agent in the *Academy Players Directory*, anyway.

ANSWERING DEVICE

All in all, we suggest getting an answering machine over a service. It's cheaper—you pay for it only once (an answering service will charge by the month). And if you forget to turn on the machine, missing a message, you can have a jolly good time kicking yourself in the pants . . . but finding out who missed your message when you have a service is only slightly easier than finding out who shot Cock Robin.

COMPOSITES

This is not an expense you need to worry about until you've gotten a commercial agent (see our chapter on composites in the "Commercials" section of the book).

GOOD STATIONERY

The better your stationery looks, the more replies you will get.

THANK-YOU NOTES

Aside from simple courtesy, if you're a smart actor, you'll send these out every time you get an audition, interview, part, or shake of the hand, if for no other reason than it puts your name in front of the person one more time.

CARD FILE

It's good practice to keep a file on every person you meet, the where and why of the encounter, perhaps even your feelings about how the encounter went.

Also, you might record various statements you hear about these people regarding their approach to their work, as well as any statements they make at seminars, in publications, etc. You'd be surprised at how much information you can put together about, say, a casting director—and the more you know about his or her preferences (and yes, quirks) the better.

BLANK LABELS

These are the labels you stick onto manila envelopes when sending out résumés and résumé shots. They're not vital, but they are inexpensive and they make the envelope look a trifle nicer.

LABEL SETS

The same Breakdown Service that provides casting breakdowns to agents (see "Theatrical Agents—What They Are and Do," Chapter 10) also provides services to actors. Among them, for just under $16, is a set of labels preaddressed to all the casting directors in town; for about $21, they'll send you a set for all agents; for $7.42, a set for commercial casting directors. Certainly saves a lot of work. (This is not to say that this is the only such service: check *Drama-Logue* for ads by others if you want to comparison-shop.) For other Breakdown Service offerings, see "Publicizing

Yourself, chapter 28"; for the phone number, see "Lists" section in Appendix B.

SAG AGENCY LIST

For free if you're a member, for twenty-five big pennies if you're not, you can get the complete list of agents franchised with SAG—and you don't want to get involved with any other kind of agent. Just go down to SAG and ask for a copy, or use ours in the back of this book. SAG also has available a list of casting directors and their telephone numbers, which it updates every couple of months.

GEOGRAPHICAL CASTING GUIDE / BREAKDOWN-SERVICE GUIDE

The *Geographical Casting Guide* is a small booklet that lists names, addresses, and phone numbers of all casting directors. There's other handy information in it as well. Its great feature is a listing of casting directors in geographical, as well as alphabetical, order. This enables you to start, say, at the 9000 block Sunset Boulevard and work your way east, dropping a résumé and photo at every casting director's office along the way. Is it worth it? Wouldn't hurt. Just wear soft-soled shoes and bring along plenty of dimes for all those parking meters.

You can pick up the Guide at many newsstands and at Larry Edmunds or Samuel French, Inc., drama bookstores for $3.50.

For those who want absolutely up-to-date information regarding casting directors (they move around a lot, and the *Geographical Casting Guide* is printed only twice a year), you can subscribe to the Breakdown Service's Casting Director List Service. Their directory also is alphabetical and geographical, but it is published every three months, *and* you are sent updates every two weeks. A one-year subscription costs $31.80.

(Note: in the budget, we used the higher figure of the Breakdown Service subscription, but whether you use it or the Guide depends entirely on you.)

PRODUCERS GUIDE

This is an absolutely super little booklet called *The Producers: A Descriptive Directory of Film and Television Producers is the Los Angeles Area.* In addition to the names, addresses, and phone numbers of the major production companies and the industrial film producers, it includes descriptions of the kinds of work each does. It costs $4.95 and is available at Samuel French and Larry Edmunds bookstores. You can also order direct from the author: Richard Burger, P.O. Box 25165, Los Angeles, CA 90025.

THE STUDIO BLU-BOOK/PACIFIC COAST STUDIO DIRECTORY

Put out by the *Hollywood Reporter*, it costs a rather expensive $25, but it includes personal managers, business managers, directors' agents, stars' agents, stores that sell stage makeup, and more. Sooner or later, it'll come in very handy. Available at the above and other bookstores.

A similar resource that can be a little or a lot cheaper, depending on how you cut the deal, is the *Pacific Coast Studio Directory*. It costs $5 per issue and contains much of the same kinds of information as the *Blu-Book*. However, it is a quarterly, as opposed to an annual. By subscription it costs $15 a year. They also offer a chart of where many of these companies are located, for $5 at bookstores, or $3 if purchased with a subscription (a total subscription price of $18).

Again, we've used the higher figure in the proposed budget.

THE LOS ANGELES ACTORS GUIDE/DRAMA-LOGUE GUIDE

The *Los Angeles Actors Guide* is another of those handy annual directories lovingly put together by one author, in this case Noreen Sims. It includes detailed information about various agencies' and theatres' policies, workshops, photographers, even where to get a personalized makeup/hairstyle session. Costs $6.95 at the drama bookstores and others.

Information on theatres and workshops can also be found in the *Drama-Logue Guide to Southern California Theatre*, an annual insert in that weekly paper (Christmas issue).

TRADES SUBSCRIPTION

There are, basically, four trades: the *Daily Variety*, the *Hollywood Reporter*, *Drama-Logue*, and *Entertainment Monthly*. We have included a subscription to one of these in your budget.

- *Drama-Logue:* This weekly newspaper is an excellent source of information as to who's casting what. It is invaluable if you are trying to get into a stage play. It also runs features, news, casting announcements for student and other films, and ads by photographers, acting workshops, voice coaches, and the like. The staff admits there have been times when subscribers have gotten their issues too late to audition for some shows. This is apparently a post office problem, but it's probably best to get your copy at the newsstand. It comes out Wednesday evenings at some newsstands, Thursdays at most.

- *Entertainment Monthly:* This is a general information periodical that comes out monthly. It contains interviews and features on people and companies involved in commercial production and is a great source for learning more about that aspect of the industry; however, it is moving into other areas, too, especially cable. Subscription or newsstand.

- *The Daily Variety/the Hollywood Reporter:* These are the daily newspapers for anyone involved in show business on the West Coast. They contain news stories; articles; box-office records; ads for actors, agencies, etc.; and reading at least one of them can be invaluable. We won't get into the continuing debate as to which is "better," but we will say you needn't subscribe to both. Above all, on Thursdays both papers print a list of television shows (staffs, producers, directors, casting directors), and on Fridays they print the same sort of information regarding motion pictures that are in (or about to go into) production.

POSTCARDS

When you are going to be in something, or you want to call attention to, say, a change in agents—or merely want to remind people of your existence this is one form of doing it.

It's simply a photo of yourself, cut to postcard size, with a photo on the front and blank space on the back for you to write or have your message printed.

We used to be really enthusiastic about this method of publicizing yourself. It was cheap and effective. However, with widening use, postcards may not be as useful as they used to be. "I get so many of these a day," says casting director Ron Stephenson. "You want my honest opinion? It's a waste of a lot of stamps." Add to this the fact that they're no longer inexpensive (right—what is?) and we have to admit our enthusiasm has waned a bit. Still, they remain the most practical, unpesky reminders actors have to work with.

GOOD TYPEWRITER

Besides eliminating the need to have your résumé typed by a pro each time you get a job, a good typewriter is a darn good investment. Your letters will look better, and you'll feel better about sending them. Also, there are tax advantages (see Appendix A, 4). Sounds pretty good to us.

DESK

This is more for your attitude than anything else. After all, you can work from the kitchen table if you want to. It's just nice to have a spot of which you can say, "This is where I go to work on my career." In any case, it will help to designate some area of your apartment as your "career area," preferably near the phone.

CALENDAR DATE BOOK

At this stage in your career, you'll probably find it hard to believe that you might forget an appointment with an agent or casting director. However, as you move through your career, you'll find that it *is* possible—especially if you're going out a lot and seeing a lot of people.

An appointment book will prevent this dire event from crossing your karma.

Furthermore, you will see later how vital that book can be in regard to your income tax return.

By the way, SAG puts out a wonderful datebook at the beginning of each year. Besides the calendar date section, it includes many rules, regulations in regard to payment, work, etc., that you should find an excellent reference guide. The going price in 1983 was $7.50—but get one as soon as it's published (November-December of each year). They go fast.

VIDEOCASSETTE

Whenever you are going to appear in something on television or motion pictures, have a videotape copy made of your performance—regardless of the size of the part.

Increasingly, these videotapes are being used by casting directors, producers, agents, and directors in the decision-making process as to whether to cast you or take you on as a client. After all, a videotape doesn't require making an appointment with the actor; the interested party can view your work at his convenience, without the added pressure of your presence. In short, having a videotape of your work is becoming as important as having a good résumé shot.

- *If the part is on a television show*—*"air checks"*: Notify, in advance, any of the many companies capable of making videotaped copies and tell them you want an "air check." They'll need to know: the name of the show, the day, time, and approximate length.

When the show airs on TV, they make a copy for you. Later, you'll have this copy-edited down to include only your scenes, the name of the show, and your billing (if the billing was special). Nobody wants to sit down for twenty minutes, waiting for you to appear.

- *If the part is a motion picture:* If you don't want to wait the year or so that it will take for the picture to be aired on television, or if you are in something that will never be on TV (industrials, out-of-town commercials, student films, etc.), try to get a copy of at least your scenes from the producer or director. Most companies capable of doing air checks are also capable of transferring film onto tape.

  Unfortunately, if the movie is a major one, the chances of your getting a copy are two: slim and none. You'll probably have to wait until the film is televised. If the motion picture is an industrial or a student film or tape, your chances are much better. Indeed, if it is a student film or tape, you'll be working for free—and asking for a copy as part of the deal is not unreasonable.

- *Presentation tapes:* Once you've been around long enough to accumulate a number of scenes from different movies or TV shows on tape, you'll want to have these scenes re-edited into a "presentation tape."

  This is a ten-minute tape that shows you doing many different characters in quick succession, in order to give the viewer an idea of your range and abilities as an actor. Thus, as you go through your career, tape everything, regardless of how small the part and regardless of how you think you did—including commercials. You'll be surprised at how a bunch of bit parts can impress when edited properly into a presentation tape.

- *Some additional thoughts:* It's not a good idea to have a pal do the taping unless he's a pro with professional equipment. Besides the irreparable mistakes that can happen, you should know that all your tape should be on three-quarter-inch videotape—not half-inch videotape (and most home videotape machines are half-inch).

  The industry is just as interested in the quality of the tape itself as it is in your performance(s). If your tape is of poor quality, they will consider it unprofessional and simply won't watch it.

  Speaking of quality, there are many companies that will videotape a three-to-five-minute scene you have prepared with an acting partner. Since these companies charge $300 and up, and since the quality of the work often leaves something to be desired, we recommend against doing this. Most of the industry people we interviewed said they were interested only in seeing tapes of professional work, done under professional conditions (lighting, sets, etc.—though student films are acceptable). If they want to see you doing a prepared scene, they can simply call you in and have you do the scene live. Finally, as Susan Glicksman, Director of Casting, West Coast, ABC-TV, suggests, "Have your best things first." You won't want to risk a busy executive turning you off before you ever got "on."

We've included this information on the first year's budget just in case you get really lucky and win that first job in your first year.

THEATRE AND CLASSES

As we said on the budget, only you can decide what you need and what you can spend.

That's it. Once you've got all these supplies, save for postcards, composites, and videotape, which probably will come later, you're ready to get started on your career—except for one other supply item: your attitudes.

9 ATTITUDES: NEED—THE CAREER KILLER

Have "screw you" money.

Barry Shear, Producer/Director

You are about to read what we feel is the single most important sentence in this book. It is our *best* advice.

Don't need the work. If you need the work, you won't get the work.

Time and again we hear stories concerning how actors got their jobs, and after boiling these stories down, we discovered that the reason most actors get jobs has something to do with a lack of need—a lack of desperation and a sense that the job just wasn't all that important to them.

Now, for most actors, the problem is not so much in the understanding of the concept, but in the practice of it. After all, the hardest thing (especially for honest people) is to pretend you don't need something when you really do. Thus, the key to this is not so much in *pretending* that you don't need the work but in honestly *not* needing it.

How do you honestly not need the work? Okay. First, as Mr. Shear put it (although a bit more strongly)

HAVE "SCREW YOU" MONEY

Earlier, we mentioned that the starving-actor routine was a lot of nonsense and could be harmful to your career. Now we'll take that a step further and say that it *will* be harmful—disastrous. Starving actors only continue to starve.

Producers, directors, and casting directors are all looking for people who can handle pressure. The actor who needs the job to pay his rent has additional pressures on him that have nothing to do with the "shoot." Consequently, the actor blows takes and readings—not because he's a bad actor but because that job is too important to him. It shows, and he doesn't get the job.

Besides, you can't make intelligent decisions when you're hungry. For example, sooner or later, you're going to want to advance up the ladder. This might mean turning down a two- or three-line "day player" part. (It's said that careers are made in this industry by how many times an actor says no.) If you keep accepting these kinds of roles, you may wake up one morning to discover that's how the industry views you—as a "day player." But how can you turn down a part if that's all that stands between you and eviction?

There are hundreds of examples we could use, all leading to one conclusion: work for it; beg for it; "glumb" it from your parents—but *don't need the money.* "Have a backup," says Mark Locher, associate editor of Screen Actor Publications (of SAG). "Have a sideline or some other source of income so that you'll have something to fall back on when acting gets thin, because it certainly does for everybody." And, as Georg Duuglas, special assistant to the president of AGVA, put it, "Be financially stable so that you're not vulnerable to all the nonsense that goes on in this town."

HAVE OTHER INTERESTS

If you were to take a survey of working actors, as we did, you'd learn that when they got jobs, it was often because the jobs or auditions "got in the way" of something else they were doing, usually having nothing to do with acting.

When they went to the audition, their minds were more on that "something else," and they were more relaxed and didn't try as hard. The producer or director saw actors who weren't desperate and hired them, little knowing it was concern over who should play first base in the next Little League game or a nagging problem with a sick begonia that kept the actors from being nervous.

Now, we aren't saying don't pursue a career. Certainly, you must make those calls, visit studios, send out photos and résumés, etc. We are saying that there is a difference between dedication and obsession. There are more important things in life than film running through a camera.

Have an avocation. Do something that brings in an extra few bucks on the side. Learn a trade that you can do free-lance, making you your boss for life. Have a hobby. Smell the begonias.

HAVE COURAGE

"Dare to be hated."   Bette Davis, in a TV interview.

We've been to many gatherings of actors where the atmosphere was that of a group of desperate, whipped puppies, gathered together to yap about their "masters" (producers, etc.).

Well, you can join the kennel or learn, early on, to retain your self-respect.

This industry, as every other, has its share of petty, bullying bureaucrats who enjoy "doing a number" on actors. You owe it to yourself not to allow these people to push you around. If someone is rude to you, you don't have to sit there and take it because you're "only an actor" and need the work.

Now please understand that we're not talking about walking around with a chip on your shoulder—then you're being the ugly bully. We're talking about refusing to allow yourself to be somebody's doormat.

If you allow yourself to be walked on, you'll soon get frustrated, hurt, and angry. Frustrated, hurt, and angry actors don't work.

KNOW YOUR PRODUCT

"Most actors don't know their product."   Mac St. Johns, Publicist

. . . And, even more important, try to understand that you *are* a product.

Know what your strong and weak points are. Remember, no actor is right for every part. If you look like "Auntie Em," don't try to sell yourself as the next "Dorothy" and then complain about what a rotten business this is when nobody buys.

It's not an easy thing to do, but try not to take rejections personally. If you were selling a Mercedes but your customer was in the market for a Cadillac, we doubt you'd take that as a personal affront.

When you don't get that part or agent, it simply means that they weren't in the market for a Mercedes that week.

KNOW YOU KNOW IT

"Know your craft."   Ralph Senensky, Director

There's no way around it. Some dues will have to be paid.

You're going to have to study hard and work at your craft. You're going to have to go through the pain of doing badly before you do well. Far better that you make your mistakes before you declare yourself a pro.

Sooner or later, you'll be asked to show what you can do, either at an audition or in a professional job. If you need knowledge and experience, a little voice from somewhere inside you will scream, "Dear God, I'm not ready for this."

Know you're ready—know it in your gut.

SET DAILY, CONCRETE, AND ATTAINABLE GOALS

"Try to do at least one thing a day to help your career."

Merritt Blake, Theatrical Agent

Taking off for weekends and holidays, if you do what Mr. Blake suggests, you will have done 250 things to help your career at the end of your first year. That's about 248½ more things than many of your fellow actors will have done. Why?

Well, ask an actor what he really wants, and he'll most likely say, "To be a working actor." Ask him how he intends to achieve that and his eyes glaze over.

Most actors spend a lot of time spinning their wheels because they don't really know where they're going. Their goals—if they have any—are usually very foggy in their own minds.

It's a lot smarter to say, "Okay. At the end of my first year, I want to have obtained all the supplies I need, gotten an agent, and gone on one interview."

Then, if you're really smart, you'll break that list down into monthly, weekly, and daily goals.

Don't try to set "goals for life." They're not concrete. There are too many unknowns out there that can completely change your life. Make your goals *concrete, attainable,* and *daily.*

We once talked to a recovering alcoholic. This is what he said: "If I thought I could never take another drink for the rest of my life, I'd be back on the booze in a minute. I couldn't deal with that. The only way I can stay sober is to do what Alcoholics Anonymous teaches—I take it *one day at a time.*"

GET OFF YOUR OWN BACK

"Don't worry about it. Alfred Hitchcock always used to say, 'It's only a movie.'"

Angie Dickinson to an actor
who had just blown a take on the "Policewoman" set

One of the most therapeutic things an actor can do is to take a cold reading class. Why? Because, by watching others, he learns that he's not the only one who ever screwed up a reading.

We actors are amazing. If we're not yelling at our agents, we're inwardly screaming at ourselves. *Everybody* seems to be working more—and working better.

Try not to get down on yourself. If you make a mistake or do a bad audition/interview/performance, go home, kick a door, and forget it. Nothing is life or death. Everybody screws up.

Remember that Babe Ruth struck out far more often than he ever hit the ball . . . but also remember what he is remembered for.

Sooner or later, you'll get "good wood" on the ball.

NONWORKING ACTORS

"Earlier, I heard you say not to hang around with nonworking actors. I'd like to hug you for saying that."

Fran O'Bryan, Theatrical/Commercial Agent

Welcome to Negative City. Population: thousands. Points of interest: none. (After all, it can't be done.)

The greatest spur in the butt is to be around people who can do and are doing. They'll inspire you to do more, if for no other reason than that they are living proof that things *can* be done.

The only things you'll learn from people who are failing is how to fail. They're magnificent at teaching all the ways things can't be done. Worse, stated or not, they don't want you to succeed. They'll "commiserate" you into doing nothing.

Birds of a feather . . . need together.

ALWAYS ACT SUCCESSFUL

Q: "What mistake do you continually see actors making?"
A: "Being too hungry."

Ruth Robinson, Associate Editor,
Hollywood Reporter

This doesn't mean be cocky—that's just a mask for the insecure. And it doesn't mean you've got to drive a Mercedes and wear Gucci loafers.

It means giving those in the position to hire you a feeling that they can be confident in you because you know your value.

Agents should feel that if they don't take you on they're making a big mistake. Casting directors, producers, and directors should get the impression that you just never stop working. Present yourself as a successful working pro, even when times are tough. Act as if you've "made it" long before you have.

As actor Edmund Gilbert puts it: "Be there before you get there."

AVOID NEGATIVE BEHAVIOR

"No matter what, try to be positive."

Jack Rose, President, Jack Rose Agency

There's an old salesman's creed that goes: "To be enthusiastic, act enthusiastic."

If that sounds corny to you, go to a commercial audition sometime. There you'll find a roomful of actors who know that they have to be bright and "up" if they want to get cast. And because everyone is acting so happy and perky, you'll find it very hard to be negative or "down." Enthusiasm is catching.

Conversely, so is negativity . . .

You're going to have to be constantly on your guard against negative behavior—whether in others or in yourself.

Consider this quote from an actor friend of ours: "I never read the trades. The trades make me feel that everybody in this town is working but me."

He has a point. If you find yourself getting upset at all that work out there that you're not getting, then don't read the trades. Not until you can read them again for the positive information you can actually do something about. Too often, actors will read something about a film that has been cast, decide that they weren't up for the part, and immediately pick up the phone to chew out their agent. That's one long series of negative behavior.

Here are some other things to be on the lookout for:

- Don't read reviews of a show you auditioned for and didn't get. (No matter what the reviews say, you'll just get upset. Face it—you're being perverse.)

- Don't go to see a movie, TV show, or play you were "up for" and didn't get (more perversity).

- Don't listen to stories about how a fellow actor didn't get a part or an agent. What a downer! (Our favorite way of handling this was the following overheard conversation: First Actor: "I'm really miserable. I was up for a part and I didn't get it because . . . Second Actor (interrupting): "At least you were up for it, baby.")

- Don't listen to anyone who says you'll never make it. (Unless they've shown a remarkable propensity for walking on water.)

- Don't read bad reviews of a show you are in. (Talk about perversity!)

- Don't fall into "bad mouth" sessions about anyone or any group. (Ever felt better after one of these?)

- Be sure your acting teachers are trying to help you with their criticisms—and not just trying to keep the bucks coming in from a lot of perpetual students or enjoying playing games with your emotions.

- Don't dwell on the mistakes you made. Dwell on what you learned from them.

- If you're not a beginner, stay away from people, groups, or situations that cast you in that light.

- If you're at an audition, don't assume you're wrong for the part. If you're there, you're right for it.

- Don't get secretly mad at your agent because he has other clients. That's what keeps him in business.

- When you are being criticized, always ask yourself first what the other person's motives are.

- Don't enjoy someone else's misfortunes.

- Don't listen to doomsayers.

- Don't work for compliments work for money. (By this we mean, don't keep working at the same theatre or acting class because everybody there thinks you're soooo good. You're nesting if you do that, and you know it.) "Working for the money" means working to improve your pocketbook, your opportunities, or your skills—not merely to get stroked.

Finally, as AGVA official Georg Duuglas said, "My comment to every person who walks into this office is they must keep their self-respect and their dignity."

And, above all . . . *Don't need the work.*

III
THEATRICAL AGENTS

10   What They Are and Do
11   Seeking a Theatrical Agent
12   Choosing a Theatrical Agent
13   Dealing With / Motivating an Agent
14   Changing Agents

10 WHAT THEY ARE AND DO

Nobody pays me to keep people out of work.

Jim Gibson, Theatrical Agent

Do you need an agent? Only if you want to be considered a pro, get paid more than union scale, and have a shot at better billing. And only if you want to work.

When casting, the studios, casting directors, producers, and directors of Los Angeles hate crowds. (It's hard to be laid back in a mob.) Consequently, they've set up elaborate systems to keep the general acting population *uninformed*. Without an agent, with the exception of an occasional hot tip from a friend or the trades, you'll miss out on most jobs simply because you won't know they're there.

Perhaps most important, however, once you get an agent to represent you, you cross a very important psychological barrier. You become a legitimate professional; someone (else) in the industry believes in your talent. One producer said out loud what most industry people feel when he said, "I get leery of actors without agents."

There are about six different kinds of agents, each handling performers in different areas of the business. No matter what his special field, he is still a salesman whose product is talent:

- *Theatrical agent:* Television and motion pictures.
- *Commercial agent:* On-camera work in commercials.
- *Legitimate agent:* Theatre.
- *Voice-over agent:* Radio and off-camera work involving only the actor's voice for commercials, cartoons, announcing, and radio drama.
- *Modeling agent:* Models, and often print work (magazine ads, billboards, other print media), although this can be handled separately.
- *Variety agent:* Nightclub work, personal appearances, etc.

Your main concern, if you're like most actors, will be to obtain a theatrical agent and a commercial agent—that's where most of your income as an actor will be found.

In Los Angeles, you may sign with only one agent per category. (There is no such limitation in New York.) That is to say, you may sign with one

89

agency to handle you in all fields, but you may not have several commercial agents, several theatrical agents, etc.

WHAT A THEATRICAL AGENT DOES

The typical theatrical agent has about fifty actors in his "stable." (That's the term. Well, it *is* a horse race.) Each morning, between slurps of coffee, the agent looks over one of his primary tools for finding his clients work: the Breakdown Service.

Since acquiring and reading entire scripts is extremely time-consuming, this service has become invaluable in providing agents and personal managers with a summary of all roles found in scripts about to go into production. The information includes a list of parts, the size of every part, and a brief description of every character. The service is not available to actors. It is also no guarantee that any role listed has not already been cast.

From the descriptions found in the Breakdown Service, the agent decides which, if any, of his clients are "right" for the various parts.

With a typewritten submission sheet and pictures and résumés of the actors whose names he's submitting under his arm, the agent then visits the casting director, or has his submissions delivered.

The casting director checks the submissions and says yea or nay based on his reading of the script and what the producer and/or director has told him about the part. Most often, the answer is nay: the part has been cast; or the casting director thinks the actor is wrong for the part; or the casting director doesn't know, like, or trust the agent. (It isn't uncommon for an agent to be unable to see some casting directors.)

Faced with a turndown, the agent may try to change the casting director's mind, or he may submit another actor for the part (theatrical agent Colee Viedelle calls this "the Fuller Brush approach to agenting"), or he may fold his tent and slip away. Rarely will an agent go over a casting director's head to the producer or director, as he knows this won't exactly endear him to the casting director, with whom he must deal again on other projects.

If, however, the agent gets a yea, a time is set for the actor to audition. If the actor gets the part, some serious dickering will take place between agent and casting director, primarily over salary and billing. The actor won't take part in the actual negotiations; the agent will call him only to get a thumbs-up or thumbs-down on the deal.

After the actor does the job, his agent receives 10 percent of his *gross* earnings. He is *never* paid in advance. When the actor is paid, the agent is paid—*and not a moment before.*

The rest of the agent's day is one long series of phone calls from clients, reading contracts, interviewing potential clients, strategy meetings with fellow workers, etc. But when the sun sets in the west, he gets to go home, right? Wrong. He's off to see one of his clients perform in a play. These dervishes really whirl.

ABOUT LEGITIMATE AGENTS

These are the agents who handle stage work. The problem here is simply the lack of paying work within the city. "The opportunities to make a living in L.A. theatre are almost nil," says legitimate/theatrical agent Larry Fonseca. If you sign with a legitimate agent, he'll probably want you to agree to go out of town if you are cast, as that's where most of the work will be. But while you're strutting the boards in Birmingham, the rest of your career will be on hold. You take the money and make your choice. In any case, the information in this section basically holds true both for theatrical and for legitimate agents.

A WORD OF ADVICE

If you don't have the right qualifications—good photos, a decent résumé, and a SAG card—unless you're under twenty-one and look it, you're wasting your time. As one agent bluntly put it: "What makes an actor think he qualifies for film work when he's done no films and has few or no theatre credits?"

Postpone the Great Agent Hunt until you've gotten some experience. In the meantime, if you have a good smiling photo, you might try for a commercial agent. Since many commercials don't involve lines, commercial agents are more receptive to a beginner who has no credits but has a look or personality they think will sell. (Again, unless you're a youngster or have a *very* special look, you'll probably need a union card, at least AFTRA.)

Too often, we've heard actors in a beginning acting class talk about how they need to get an agent. A one-year-old horse doesn't need a jockey. He needs a trainer.

11 SEEKING A THEATRICAL AGENT

*The relationship between the actor and
the agent can be summed up in two
words: hot pursuit. It's the actor's job to
attack and attack again until he gets the
attention of someone in the industry who
can do him some good.*

Michael Campus, Producer/Director

Put on a hard hat 'cause some large chunks of stone wall are about to
bounce off your head. Agents have far more experience turning you down
than you have convincing them to sign you. When you're starting out,
merely getting one to see you will be a time for buttered popcorn all
around.

When you hear the dusty old line "Sorry, we're not taking on any new
clients at this time," however, bear in mind that agents are always/never
taking on new clients, and there's no room/plenty of room for you. (Let
Paul Newman walk into an agent's office, and room will be found for him.)
If you can act, have experience and a SAG card, there is an agent for you. It
just might take many miserable months to find him.

A WORD OF WARNING

To avoid getting ripped off, never sign with any agent who isn't union-
franchised. A franchised agent has agreed to abide by all union regulations,
and you'll be protected from most unethical practices. Once you're union,
in fact, you aren't allowed to sign with a nonfranchised agent even if you've
gone too long without a sun hat and want to.

If you are interested in a particular theatrical (movies/TV) agency, check
your list of franchised agents. If its name is not included, call SAG (ask for
"Agencies"); perhaps the agency received its franchise after the list was
published. If the agency you want is legitimate (stage), call Equity.

Most agents hire additional personnel, called subagents. SAG and Equity
list them as such, and they need not be franchised as long as the agency for
which they work is franchised.

A word of warning: in your hunt for an agent, you may run across so-
called "agents" or "agency-finder services," often using impressive-sound-
ing names like "Galactic Representatives International." They prey on the

unwary actor. They guarantee jobs; demand money for ads in their "magazines," which, they promise, will be seen by everyone in the industry from Louis B. Mayer (So what if he's dead?) to the washerwoman at William Morris (Who knows? She may be casting something next week); set you up with photos for a mere $500 or so; offer acting classes that teach you to stand in a corner scratching and moaning. The very worst of the lot can even be fronts for prostitution. How can you avoid the sharks in the water?

If an "agent" ever asks you for money, run, don't walk, out of his office. An agent on the up-and-up makes his money from one source only: *10 percent of what you make, after you make it.* Your best protection is that franchise. If the agent isn't franchised, don't sign. Period.

THE SIMPLEST WAY

... To get an interview with any agent is to have a producer, director, or casting director put in a good word for you. Even a represented fellow actor can sometimes help. If you're an acquaintance of anyone in the industry, *ask.* A referral won't guarantee the agent will sign you, or even see you, but it can't hurt.

THE DIRECT WAY

This method isn't a lot of fun, involves a lot of work, and gets old fast. It's only got one thing going for it. It works.

Take the list of franchised agents, scratch off the top dogs such as William Morris and ICM, and mail your picture, résumé, and a cover letter to the first ten of the remaining agencies on the list.

Here's a sample—not the only way to do it.

Dear ___:

> Your agency has been recommended to me a number of times in my search for representation in Los Angeles. A look through the *Academy Players Directory* seems to indicate you have no one quite like me, so I enclose photos and résumé for your consideration.
> I'll call in a week or so, and hope we can get together for a chat.
> Also, do you have a favorite Equity Waiver theatre?
>
> Very truly yours,

You'll notice the letter is brief. Use just about any approach that's comfortable to you without getting silly, negative, braggadocious, or giving the impression you can outgush Ol' Faithful. And remember, your letter reveals something about your common sense. "Anyone who can't spell 'Dear Mary Spencer' is out," dryly notes Ms. Spencer, a theatrical agent.

The following week, pick out the next ten agents on the list, send them letters, résumés, and photos, and start calling the original ten agents you wrote. For the next six months or so, you'll be calling and mailing to ten agents a week. Expect 99 percent rejection. And a few "Can you call us back?" responses. And back . . . and back . . . and back. . .

Sound awful? It is. That's why there are more unrepresented actors than represented ones. Many actors try this approach for a week or so, quit, then wail, "Ya can't get an agent."

A variation is the old dropping-in method. Most often it doesn't work, but you never know. You may not get to see an agent, but you can leave your photo, résumé, and a personal impression—if only on the receptionist. And all that walking is a great way to lose weight.

Whether you're dropping by or phoning, you're going to be talking to a lot of secretaries. This brings us to . . .

SECRETARIES AND THE BRICK-WALL SYNDROME

Today's secretary is tomorrow's agent, casting director, or producer, and taking them for granted is like eating ice cream on a diet. You'll be aghast at where it shows up later.

Secretaries control access to agents, casting directors, and producers. Whether they throw broken glass or roses in your path is up to you.

Begin by understanding that they're constantly dealing with actors, in person and on the phone. Consequently, they've developed pretty good defenses. You'll sense that tone of indifference the minute you start talking. Without getting obnoxious, find a way to catch their attention. Learn and use their names. Ask questions. Try to involve them in conversation. Most of the time they'll be too busy to talk and, if they are, leave or hang up. Every once in a while, though, you'll catch a secretary during a lull. Then it's time to make a friend.

What you are striving for, remember, is a businesslike amiability—a scaredy-cat "I'll-just-die-if-you-reject-me" air isn't going to sell you any better than the hotshot bullyboy approach. As casting coordinator Tawn Holstra put it: "The thing about telephones is that the fears of the people on the other end come through. I mean, I'm not going to bite you. You can ask me things and you don't have to be afraid of me. There's nothing I can do to you on the phone. Nothing."

And regardless of whom you wind up speaking with, bear in mind these two tips from theatrical agent Vikki Bandlow: "When the actor calls, he usually calls in slow motion. Get it out." And: "Everything's so heavy in this business. If someone can get me to laugh on the phone, I'll have him in. I love to laugh!"

It is going to be much easier having a business conversation, of course, if you have specific business to talk about. Which brings us to:

PERFORMING YOUR WAY TO AN AGENT

By this we mean performing in something the agent can see and like.

Theatre: We can't stress too strongly the importance of doing theatre in Los Angeles. We know many actors who have gotten agents, roles, even that proverbial big break while emoting before a full house of twenty people. You "old pros," new only to the Hollywood scene, may balk at this. You may feel you've proven yourselves on stages all over the country, and advice to do more stage work—in small theatres no less—is insulting and a waste of time. After all, you came to Hollywood for film work! Do it anyway. Nobody wants to buy a ham in a poke—unless they see you act, how do they know if you're an experienced, interesting actor or one who's merely left audiences comatose from coast to coast?

As opening night approaches send out letters or postcards to every casting director and agent in town. A sample:

Dear _____ :

This is to invite you and a guest of your choice to the upcoming production of ___PLAY___ at ___THEATRE & ADDRESS___ . We open on ___DATE___ and close on ___DATE___ . All performances start at ___TIME___ .

Consider this letter as your "tickets" for any night of your choosing. (Please do call and make a reservation to ensure we hold two good seats for you.)

I play ___CHARACTER___ , and appear ___ONLY IN ACT I,___ THROUGHOUT THE PLAY, ETC.___ .

Please do come. I believe you'll have a thoroughly enjoyable evening.

Sincerely,

If the theatre won't grant complimentary tickets, make an agreement with the box office that you'll pay for any tickets given away to people using these letters.

- *Equity productions:* If you are cast in an Equity show in Los Angeles, you may assume that there will be industry professionals in at least some of your audiences. Unfortunately, because there's so little paying theatre in the city, you've probably got a better chance of being cast in a movie or TV show.

- *Community theatre:* You already know this is off limits to union members. If you do it anyway, bear in mind that getting industry people to community theatre may be difficult. Agents aren't all that interested in seeing a cast composed mostly of insurance executives doing theatre as a hobby; their chances of picking up a client are slim. Still, you might get lucky; someone may come to the show because he's a friend of a cast member. Be sure the theatre keeps a guest book (buy one for them if they don't), and check it every night.

- *Equity waiver:* You may do this kind of theatre whether you are union or not. (More on this in Chapter 26.)

  The theatre will seat 99 or fewer, you'll probably be unpaid or even charged dues, but if it's a good production and well publicized, your chances of being seen by industry people are decent to excellent, depending upon reviews and the reputation of the house.

- *Movie or TV show:* Are we kidding? No, actors do luck into these even without agents. Just be sure you've got lines—extra work doesn't count. If you're in a movie, you may be surprised to find it does you little good before it opens; when it does, however, send out your letters or postcards, wait a few weeks, then call back. If it's a hit, work hard and fast—everyone connected with such a film is to some degree hot, a profitable state of affairs both rare and fleeting. Don't waste such an opportunity—it may be five years before you get another like it.

  If you are in a TV show, include the day and time of the show in your letter. You can get this information from the producer's office. Television books well in advance. Also include approximately when you'll make your appearance; no one wants to sit through fifty minutes waiting for your three-minute part. Call every agent a day or so before the show airs to remind him. After it airs, call back and ask for an appointment. We know—aargh. But it works.

No matter what your vehicle, don't make the romantic (or lazy) mistake of sitting back, waiting for agents to contact you. Go after them.

OTHER METHODS OF GETTING AN AGENT

Showcases

You and a partner prepare a scene, audition it, and, if accepted, perform it later before a small but choice audience of agents, casting directors, and the like. The best known of these is "Performers Audition Showcase" (980-

2740). They charge $85 per person. There are other showcases, of widely varying quality; to find them, see *Drama-Logue,* but check them out before you pay a dime. A good showcase (one well attended by the industry) can be a potent boost to your career. A bad one merely lines someone else's pockets with your money.

Classes/Seminars

Attending seminars with agents as speakers can be helpful. Ask questions. Make the speaker notice you. Afterward, go up and introduce yourself, and see if you can wheedle an appointment. We've seen it work.

You can also take an acting class and, once you've proven how good you are, ask your instructor (especially if he's a casting director) or even a fellow student for a recommendation. Be aware, however, that the teacher is usually flooded with such requests and has only so many favors he can ask of his connections.

If you are already well trained, you might take a class that invites industry people to come and watch/teach/comment. (These are not to be confused with classes that *promise* jobs or recommendations—avoid those!) On the whole, however, take classes to learn, to stretch, to take chances in private, away from judgmental industry eyes—not to impress in hopes that someone will do something for you. Besides, if you're not "ready," the play can backfire, emphasizing your limitations instead of your strengths. You are, after all, presenting yourself as a student, a rather weak introduction for a "future star" unless you are very young.

Serendipity

Finally, there are as many different ways of seeking an agent as your imagination can come up with, from sending flowers (it's been done but is rather obvious) to taking out a billboard on Sunset Boulevard (also not recommended—it's silly). A genuinely fresh approach can be charming, such as that offered by publicist Barbara Best: to a single agent of your choice, send one genuinely funny greeting card every day for 30 days. When you're done, he should certainly be interested at least in meeting you! And, of course, socialize; make friends and contacts.

All these methods have worked and will work—if you really go at them. That's the key: how hard you try.

INTERVIEW WITH A THEATRICAL AGENT

Lo and behold, you have an interview. Unless the agent is merely doing a friend a favor in seeing you, the thing to bear in mind is that, while he isn't ready yet to sign on the old dotted, you have at least piqued his interest. There's something about you, your pictures, résumé, and/or performance that is "special" and can possibly fill a gap in his client list. Now he wants to size you up as a professional. Do you have craft? Intelligence? Knowledge? Common sense? Can he send you out on a job or interview without your making a fool of yourself—and him? He'll want you to be confident—not cocky—and to come through with poise when you meet important people or when the cameras roll. And he'll want you to be pleasant to be around— the last we heard, "Grumpy" still doesn't have an agent.

If he hasn't seen your work and you have no videotape on yourself, the agent may ask you to do a "cold reading" or an "office scene" for him. (More about interviews, cold readings, and office scenes in the next section; they are crafts in themselves, and you'll be doing a lot of them for casting directors, producers, and directors as well.)

O.K. The interview went smoothly. A few days or a week has passed, the agent has done his thinking and discussed you with his associates, and he has decided he wants to take you on. Now the question is: Do you want *him?*

12 CHOOSING A THEATRICAL AGENT

Just because someone shows an interest in you doesn't mean he's necessarily the best person for you.

Jerry Cohn, Personal Manager

It's hard to relate to "Choose your agent carefully" when you're thinking "I'll be glad to, as soon as I can get one to talk to me." And, when an agent shows some interest, it's even harder not to leap into his arms screaming "Take me!"

If only one franchised agent is interested in you, sign with him. Still, find out who you're getting involved with. A franchise tells you only that the agent is basically on the up and up. It doesn't say that he's any good or that he's right for you. Even if you were buying the last car on earth, you'd still want to know how it runs.

CHECKING OUT AN AGENT

There's no Better Business Bureau for agents; but fellow actors, instructors, and other industry people you know can be of help. If you run across a client, you might ask him if he's happy with the agent; if he gets out on interviews; if he's treated courteously; if he has easy access to the agent. Bear in mind that every agent is hated and loved by someone. No one opinion should be considered absolute.

Conflicts / clients

When it comes time for submissions, you won't want your agent choosing between you and another actor who also fits the part. That's called a "conflict."

Conflicts are not so crucial in commercials, and commercial agents usually have several clients of every type. Theatrical agents, however, often will turn you down if you are a direct conflict with one of their clients. With those who are not so scrupulous, a little checking can save you grief. You have enough competition *outside* your agency!

Find a copy of the *Academy Players Directory* and turn to the section that displays your glorious mug. If you spot a conflict, mention it to the agent. The conflict may have left his agency. Or the agent may see you differently. Can you live with that viewpoint? If not, don't sign.

It's also true that agencies get typecast too; some are known for handling character actors, others for "beautiful people," others for ethnic groups, and so on. Some agencies mix their talent. You'll want to be compatible with what they're known for; if not, when a casting director is in a desperate hurry for your general category of actor, he won't be calling your agency first.

While you're looking at the directory, try to get a general impression of the agent's clientele. Do his clients look sharp? Professional? Have you ever seen any of them on screen? How about the quality of the photographs? A spate of poor pictures indicates: the agent's ability to pick people who know what they're doing is suspect; the agent doesn't bother to check the directory and insist his clients change those poor photos; or at the very least, the agent can't choose photos. That may not knock him out of the box, but it does tell you something about his taste.

Number of clients

According to SAG rules, all agents must present their client lists to prospective clients on demand. If you want to be more diplomatic, however, pop over to SAG and ask to see the agency's client list.

No theatrical agent can adequately handle more than about 50 people. (If there are two theatrical agents in the agency, they can handle 100 actors; three can handle 150; and so on.) Fewer clients are better, but agencies who take on newcomers are gambling and seeking fiscal safety in numbers. More than 50 clients, however, and you're not signing with an agent; you're signing with a meat market. The agent's probably hoping you get lucky finding work on your own.

It's irrelevant how many people are signed in other departments of your agency, such as the commercials department (which, by the way, can legitimately handle more clients per agent than the theatrical department). Therefore, when you look at SAG's list, check the code sheet: next to each actor's name will be a number corresponding to a number on the code sheet, which will tell you in what department he is signed.

Office/employees

You can learn a lot by keeping your eyes and ears open when you go for your interview. What is the general atmosphere of the office? Dead? Alive with activity? Are the people warm or cold? Polite? Rude? Happy? Miserable? Does the receptionist seem to know what she's doing, and does she

treat you with courtesy? The appearance of the office: is it neat or sloppy? Cheap? Gaudy? How about the agent's stationery—does it show class? All these things are direct reflections on the boss and will tell you a great deal about how you'll be treated as a client.

INTERVIEWING THE AGENT

Once the agent is finished interviewing you, you'll want to gently "interview" him by asking . . .

How he sees you

If you're thinking in terms of Sean Connery roles and he's talking Quasimodo, something's wrong. Within bounds, there should be agreement on the kinds of roles he'll be submitting you for. If he's too far off the mark, you might do better passing.

How often he wants or expects you to contact him

We know an agent who answered that question by saying, "My clients are only to call me between 9:20 and 9:40 A.M." Well now, wait a minute— who's working for whom? It's one thing for an agent to ask his clients to call him only in the morning or in the late afternoon; it's quite another to give a 20-minute time span. That agent's answer told us he was not only a bureaucrat but a bully as well.

A good agent will tell you he wants to hear from you. He welcomes ideas. He won't want you to call every day, but he will be open to suggestions. If you get the feeling an agent "doesn't want to be bothered," don't "bother" him by signing.

How much independent seeking of work/auditions/contacts he expects you to do

When you're starting out, your agent will expect a lot. As you move on, perhaps a little less. But neither party should ever be expected to do it all. Some agents will tell you not to seek interviews on your own, as they feel this is "bad form." If so, go along. Wait a few months. If the interviews are coming in, fine. If not, go back to work. You can starve playing by someone else's rules.

After the interview, it's time for a mull or two. Was the agent straight with you? Did you catch him in any lies? Did he ignore you? (We know an actor who went to lunch with a prospective agent and his subagent. They spent the entire lunch talking about what a great deal they had just gotten for another actor.) Was there a degree of rapport? A sense of humor? You don't have to love your agent—perhaps not even like him—but at the very least you should be able to respect him a little.

And go with your gut—agents do. Often, they'll accept or reject an actor strictly on gut instinct. If a small voice tells you something's right or wrong— something's right or wrong.

OTHER SUGGESTIONS

- *Agency Size:* If your agent handles Barbra Streisand, who makes millions per movie, and you, who makes $400, who's he going to work for? There's even an expression for this: "Buried in your own agency." While the William Morrises and ICM probably won't even want to talk to you, you'd likely be making a mistake to sign with them when starting out anyway. Until you've made a name for yourself, you'll want a small or mid-size agency that is excited about working for you.

- *Try not to sign with one individual in more than one category of representation:* No single soul can adequately be a commercial agent and a theatrical agent at the same time. For each category, it's best to have a different person representing you. This doesn't mean you can't have a commercial agent and a theatrical agent in the same agency, of course—as long as there's a different person doing each job.

- *However, it's also best to sign with different agencies for each category:* Things can get a bit sticky if you're happy with your commercial agent and unhappy with your theatrical agent, and they're both working for the same agency.

- *Verbal agreements:* To put it bluntly, if your prospective agent tells you, "We won't have a contract; we'll just have a verbal agreement," you don't have an agent. He's waiting: if you fall into a part, he'll be glad to take 10 percent. As Samuel Goldwyn is said to have put it, "A verbal agreement ain't worth the paper it's printed on."

  On the other hand, if that's all you can get at first, take it—but keep looking for an agent willing to put it in writing. SAG says the verbal agreement is good for three months, but you are unlikely to have problems if you want to sign with another agent within that time. (In practice, the agreement can last as long as you and the agent can live with it.)

  Write the agent a letter confirming your verbal agreement, with a copy to all the unions, and list him as your agent in the Academy *Players Directory.* This way, potential employers will be able to find your representative, and you will appear more professional.

- *The agent's enthusiasm:* Key ingredient in choosing an agent: the excitement factor. An agent's enthusiasm over your potential can cover a multitude of sins. If all his clients hate him, if he doesn't work for anybody else, if he's not very pleasant to be around, but he's excited about you and works for you—you've got a good agent.

Having said all this, we must go back to the advice we gave you at the beginning of the chapter: when you're starting out, sign with any franchised agent who wants you—and if you're unhappy, keep looking for another, better agent. A cardinal rule of show-biz psychology is: It's easier to find an agent when you already have one.

Besides, you have an out in . . .

THE CONTRACTS

Lurking in all three contracts you'll be signing with your theatrical agent is a provision that basically says that *if you don't get 15 days of work in any*

91-day period, you or your agent may terminate the contract (Paragraph 6).
There's your "out." It came about because actors didn't want to be saddled with an agent for a year if the agent obviously was not working for them.

There's also a provision in the two SAG contracts that says if the actor has a multiyear contract with an agent, he can fire the agent on the yearly "anniversary" (the day he signed) of the contract, regardless of whether or not the actor is working. (This last provision is *not* in the AFTRA contract, by the way.)

These provisions are there for your protection, and there's nothing to stop you from signing with an agent you're not crazy about only to turn around and look for someone who suits you better, safe in the knowledge that you'll be available in 91 days. It's not the most pleasant thing to do, but neither is looking for an agent when you don't have one.

(Note: The above isn't necessarily true when you sign with a commercial agent. It depends on whether you initial a box on the main contract or a "commercial rider." With the former, it remains the same—15 days' work in 91 days. With the rider, however, this changes to: You must earn $2,000 in any 151-day period. The rider, in other words, holds you to your commercial agent for a slightly longer period of time. In any case, we discuss all agency contracts in more detail in Appendix A.)

13 DEALING WITH/MOTIVATING AN AGENT

Q: When it comes down to it, does the actor work for the agent, or does the agent work for the actor?

A: Well, ideally, both.

Interview with Sandra Siegal,
Theatrical Agent

Overheard conversation:

First Actor: "What should I get my agent for Christmas?"

Second Actor: "A cattle prod."

All of us like to think of ourselves as special, and we tend to get a little bitter when we discover our agent actually has the audacity to sleep at night when we're not working. And when enough sleep-filled nights go by, we start thinking about cattle prods.

Well, that's not the solution—at least, not exactly.

Assume for a moment that your agent has thirty clients. Assume he works ten hours a day. If he treats every client equally, the most he can spend on your career—submitting, talking about, meeting with you, negotiating for you, and so forth—is twenty minutes per day.

Naturally, the amount of time he spends on your career on any given day will vary. But if he takes more than twenty minutes, another client will lose out completely. In other words, there will be many days when your agent simply won't be working for you *at all*.

No matter how hard you work at building a good relationship with your agent, he'll never work as hard for you as you'd like him to. He's not your savior. He's not a career maker. As one agent summed it up: "The prime job of an agent is not to help an actor seek work. It is to negotiate contracts and to open doors."

If you're not working and are thinking of cattle prods, you'll ultimately be a lot happier if you turn them on yourself.

WHAT YOUR AGENT LEGITIMATELY SHOULD EXPECT FROM YOU

- *To get work on your own:* Especially when you're new. Frankly, when you're starting out, you'd do best thinking of your agent as the person you call after you've gotten the job—to negotiate the deal. That way you won't be disappointed when he doesn't call and pleasantly surprised when he comes up with an interview or two.

- *To be active and visible:* Spending your life on the beach will net you two things: a nice tan and no work. Show your talents: do plays, showcases. Stay fresh: take all sorts of classes and seminars. Publicize your activities: if you're in something important enough, take out an ad in the trades *(Hollywood Reporter* and/or *Variety).* If it's a play, send out postcards, résumés, and résumé shots. Theatrical agent Vikki Bandlow says, "I get inspired by someone who's out there doing."

- *Be a fantastic auditioner:* This includes office scenes, cold readings, interviews, look-sees, callbacks, etc. You're entitled to do badly only every once in a while.

- *Be on time and don't miss interviews:* As agent Doris Ross said, "There is nothing worse after you've built up an actor to a casting director for him not to be available for an interview." Your regular job isn't your agent's concern. He's not going to understand that your boss can't spare you from the typing pool.

- *Be "reachable":* That's where answering services, call-forwarding services, and message machines come in. Your agent should be able to talk to you in person no later than thirty minutes after he places his first call to you. "The first time you don't check your service or machine—as God is my witness—is the day you get the call," says theatrical agent Mary Spencer. If you're out, it's best to call the receptionist at your agency (or your answering service) and ask him to check if you're "clear." Also, be sure to notify your agent if you're going out of town.

- *Keep your agent well heeled in résumé and résumé shots:* Periodically check with him to be sure he won't suddenly get caught short.

- *Keep your* Academy Players Directory *listing current.*

- *Keep in touch:* On the average, no more than once a week; no less than once every two weeks. As personal manager Mel Becker commented, "If every client called his agent once a day and spoke to him for five minutes, he'd spend all his time on the phone talking to clients and never get any work done."

- *Come up with ideas:* If you read that a show is casting and you know the producer, it's a good idea to remind your agent. He might not have known that or he may have forgotten.

- *Pay him his commission:* If you get a check directly, remember he's partly responsible for it.

WHAT YOU CAN LEGITIMATELY EXPECT FROM YOUR AGENT

- *To be submitted and talked about:* At the very least! If he's not doing that, he doesn't deserve having you as a client.

- *To be told the truth:* Unfortunately, a lot of smoke is blown at actors—not only about submissions (a very difficult thing for you to check up on) but in the entire actor-agent relationship.

- *To be submitted singly:* If you find that a fellow actor from your agency is auditioning for the same part, check to find out if he was called in by the producer, director, or casting director—or if he was submitted along with you. If the latter is the case, your agent isn't playing fair—not by a long shot.

- *To represent and negotiate for you not only well, but in good faith:* When the agent submits you for a part, he is a salesman. However, when you get a part, suddenly he's got to grow fangs and battle for every dime and piece of billing he can get. But he can't negotiate in a vacuum. He knows that, sooner or later, he's going to be back knocking on the casting director's door with résumé shots in hand, acting like a salesman again.

   Further, you're not his only client. Therefore, Truth, Justice, and the American Way end at the point where the agent is in danger of getting a casting director, producer, or director mad at him. He's going to be somewhat circumspect about going out on a limb for you because if the limb breaks, his entire client list falls down with him.

   This is especially true when it comes to casting directors. According to theatrical agent John Mekrut: "The agent–casting director relationship is funny, subtle, strange . . . you can push them, but you can't push them too far. That's who's going to buy your actors from you and you can't force them to slam the door in your face—which they'll do—ultimately to the detriment of all your clients."

   It's not good strategy to ask your agent constantly to stick his neck out for you, but he shouldn't act like Chicken Little all the time either.

For example, continually asking your agent to go over a casting director's head to the producers you know places the agent's entire client list in jeopardy with the casting director. But if you know a producer will see you for a part and the casting director has refused to call you in, as long as you don't make a habit of it, you'd be right to press your agent to call the producer. If he refuses, he may be too worried about irking people when that could be just the ticket. After all, this is no business for irk-shirkers.

- *He should keep an office, and it should be organized and decent-looking:* Frankly, we're leery of an agent who operates out of his home. It's just not professional. Further, if his office has pictures scattered all over the place, we'd worry about how organized he is and whether we would get lost in the shuffle.Yep, neatness counts. On his stationery, too. And in his submission. And even in the way he dresses.

- *He should return your calls and inquiries:* Unless you're constantly bugging him, of course. We're talking about respect. As one agent remarked: "A lot of agents don't want to hear from their clients—ever. That's notorious in this town. Actors say, 'Well, they didn't call me back at William Morris; now they're not calling me back at ICM.'"

- *He should follow up on your suggestions:* Nothing is more maddening than occasionally to suggest an approach to your career only to have an agent greet it with an excited yawn.

- *He should be interested in and see your work:* When you do a play, movie, or TV show, he should be in the audience. When you put together a $200 presentation tape of your work, he should look at it.

MOTIVATING AN AGENT

. . . Isn't any different from motivating anyone else—treat him as a human being. Take him to lunch and *don't* talk about your career. Try to make at least a business friend out of him. Be honest, but not brutally honest. Try to see his viewpoint. Make him laugh. Give him a hot tip on a good horse in the ninth. Treat him with respect and demand that he return the favor.

Personal manager Cathryn Jaymes suggests: "Ask your agent: 'What can I do to help you help me?'"

Another tip: Whenever you visit your agent, wear different outfits. Various looks will suggest a range of casting possibilities.

And another: How about thanking your agent for getting you an interview? As one agent said, "I almost never get thank-you notes from actors—when I do, I remember them."

However, you may kill yourself trying and still not make a dent in your agent's consciousness. Our favorite story about this problem was told by Sylvester Stallone one day on a TV talk show. Stallone said that whenever he walked into one agent's office (before achieving *Rocky* fame), the agent would say, "Oh, we were just talking about you." Stallone would look down on the agent's desk, and sure enough, he'd see his picture lying on it—with a coffee ring on his face!

Your relationship with your agent will be as good or as bad as the two of you make it or are willing to make it. It's a kind of wacky marriage—preferably one made in heaven, not in Japan.

Still, it's probably best not to expect too much from your agent. Sure, technically he's your employee. The better agents take that to heart; the other agents merely pay lip service to it. After all, when push comes to shove, you need your employee more than he needs his employer. But even the best agent can spend only those 20 minutes on your career. You can spend 24 hours if you like.

14 CHANGING AGENTS

*Changing agents is like changing chairs
on the deck of the Titanic.*

Olde Hollywoodye Saying

"Who's your agent this week?" is a fairly common, if not very happy, joke in the film industry. Some actors change agents as often as other people change socks.

Well, agent hopping is an exercise in futility. It speaks poorly of the actor's judgment and tends to frighten off prospective agents. After all, commitment is a two-way street. Establishing a relationship with an agent will help a lot more than constantly moving cards around in a card file.

Besides, as casting director Marci Liroff put it, "Basically, if someone wants you, it doesn't matter who your agent is."

Agents know you can leave them at the drop of ninety-one days, and this may create an understandable lack of drive. We once asked an agent if it drove him crazy to work for a client, only to have the client suddenly drop him. His answer was very telling: "No. I expect it."

Still, actors do outgrow their agents (and vice versa), and agents can "cool off" on a client or not work for him at all. So the trick is to know . . .

WHEN?

A tough call. Your agent needs time to get you moving, but you can't sit around forever waiting for him to start the car. We'll give a basic time limit, but bear in mind that union strikes, hiatus (the slack season, which lasts roughly from April through June), bad economic times, and other factors should be taken into consideration before you impose it. Also, if you're *certain* your agent hasn't been working for you, there's no need to wait for any time limit to pass in order to be fair—he's not being fair with you.

OK.: All things being equal, give him a year, then ask yourself two questions. How many interviews have you gotten and how far up the ladder have you moved?

If you haven't been out at least a few times, something's wrong. And, if you've been with an agent for years and are still going out on three-line bit parts, it may be that the agent doesn't have enough "clout" to get you anything better.

Clout

Agents vary in the influence they have, depending on how many in-demand name actors they have in their client list. Although some agents and casting directors may not like to say so, there *are* such things as "day-player agencies" (small agencies a casting director will think of primarily when casting bit parts that will take only a day or two to film). If your agency can't or won't progress beyond this category, you may not either. One method is to think of all agencies as being "A," "B," "C," or "D" list agencies. An "A" list agency is a giant such as William Morris, CAA, or ICM. They handle not only major stars but major directors, writers, and other industry craftsmen to the extent that whole movies can be, and are, "pack-aged" almost entirely from within that agency alone. A "B" list agency is almost as big, with mostly name actors and, possibly, directors and writers among their clients as well. A "C" will handle some guest stars and many supporting players. A "D" is your basic day-player agency, top-heavy with newcomers.

Ultimately, it's best to sign with the biggest agency that won't bury you. Word of mouth, a check of the *Academy Players Directory,* and the location and look of the office can categorize most agencies for you. After you're signed, the attitude of the agent and the kinds of roles you're offered over a period of time will tip you off as to whether you're with a *D* agent capable of rising through the ranks or one who is happy to be no more than what he is. It won't hurt to ask yourself periodically where you are and where your agency is. The twain should meet.

One very important caution: *Agencies can grow with their actors.* As theatrical agent Jim Gibson said, "I'm not a farm club for William Morris." If you're thinking of leaving an agent who's working for you and getting the job done, have you thought about a cold shower?

Dickering ability

As you work, your agent should be getting you more money and better billing.

First, money. When you are starting out, you probably won't get much more than "scale plus ten." This means you're paid union scale plus an additional 10 percent that serves as your agent's commission. Your agent won't be able to increase your salary by leaps and bounds. All studios and casting directors keep a record of what you've been paid, called "your quote." This information is passed around liberally, and if a casting director wants to find out what your quote is, he can do so, even from a different studio. Expect a maximum increase of about $50 to $100 per day and $100 to $300 per week when moving from one job to another. If you or your agent ask for much more, the deal may fall through. After a year, though, there should be some increase in wages. If not, your agent may be a lousy dickerer.

The same goes for billing. There ought to be movement in that area too. Just bear in mind that billing is dickered over as fiercely as money, and an increase in billing is often used as a substitute for higher pay. That last point is crucial. If your agent concentrates solely on money, ultimately he's hurting you.

Is he working?

Your agent keeps telling you he's submitting you—but you aren't getting any interviews. Is he telling you the truth or just "feeding you wolf cookies"? One way to check is to give your agent photos in relatively small numbers, twenty-five to fifty, and see how long it takes him to ask for more. If you gave him fifty photos a year ago and there are still forty-nine on the shelf, some of those "submissions" are phantom.

Is he REALLY working?

Finally, there are submissions . . . and then there are *submissions*. When an agent says he's put you up for a role, try to find out specifically what that means. Did your agent send your picture along with forty other pictures? Did the agent call the casting director and say, "What about so-and-so?" If the casting director didn't know you, did the agent talk to him enough about you to get you a chance to meet him?

As one casting director said, "You've got to be a little realistic . . . if you're just starting out and your agent puts you up for the lead in 'Quincy,' more than likely it ain't gonna happen. That's one thing that does annoy me about agents . . . they'll get a breakdown [for the lead in a new series], and you know the guy's gonna be George Peppard, and the agent submits somebody that was just in *The Owl and the Pussycat* in Glendale."

HOW?

It's not too hot an idea to go storming out of your agent's office yelling "You're fired!" It might make you feel better for a while, and it's certainly dramatic as all get out to slam the door and disappear in a cloud of dust— but when the dust settles, you'll be the one who's left high and dry. Before you fire that @#!!?$*, you'll be in a much better position if you've got another agent waiting in the wings.

When interviewing with a prospective agent, if you feel the urge to bad-mouth your old agent, lie down till it passes. All the while you're talking about what a rotter your current agent has been, the new guy is going to be wondering what you'll be saying about *him* in the next few years.

It's also wise to avoid saying you got all of your jobs yourself, even if it's true. The prospective agent has no way of knowing that and might figure you're unwilling to give credit where it's due.

Actually, it's probably best simply to say something like "Well, my agent is wonderful for many of his clients, but for me, it just doesn't seem to be working out" and drop it. As one agent says, "When an actor says, 'My agent is terrible,' I think the actor is terrible."

When you are finally ready to make the change, write your old agent the following letter:

Dear _____:

This is to inform you that your services as ___TYPE OF___ agent for me are no longer required as of this date.

If your contract is still current, but those fifteen nonworking days in three months have gone by, insert "as per Paragraph 6." If you're using the one-year-anniversary-date clause (SAG only), insert "as per SAG contract Paragraph 10."

Sign the letter, date it, and mail it to your old agent, with copies to both SAG and AFTRA (whether or not you're a member of both unions), to your new agent, and keep a copy for yourself.

Notice no angry screaming in the letter? If you want to include a brief informal private note to your old agent, that's okay, as long as you've got something nice to say. The simple act of firing the agent is a sufficiently eloquent statement of your opinion of his performance.

Just remember, as there are good and bad salesmen, there are good and bad agents. A "bad" agent can set your career back; a good one can be a godsend. But no agent will ever be as good a salesman of you as you.

IV
SEEKING WORK

15   The Buyers of Talent
16   The General Interview/Look-See
17   The (Almost) Cold Reading
18   Office Scenes

15 THE BUYERS OF TALENT

As far as actors are concerned, casting directors are the keys to the kingdom.

Noel Black, Director

Know a gaffer? He might be of help. Does your dentist's cousin Zelda work in the mailroom at Universal? More potential help.

Still, the most important contacts you'll make are the buyers of talent: network executives, producers, directors, and, especially . . .

CASTING DIRECTORS

Casting directors work either as independents, hired by the job, or as studio or network employees . . . but their basic assignment is the same: finding talent. You'll see them at Equity Waiver theatres, showcases, and nightclubs, peering at television programs, viewing videotapes and office scenes, and going to movies from grades A through Z.

When time comes to cast a project, the casting director suggests actors to the producer/director/network executives based on their guidelines, the script, agents' submissions, and the casting director's own knowledge of the talent pool. Actors considered "right" are called in.

When an actor is cast, the casting director negotiates salary and billing with the actor's agent as the producer's representative. Except in rare cases, the casting director doesn't hire the actor or make final decisions on what to pay or how to bill the actor. He needs the approval of those who control the purse strings.

Why not skip over this "middleman" and go right to the people who do the hiring? First, you'll rarely meet a producer or director without first being screened by a casting director. Second, a casting director may cast a half-dozen projects in the time it takes a producer or a director to shoot one. As far as you're concerned, casting directors are walking employment agencies.

GETTING INTERVIEWS/KEEPING IN TOUCH

We use the word "interview" in the same manner as the industry does: as an all-inclusive term for any of three different possibilities:

1. *Auditions:* You perform (usually a cold reading, which we will define in a future chapter).

2. *"Look-sees":* You talk with a producer, director, or casting director as part of the casting process for a specific project.

3. *General Interviews:* Same as a "look-see," but the meeting is only for possible future reference.

Naturally, all casting directors hold auditions and look-sees, but only some hold general interviews. No matter. You're trying to get to see them—the kind of interview it turns out to be becomes important only after you've got one.

Use the same techniques as those for seeking an agent (the ten calls, ten letters a week, and so on). To find the casting directors, use the *Geographical Casting Guide* or the Breakdown Service. You don't have to have an agent to do this, but you'll find you'll probably get more interviews if you do.

Since your agent, if you've got one, is your business partner, you can pick up the phone merely to remind him you're around. Do that with a casting director and he'll probably tell you to go take a flying leap. Yet as one producer put it, "This is an out-of-sight, out-of-mind business." Keeping in touch is vital.

Your agent

It's his job not only to get you interviews but also to remind people that you're around. However, you'll probably do better not to rely on him too much.

Theatre

This can be a great help, especially Equity Waiver. It's hard for a casting director not to be reminded of you if you're in a play he's watching. Plays beget parts.

Dropping by

A word of caution: in New York, regular rounds by aggressive actors are an accepted practice. In laid-back L.A., you'll need to make your rounds with discretion and subtlety—as though you are doing nothing so crass as making rounds, but rather just happened to be in the neighborhood (or on the lot for a job or audition with someone else) and thought you'd say hello.

To show you how sticky the subject of rounds can be, here's a list of word-for-word answers we got from casting directors when we asked them: "Should actors drop by?"

- "No."
- "I don't mind—if I know the actor."
- "I hate it! Don't drop by: the dialing finger is important."
- "Well . . . no. Except to drop off a résumé shot."
- "I feel terrific about it. But the studio doesn't."
- "Well, it's not too great."
- "Doesn't bother me."
- "N.G.!"
- "I don't mind, as long as they don't camp out."
- "It's the pits!"
- "It works one-hundred percent better. Not to try to get into the office for an appointment, but to drop a picture, because it's very hard to trust pictures . . . sometimes the 'feeling' of the picture isn't always the 'feeling' of the actor."
- "It's okay, as long as the visit is brief and the actor isn't persistent."

Paralyzing, isn't it? Here's what industrial film producer Don Ciminelli had to say: "There will be times when you'll feel like you're pushing, and maybe you are—but you will find people like me who will understand that that's what you *have* to do. Because if you call me at the right time, you go to work for two weeks. You have to keep campaigning."

And here's what legitimate/theatrical agent Larry Fonseca had to say: "The difference is, out here we're all 'laid back,' and in New York they go for the jugular vein. That's what I try to instill in my actors—be aggressive. Go for the jugular vein."

Since most theatrical casting directors have their offices on studio lots, you could cultivate friendships with people who can get you inside the gates, wait until you have an audition or job on that lot, or just try chugging briskly past the guard with a knowing wave and all the chutzpah you can muster.

Once inside the gates, regardless of why you came, nobody keeps track of how long you stay. It's time to go visiting. Use a casting guidebook and try to drop in on *every* casting director on the lot. Bring résumés and photos—especially if you've never met any of the casting directors you're going to pop in on. When you stop in, say hello to the receptionist/casting coordinator/secretary. Give him your "I was in the neighborhood" speech, and if he's in no mood to talk, cut it short. If he's in a talkative mood, make hay. Whichever, he probably won't get mad if you offer to leave your résumé and photo. One agent suggests, "You could be a little devious and attach a note with it that says, 'My agent asked me to drop this off.' "

While actually getting to see a casting director would be a real bonus, your prime mission is to jog memories. To keep those remembrances fond, it will help if you stay pleasant, aren't too pushy, and don't keep turning up like a bad penny.

The mails

Besides periodically sending résumés and pictures, sending thank-you notes, Christmas and birthday greetings, and, of course, postcards can also help. So can announcements of your plays, movie, and TV appearances. And, yes, even an occasional note saying "hello" is okay, especially if it's witty. Notes won't always be read, but the right reminder in the hands of the right casting director at the right time might result in Bank Night. It only takes one.

Phoning

Most of the time phoning is considered obnoxious, but if you have something specific to talk about—a play, a film, or a TV show—your call, like a letter, will be accepted as valid business. When you do phone, leave your message with the assistant if that's what they want.

Other methods

Anything from ads in the trades to asking a pal to say hello can help. For example, every studio has a commissary. Have lunch there when you can (not every week, though; that's too obvious). Try to keep in touch with every casting director you know, and add several new ones to your list, about every three to six months. If you do, you'll work. Casting directors *are* the keys to the kingdom.

PRODUCERS / DIRECTORS

After you're cast, the director will be the one who works with you. The producer will okay the deal, sign the checks, and be on the set to oversee the entire production. But they both do the hiring. Each is equally important to your career, and if either takes a liking to you, sooner or later you're going to work for him.

Making his acquaintance in a business context is preferable, but it's true that actors have gotten parts from chance meetings at parties and other social gatherings. (Again, this *doesn't* mean sleeping with anyone.)

Attempting to get general interviews with a producer or director, however, will almost always be a waste of time. As one producer remarked, "If I'm not casting, what have we got to talk about?" On rare occasions you might have some luck, but you'll probably do better spending that time getting to the casting directors. Further, when we talked about dropping by, you'll notice we excluded producers and directors. That wasn't an oversight. How do producers and directors react to actors walking in on them and dropping off pictures? Theatrical casting director Ron Stephenson says, "I can tell you right up front—they *hate* it. It's dumb. If you know that producer as a friend, that's one thing, but please don't go around bugging producers. They really hate it."

Once you've worked for a producer or a director, it's a different story. Then you can use all those "reminders of your existence." And if he's accessible, try to spark at least a casual friendship with him. Producers and directors move around as much as anyone in the industry. To keep track of them, check the production charts in the Thursday and Friday issues of the *Hollywood Reporter* and *Variety*. Producers with permanent offices can be located in the *Hollywood Reporter Studio Blu-Book, The Producers,* or even the Yellow Pages of the telephone book. The Directors Guild of America (DGA) publishes an annual directory of members with addresses and agencies of most directors. It's available only to DGA members, though we've heard of actors who have gotten copies. At any rate, you can find a director's agent merely by phoning the DGA at 656-1220, and you may be able to contact him through his agent. Unless he gives you the O.K., calling a director at home just might get an audition for you—at Murder, Incorporated.

AND NOW A WORD ABOUT THE REAL SPONSOR

Networks get involved in casting, sometimes even to the level of bit parts. They often opt for name actors, making it difficult for newcomers. However, it's often true that newcomers get their first big break in pilots. That's a major part of a network casting director's job—scouting for new stars. The catch here is, as Susan Glicksman, Director of Casting for the West Coast, ABC-TV, said: "We're looking for really unique people—for stars of series. There are always roles for thirty-five-year-old, really gorgeous guys . . . for a young, sexy girl who can do comedy."

What the heck, no matter what your "look," it won't hurt to send your résumés and photos to all network casting directors. Who knows? They may be in the market for your type this season, and one series can mean steady work for years to come.

WELCOME TO THE TEAM

Whenever you meet a producer, call an agent, write a casting director, or interview with a director, try to take the long view. You might not be right for that particular project or even the next ten, but sooner or later, if you handle yourself properly, your number just might come up.

Taking the long view, welcoming the VIP into your club of contacts rather than thinking in terms of that one job can help you come off as a relaxed pro rather than an uptight amateur.

In short, you'll probably get to "go" sooner if you think in terms of later.

16 THE GENERAL INTERVIEW/ LOOK-SEE

Think of it as having a cup of coffee with a friend.

Terry Lichtman, Theatrical Agent

You've got five minutes. You've busted your buns to get there 'cause you know that's where the jobs are. And now it's three hundred seconds of dynamite or forget it.

Most actors understand this—when it comes to auditions. But they treat interviews like spinach—something to get past to the good stuff, the dessert: the "cold reading."

Sure, cold readings (auditions) are vital, but if you think being a "good interview" isn't important, you don't understand the film industry. A large number of your jobs will come directly and *solely* from interviews. According to director Noel Black: "That small talk is very important; in some cases more important than the reading. . . . A lot of directors don't even read people. They'll talk to an actor for five minutes and base their decision on whether to cast the actor on what they think of the actor's personality."

Fortunately, interviewing, like cold reading, is a skill that can be learned—with practice.

DOING A PERSONALITY INTERVIEW

Hell and bad interviews are paved with good intentions. . . .

"They just want to meet and talk with you," says your agent.

"What the heck does that mean?" you ask yourself. "How do I behave? What do they want?"

An old high school lecture on "Proper Job-Interview Technique" comes to mind and following its dictums, you decide to take the pinstripe approach: you sit up straight, answer all questions succinctly, are *very* businesslike, to the point, give all your credits, speak only when spoken to. . . .

. . . Only one problem: The other guy gets the part.

Want to be a good interview? Tear up those high school notes, drop any preconceptions you may have had, and start with an attitude that may startle you: No matter what the actual situation, *never treat an interview as if you were applying for a job.*

The purpose of a show business interview is to meet and introduce your

123

look, type, voice, and—especially—your *personality* to the interviewer. That's all.

Forget about going to interviews with the attitude that you're a job applicant looking for work. Just go to meet and talk with the interviewer, using the techniques we'll describe below, with a friendly and relatively easygoing approach. In short, don't do a "business" interview—do a "personality" interview.

Bearing this in mind, whenever you do an interview, apply the following five general precepts (we'll show how to specifically do that as we go through the interview itself):

1. Be interesting.

2. Be interested.

3. Have a conversation.

4. Control the interview.

5. Be (the better part of) yourself.

- *Be interesting:* When we asked casting director Sally Dennison what she looked for in an actor, she replied, "A sense of humor." (Notice no talk of business, credits, etc.) Merely being polite will get you a nice nod of the head. Being a fascinating individual will get you callbacks, if not actual jobs. Don't confuse this with coming on like gangbusters. It's okay if you're naturally quiet. Quiet people can be quietly interesting. As theatrical casting director Ron Stephenson says, "I don't think coming in and bubbling all over the place and bouncing off the walls is the answer." At the same time, as producer Buddy Bregman put it, "Don't clam up. The producer or director will think, if you don't have anything to say to him, you won't have anything to 'say' in the picture. If you're shy, take a class or something because shy people just aren't going to make it."

- *Be interested:* Treat the interviewer as a fellow human being. Be interested not only in his project or what you think he can do for you (another manifestation of "applying for a job") but in him as a person. Don't talk to the title (casting director, producer, etc.); talk to the individual who's sitting there in front of you.

- *Have a conversation:* To avoid doing a monologue (boring or otherwise), and to ensure that you get a conversation going, listen to what the interviewer says about your chosen topic and ask questions. For example: your topic is skiing. As you talk about it, the interviewer says, "Oh, I love to ski." The foolish actor goes right on talking. The smart actor zooms in: "You do? Do you have a favorite spot you like to go?" Bang! A conversation. The more you involve the interviewer in your topic, the more memorable the interview will be.

- *Control the interview:* The interviewer may control the questions, but you control the answers. As we'll see, how well you exert this "control" will go a long way in determining whether your interview is successful or not.

- *Be (the better part of) yourself:* "On an interview, don't try to be something you're not," advises theatrical casting director Jerry Franks. Exactly. Bear in mind that you don't have to *try* to be yourself. You already *are* yourself. The trouble starts when you try to be anyone else. If you're a naturally dour Walter Matthau type, don't try to act like Cary Grant, and if you bubble like Goldie Hawn, don't try to be a cool, aloof Faye Dunaway—no matter what you think they're "looking for." (An actor hears he's being interviewed for the role of a villain. He applies for the job. Immediately he starts trying to act like Boris Karloff. The interview is a disaster because he comes off as phony and affected.)

However, you'll notice we added "be the better part of yourself." If you're a miserable rotter, we'd suggest behaving the way you did last summer on that day you were fun to be around. Acting like a spoiled child because you've decided "that's *me*," is *not* being yourself—it's being self-indulgent at your own expense.

As we said, we'll show you how to put these ideas to work when we talk about the interview. First, however:

BEFORE THE INTERVIEW

There's no dress code for an interview. Clean and neat is good. Always bring a résumé and résumé shot with you, even if you're sure your agent has already sent them along. You'll avoid that sinking feeling if you're asked for them. It's probably best to bring them discreetly tucked into a purse or briefcase and offer them only if asked, so you won't seem overeager. In general, don't bring your "book" (a book of photos, usually used by models) with you to an interview. Nothing is more boring to look at. (You might bring your "book" to an interview with an *agent,* but offer it only if asked.) Acting is not modeling.

Next, arrive early. Give yourself plenty of "get lost" and "get set" time. "Get lost" time is needed because you may get stuck in traffic or find yourself running all over the lot, looking for the right office. We've yet to understand the directions given us by those friendly, helpful guards at the gates. We're certain they write tax forms in their spare time.

"Get set" time is needed to catch your breath once you finally find the office and to start thinking about all the things we're going to be talking about.

And no matter how early you are, save your energy. Don't make the mistake of going around glad-handing any fellow actors who may be there. Sit down and start thinking.

When you're called, put out the smokes, get rid of the gum, and be prepared for anything. Although most interviews are one-on-one (generally you and the casting director, director, or producer), be ready to talk to a roomful of people if that's what you're presented with. And remember that the interview starts the moment you walk in the door. That first impression is vital. Don't mope your way in and then perk up; your smile will look as automatic as a faucet. When your hand is on the doorknob, take a deep breath and say to yourself, "Action."

THE QUESTIONS MOST OFTEN ASKED AND HOW TO HANDLE THEM—AND YOURSELF

Considering what we've already said about interviews, it shouldn't surprise you that, for the most part, these questions are no more than a shorthand method of getting you to talk. They're formula stuff, more boring to the interviewer than to you. He doesn't want to have to ask more than one or two of them, and will do so only if he feels he has to pull things out of you. Consequently, the more of these questions you're asked, *the worse the interview is going.*

"Tell me about yourself"

The dreaded question. Actors consistently wail, "I never know what to say to that!" And you can bet this question or a variation ("What've you been doing?", "What's been happening?", etc.) will be asked. In reply, actors usually counter with "What do you want to know?" (a horrible answer—answering a question with a question is obnoxious). Or they may make the mistake of "applying for a job," thus becoming the most fearsome of all creatures, the Incredible Walking Résumé, who starts reeling off his credits relentlessly to an increasingly glassy-eyed interviewer. Imagine having to listen to that litany actor after actor? If the interviewer wants to know your credits, he can read them from your résumé. And whenever actors talk about their credits, they become "businesslike"—as serious as tax auditors on a bad day. Besides, credits show need. Director Noel Black: "Don't give your credits. A lot of time you'll look too eager, as if you're distressed merchandise."

So how do you answer the question? *Any way you want.* Translated, "Tell me about yourself" means "Talk—and *please* make it interesting."

If you want the interview to go beautifully, you'll need to do some preinterview planning. During your "get set" time, pick something about yourself that's entertaining, interesting, memorable, and/or funny. Then, when that question is asked, use it. You can talk about your recipe for nut soup, how you spent your childhood in a lighthouse, or anything else that's interesting. You might choose something fascinating that happened when you were working and, better yet, involved a famous person. That's a subtle way of reminding the interviewer that you're a working actor. But your overall criteria should be, first, last, and always: *Is it interesting and does it lead to conversation?*

The only taboos are: your credits per se; acting in general; anything that reflects badly on you (or anyone else); anything that's negative, either directly or in tone; and any topic that's a bore. Use your friends as guinea pigs, and in the event that your first choice of topic seems to be putting the interviewer to sleep, have a second in reserve.

As we said, It's a personality interview. When you start talking about something you're genuinely interested in, your personality automatically comes shining through. We've seen it. And when you try to be "businesslike," you hide your personality. We've seen that too.

If you're ever tempted to "talk business," remember producer William Kayden's statement, "I look for that undefinable quality called 'uniqueness.' I'm not interested in credits." And commercial casting director Pamela Campus says, "We're interested in what you're interested in. And if we're bored, we'll change the subject, don't worry."

One other little bonus. If your conversation is interesting enough, there's a very good chance the interviewer (if he's a casting director—an agent will eventually need to talk turkey) will never get around to asking you all of the rest of the following questions. If that happens, you can rest assured that you just gave a super interview!

"What have you done recently?"

Here's the one time you will discuss your career, but it too requires a little planning. During your "get set" time, pick one or two of your best credits and find something specific and interesting to say about them. (Rambling on about finding motivations for Ophelia is dull; talking about how the technical crew conjured up the ghost of Hamlet's father could be fascinating.)

You'll notice we said your *best* credits—*not* your most recent. Since you don't put dates on your résumé, no one will know that your best or most interesting credit is not also your most recent unless the credit is obviously dated ("Leave It to Beaver," for example). If you've been idle for a while, and most or all of your credits are dated, and the interview is with a casting director, producer, or director, it's frankly time to bend the truth a little. We hate telling actors to lie, but saying you haven't done anything for six months or longer sounds just plain bad, and there will be times that this happens.

"In my opinion, it's a lot better to say you're in a play at some little theatre than to say 'I did something eight months ago,'" advised director Noel Black. Obviously, he's advising actors to do theatre, but on those occasions when you've been idle. . . .

Pick a credit that's undated (a showcase usually is the solution) and say you just "recently" finished it. If, however, the interview is with an agent, tell the truth. Never lie to an agent. If you haven't done anything recently, say so.

"How old are you?"

Answer the question and drop it. Responses like "How old do I look?" or "Well, I can play between ages twenty and thirty," or "How old do you want me to be?" tend to seem as if there's something you're embarrassed about. Should you lie about your age? That's up to you—as long as you pick one realistic number and stick to it. Don't go around telling different people different ages in the hope that you'll qualify for a particular part. They'll remember what you told them—we promise.

If you're under eighteen, don't lie about that. There will be all sorts of legal problems when the truth comes out, and it will. It's also not a good idea to tell people you're older than you are even if you are past eighteen— eventually that's going to haunt you.

"What brought you to L.A.?"

Saying "My mother" or "This is where my boyfriend lives" doesn't exactly make you look committed. The best answer? Something along the lines of "This is where the action/business/work is."

"Do you have any film on yourself?"

They mean a videotaped record of a film or TV appearance. If you don't, simply say "Not yet."

"Do you have an agent?"

With a casting director, a producer, or a director: If you've got one, say who it is, but don't proceed to bad-mouth him if you're unhappy. You may be talking to the agent's best friend, and only nonworking actors are unhappy with their agents. Either say something nice or don't elaborate.

If you're interviewing with an agent, simply say you have no agent, if that's the case. And try to avoid crying hysterically.

Questions about your résumé

Once again, that "get set" time is invaluable here. Use it to go over your résumé. Be prepared to say something positive and interesting about every item on it. And be sure you know who produced, directed, and cast every production mentioned. We know one casting director who said she'd never cast any actor who didn't know this. That's a bit extreme, but knowing who you worked for eliminates a lot of stammering.

"Can you (do a skill: ride a horse, affect an accent)?"

As we've said before, answer "yes" only if, in fact, you can do the skill. That's the way to build trust in you. If you're asked if you can do an accent, however, don't fall into the trap of replying in that accent. Looks too eager somehow, and you'll invariably blow it.

Other questions can include:

- "Where are you from originally?"
- "What made you decide to become an actor?"
- "Whom have you studied with?"
- "Are you studying with anyone now?"
- "Have you done any theatre in L.A.?"
- "Have you worked only on stage?"

Naturally, how you answer these questions will depend on your personal circumstances. But be ready to handle them. Only Mortimer Snerd should go into an interview not knowing what he's going to say ("I don't know, yup, yup"). This doesn't mean having a set spiel, by the way; that's going to sound as if you're a walking tape recorder. Basically, just know what you want to say.

OTHER RULES OF THE GAME

Don't be negative

Laugh and the world laughs with you; cry and the other guy gets the part.

Each negative remark lessens your chances; each positive word increases them. Be especially aware of how you talk about yourself; we've seen actors with credits as long as their arms talk as if they've never done a thing. Question: "What have you done recently?" Answer, from an actor who has just finished a guest-starring role on a major TV show: "Oh . . . not much." Or "Well, I just did a small/nothing/tiny/silly little/nonexistent role on Broadway." Think we're kidding? Those are word-for-word answers we've heard.

You'll be treated exactly as you tell people to treat you; and they'll consider your previous work exactly in the manner in which you explain it. You needn't "hype" yourself or your credits, but be proud of them and of yourself.

Don't be hostile

According to many industry people, this is a surprisingly common problem. Well, if you've got a temporary mad on, go kick a garbage can. If it's permanent, go yell at a psychiatrist or take up linebacking for the Green Bay Packers. As theatrical casting director Susan Sukman observed: "Your attitude has to be positive at all times because negative vibes will come out whether you know it or not."

Don't talk in a vacuum

An interview is a conversation, not a monologue. We've seen interviews in which the actor gave the impression that the interviewer could get up and leave and the actor wouldn't notice.

Don't try to be Henny Youngman

There's a difference between having a sense of humor and having an act. Also, never make yourself the butt of a joke; like Rodney Dangerfield, you won't get no respect. And be sure your sense of humor isn't negative, cruel, or so off-the-wall that people will think you're weird. And don't get glad-handy or act like an Uncle Tom. All of these things hide you as much as sitting there like a bump on a log, and they're even worse because bumps don't usually annoy people.

Know when to leave

When the interviewer rises and says "Thank you for coming in," the performance is over. Skip the exit speech and split.

SPECIAL NOTES

The techniques we've talked about will work with anyone, with the following differences only:

If the interview is with an agent

Ultimately, the agent will want to talk about your career. Still, at the beginning of the interview, we'd advise picking your topic(s), talking about it, and letting the agent steer the conversation to business. He still wants to see you be interesting.

If the interview is with a producer/director (a "look-see")

Besides the minor differences we've mentioned, there is a good chance he may start talking about his project. When that happens, bad interviewees sit listening dumbly, as if to say, "But what about me?" Good interviewees might ask where the producer or director came across the project, how he intends to shoot a specific section of the script, etc. Not only are you conversing, and on a subject dear to the heart of the interviewer, but the answers are almost always fascinating. In short, show an interest in the project. Don't, however, say or ask anything that seems as if you're asking for a part.

Also, as casting director Marci Liroff pointed out, "Some directors love you to say 'I liked your last movie'; others hate it." We'd advise not saying anything. Makes you look too much like a fan or as if you're applying heavy butter.

A word about nerves

General interviews/look-sees are admittedly nerve-racking, but most industry people will go out of their way to relax you. "When I see an actor is nervous, I'll tell him, 'I just did two loads of diapers this morning,' " says one casting director.

Granted, it's hard to be blasé, especially if you walk into an office and there, seated on a sofa, is your all-time favorite director. Unfortunately, you just can't come off as a nervous Nelly; the director or casting director will worry that if you can't handle your nerves on a simple interview, you sure won't be able to handle the pressure on a set. "If you go in very shy and inhibited and very insecure about what you're doing there in that office, they're not going to feel very respectful of your talent, unfortunately," says theatrical agent Maxine Arnold.

Remembering not to "apply for a job" can help; so can remembering to treat anyone you meet as a fellow professional, not as some god you can't wait to worship. Nobody hires fans. And then, there's practice. If you can't afford a class in interview technique, set up some empty chairs and a tape recorder and pretend you're being interviewed. Enlist a friend to help; have him ask all the questions we've mentioned. Then listen to the playback of your answers, bearing in mind all we've talked about. (Access to videotape is invaluable in getting rid of assorted tics and mannerisms.)

And a word about listening

You wouldn't think we'd have to mention that when the person sitting at a desk across from you opens his mouth, it's time for you to listen. You wouldn't think. Theatrical casting director Mike Fenton said:

"We were casting a film with Claude LeLouch. LeLouch speaks English but he doesn't think he speaks it very well. . . . We were having interviews. An actor would come in and sit in a chair, and I would say—per Mr. LeLouch's instructions—'Mr. LeLouch is very pleased that you've come to see him today. He is hesitant about his English. He doesn't feel comfortable speaking it, so he probably will not say a word. But what he would like to know, first of all, is: What did you have for dinner last night?'

"Well, that stumped a lot of actors. I mean they were totally thrown. They didn't know what to do. And then, *there would be a further instruction:* 'Say it as if you were very angry,' or 'Say it as if you were very joyous'; 'Say it in a sensual way'; 'Say it as if you were mad at the world.' So there were different instructions on *how* to say what you had for dinner last night. Well, it was bizarre. An overwhelming number of actors *never heard* the second instruction. They just went off saying what they had for dinner without adding to it the inflection he was looking for. So that, at least 65% of the actors who came in for that motion picture never had a chance at it because they never heard what was said to them. They never heard the instructions. It's real important to listen." 'Nuff said.

AFTER THE INTERVIEW

Examine how the interview went. What worked? What laid an egg? Did you do and say the things you wanted? How did they react to them? Was there any negativity on your part? Did you fall into the trap of bad-mouthing yourself? Was it a conversation? An interrogation? A joy? An excruciating bore? Did you control the interview?

If the interview worked, know why it did. If it didn't, know that, too, and treat it as a learning experience, not the end of the world—or your career. Which brings us to our last point.

Nobody does a *perfect* interview. And if you feel you bombed, try not to get down on yourself. As theatrical casting director Judith Holstra commented, "You're not doing cancer research, y'know."

Life will go on, phones will ring when you're in the bathtub, that movie you've been wanting to see will still be playing, your income tax will still be due on April 15—and other interviews will come your way. And your dog will still wag his tail just as frantically when you walk in the door.

Ultimately, that's far more important.

17 THE (ALMOST) COLD READING

The most distressing thing is when an actor feels the people he's going to read for are enemies. If I'm bringing you in, I'm rooting for you. The producer and director are wide open. They've got to have someone in their show and they want someone good. So you walk into a room full of people who are pulling for you. It's a room full of friendliness. We all want you to be terrific. So come in and be wonderful.

Ron Stephenson, Theatrical Casting Director

"Oh, I'm terrible at auditions," announces the famous actor, blushing. If you believe that, we've got a bridge we'd like to sell you.

In rare cases, an actor will be seen in one show and cast in another without ever having to audition. If that happens often enough, he becomes famous without ever having to read for a part. Still, how did he get the first part? By osmosis? And do you want to bet your career on that kind of luck?

Cold readings (auditions with script in hand) are the crux of an actor's career—make-it-or-break-it time. Cold-read poorly often enough, and you'll find yourself back in Sweetwater, Nebraska, being the plumber your father wanted you to be in the first place. Cold-read well often enough and you might just become famous enough to demur, "Oh, I audition terribly."

FOR WHOM THE PHONE RINGS

When your agent (or, in rare cases, a casting director) calls, get the particulars about the appointment (when, where, and for whom), and repeat them back to make sure you've got them right.

Then find out as much about the character you'll be "reading" as possible. Ask your agent to read the description from the Breakdown Service, and ask about any other particulars given him by the casting director. (Occasionally no one will know anything.) When possible, scripts are supposed to be available to actors 24 hours in advance of the reading. If they are, go down to the studio and get one. If there isn't a complete script available, see if you can at least get the pages you'll be reading, called "sides." The more you know . . .

Now it's back to the closet. Whenever you go on a theatrical cold reading, you'll want to dress to *suggest* the part. If you're up for a construction worker, perhaps jeans and a workshirt. But you won't need to wear a hard hat, carry a lunch pail, or go out and rent a pneumatic drill.

ARRIVAL/PREPARATORY WORK

As with general interviews, be an early bird. Even if you've had the script overnight, try to arrive at the producer's office at least twenty minutes before you're scheduled to read.

When you're given your sides, sit down and read them, as if you were reading a book. Besides finding out what's going on in the scene, ask yourself:

- What type of show is this? (Soap opera means an intimate reading. A half-hour comedy means a bright, zesty reading with lots of energy. Your standard TV show or film is a little more energetic than soap opera, but not as zesty as comedy; be "energetically real.")

- What's the "feel" of the scene (stark tragedy, light and breezy, etc.)?

- What are all the characters talking about?

- What is your character's relationship to every other character in the scene?

- What seems to be your character's basic objective? What does he want?

If there's anything you don't understand, including the pronunciation of a single word—ask. Only when you're completely satisfied that you know what's going on should you start working on a scene. Sound obvious? You'd be surprised at how many thoroughbred actors chomp at the bit so hard they start to work on a scene without reading it. They leave the starting gate before they even know what race they're in.

WORKING ON THE SCENE

Find a place where you can rehearse, even if you have to leave the building. If your rehearsal area—which includes the sidewalk, if that's all you can find—is out of calling range, tell the assistant where you'll be and periodically pop in to let them know you're still nearby.

When working on the scene, you want to concentrate on:

1. Practicing listening.
2. Picking a direction.
3. Keeping your eyes out of the script.
4. Memorizing the first and last lines (only).

Practicing listening

When you work on your reading, you may be tempted to concentrate solely on your line readings. If so, you'll skip the one ingredient that can lift your reading above all your fellow actors': *listening.* "You have to remember that sometimes the camera's on you when you're not doing lines," says producer William Kayden. "Reactive readings are very important." Good line readings alone can produce a decent reading. Listening, reacting, and playing to the person reading opposite you, in addition to interesting line readings, will get you cast. When we asked theatrical casting director Doris Sabbagh what she looked for in actors, she answered typically: "*Listeners.* Don't stand there waiting for your next line."

Picking a direction

Whenever an actor asks theatrical casting director Judith Holstra, "How old is my character?", her immediate reaction is, "How old are you?"

Many actors assume that picking a direction means trying to develop a character totally foreign to themselves. It doesn't—not in film work. When you act in theatre, you merge and adapt yourself to the character; when you act for the camera, you merge and adapt the character to yourself. Forget playing the character with a limp; aging the character up or down; finding speech patterns, accents, and so forth. Essentially, play yourself. Simply ask yourself: How would I react to this situation?

As with any "rule," there are exceptions. If you're asked to do an accent, for example, do it—but, in general, follow director Gary Nelson's advice: "I look for naturalness, not 'acting.' Don't hide behind a character. When an actor comes in and acts and talks one way and then, when he picks up a script, acts and talks differently, I get scared." It might look phony on camera.

However, there are a lot of "yous," and that's where picking a direction comes in. "You" can be a doctor, lawyer, or Indian chief. "You" can be angry, loving, murderous, shy. Find a way to play the scene, as you, and go with it. Don't worry if the direction you choose is "wrong." It's a lot better to do an interesting reading that misses the mark than one that is vague and undefined. The former can be corrected by the producer, director, or casting director. The latter is too boring to bother with. As director Harvey Laidman says, "I look for intelligence, good choices. Even if you're wrong, be interesting. I'm looking for people to keep me awake."

One caution. As casting director Barbara Remsen put it, "Don't make two lines more than they are." Don't read a love scene and decide he secretly hates her. He doesn't. As Judith Holstra says, "Don't look for hidden meanings . . . they just ain't there, folks." Play what's obviously there on the page.

Keeping your eyes out of the script

One sure way not to get cast is to audition with your nose stuck in the script. If they can't see you—especially your eyes—your acting ability is irrelevant. The shorthand term for this is "eye contact," but it involves more: listening, reacting, and playing to your fellow actor. When you're rehearsing, concentrate on looking out at an imaginary fellow actor, especially when that fellow actor would be saying his lines.

Don't fall into the "reading trap"; reading the other person's lines as he speaks them. If you are listening, you won't need to. These are the moments you want to be out of the script, so that the viewer can see your reactions to what is being said. Don't worry about losing your place. If you wish, run your thumb down the page as you audition—but we guarantee that if you simply learn to trust yourself, your eyes will go to the location of your next line. In any case, no one is going to jump down your throat if you take an extra beat or two to locate your line. You won't lose your audience if you remain poised and in character.

If you want the part, look up and listen.

Memorize the first and last lines (only)

You want to be looking away from the script at the very beginning and the very end of your reading. It will ensure a strong first and last impression.

Don't assign yourself too many tasks

Every time you make a decision to do something in a reading, you're giving yourself another job to do. The more jobs, the worse the reading will go. Lewis's law postulates that under the stress of a cold reading, the human mind can handle only so many tasks before it blows a gasket. For example . . .

Don't try to memorize all of your lines

Ever been to a first rehearsal "off book"? It's a disaster. You can't act and be worried about lines at the same time. Some cold-reading classes stress the so-called importance of memorizing your part to guarantee you'll keep your nose out of the script. Balderdash! Staring at your partner with glassy eyes as you try to remember your next line *isn't* listening. You'll just look as though there's nobody home. If you have only a couple of lines, or if you're one of those rare individuals with a photographic memory, go ahead and memorize. Otherwise, forget it. Cold readings are not line-memorization contests. "As a matter of fact," says Susan Glicksman, Director of Casting, West Coast, ABC-TV, "We discourage actors from memorizing lines because they get too involved with remembering the lines."

Ignore stage directions (yours or the script's)

Forget pantomime, blocking, or nifty ideas for business. All that will only get in your way. The most effective readings almost always are those in which the actor does the entire reading seated. Movement inherently distracts the viewer from your most important selling point: your eyes. If you're uncomfortable sitting, stand—but stand relatively still.

If the script says, "He lights a cigarette" or "She grabs him and shakes him," forget it. All that business is not only unnecessary, it's distracting; in the latter example, *very* distracting. No casting director wants you to suddenly start rattling his brains out.

In the same vein, you needn't read a line "demurely" just because the writer put that word in parentheses. Nor do you have to ask the producer to let you sit behind his desk because your character is at a desk in the scene. Simply sit in a chair, or stand, and listen.

Speak the lines out loud

Find yourself a rehearsal area where you can talk out loud without disturbing the secretary's typing. Regardless of how you plan to interpret a line, the first time you say it aloud it simply won't come out the way you planned. In fact, the sound of it may throw you. Have the shock come when you can work on your reading: in rehearsal.

If you haven't quite finished rehearsing when you are called in, ask for more time. Never read before you're ready. On the other hand, if you have finished rehearsing and they're not ready for you yet, sit quietly and keep your mind on your reading. Don't clown around with your fellow actors. Save your energy. You're there to get a job, not to make friends.

THE "I'M NOT RIGHT FOR THIS" SYNDROME

Theatrical casting director Bobby Hoffman says, "A part isn't born till an actor gives birth to it." One of the errors actors consistently make is to decide they're not right for a part, based on a character description in the script or the look of other actors at the audition. It's a silly mistake that can destroy your reading. Don't be your own (negative) casting director. You have no sure way of knowing how they see the part. If they like your reading, they may even change their original concept of the character. Always assume: *If you've been called in, you're right for it—period.*

A WORD ABOUT NERVES

Telling you not to be nervous is as helpful as saying "Try not to breathe." But you can learn to deal with those nerves by channeling your mind away from them. Don't give yourself the mental time to get nervous; spend your time thinking only about what you're trying to do with the reading, rehearsing, going over your objectives. When you feel those nerves on the attack, fight back by going to work.

INTO THE BREACH

When you're called in, take a deep breath, put on a confident face, and , , ,

Expect the unexpected

You may walk into a roomful of people or see one lone, slightly embarrassed-looking director. They, or he, may show you to a chair smack in the middle of the room or point to a far sofa. You may be asked to start your reading immediately or even have a producer say, "Let's not read; let's just talk." The atmosphere may be funereal or "Hey, Joe, you got gum?"

No matter—don't alter your reading because of the atmosphere in the room or because of the room itself. (Put actors in a small room, and, for some reason, they all get a terminal case of the mumbles.) Do your reading exactly as you had planned. If the reading calls for you to shout, shout; if you're doing a comedy reading, try to have fun; in short, don't pick up their "vibes," project your own.

Before you read

One of the best ways to learn a little more about what you're going to read is to ask a question about it. The best way to ask was suggested by theatrical agent Mary Spencer: "Say something like, 'I have an idea on this role, but is there anything you'd like to tell me?'" Then sit back and listen. Often the producer/director/casting director will answer the question with a long dissertation. Let 'em talk. The more he says, the more you know. If the response changes the characterization from the way you rehearsed it, switch gears and get as close to what they say as possible. Yep, you've got to be a chameleon in this business.

However, never ask, "How do you want this done?" That can lose it for you. "That's amateur night," says director Ralph Senensky. You might think that attitude is unfair—after all, is it wrong for a chef to ask you if you want your eggs scrambled or sunny-side up? Three views:

Commercial casting director Pamela Campus: "For years I thought, Gee, I'll just tell every actor who comes in, 'This is what we want, and this is how we want it.' And the actors would look at me as if to say, 'Oh, O.K.' And then they'd *still* deliver it their way. I learned the hard way. You let them deliver and see what they do, and you either like it or you don't. And if you don't like it, but you think they have potential, then you offer a suggestion— once. And if they're really good, they'll get it."

Producer William Kayden: "What we want is what you give us. We don't want to sit around and intellectualize the role."

Director Noel Black: "Some great actor may come in and have an inspiration, and for me to tell him something might be unfair . . . insulting."

We'll grant there are some directors who have absolutely no objection to your asking how they want it, but better safe than uncast. Besides all the above, they may not have the time or the inclination to direct you on the set, and they may want to be sure you can do the role totally on your own.

Don't make negative comments either—especially about the script. If they didn't write it, they chose it. Be an actor, not a critic.

If you want to sit or stand for a reading, do so, and don't ask permission. (Naturally, if someone requests that you do otherwise, do otherwise.) Bear in mind Noel Black's comment: "A lot of actors say 'Do you want me to sit or stand?' Well, it's *your* stage—do what you want." It's the difference between behaving like an obedient child and behaving like a pro.

The reading

First, take a moment to collect yourself and get into character. You're not trying to break the record for the fastest start in a reading. We don't mean stand off in a corner "preparing" for five minutes. "When someone does that in my office," says legitimate/theatrical agent Larry Fonseca, "I'll give them about five seconds and then I'll say 'Next!'" Don't waste anyone's time. A beat or two is plenty.

Next, play the scene to whoever is reading against you. Don't include the others—they don't want to be part of the scene, they want to watch. Don't upstage yourself, of course; make sure your body and hair are positioned so they can see your face.

You'll discover that 50 percent of the time, the casting director or whoever your acting partner is can't act his way out of a paper script. Play it as if he is Laurence Olivier. However, go at your pace, not his. If you feel rushed or can't hear your cues, ask him nicely to slow down, speak up, or whatever. Remember, they want you to be good, and if you're polite and pleasant, they shouldn't take umbrage.

Don't rush your reading. Do what you rehearsed unless instructed otherwise, and commit to it. This is no time to get wishy-washy.

If something happens during the reading—you flub a line, say, or lose your place in the script—feel free to ask to start over (unless you're at the very end of the scene). Don't try to muddle your way through with your mind still on that flub; it can destroy your reading. Nobody's going to get mad if you ask to start over. Producer Philip Mandelker advises: "Stop if you're doing badly. After all, you've only got one chance. If you can, try to do it humorously; what have you got to lose?"

And nobody's going to get mad if you blow a line. Never purposely change a line in order to "improve" the script, especially in a comedy. The writer(s) won't appreciate your "help." But don't worry if you flub a line and accidentally change it in the process. They'll know the difference between an accidental change and an "improvement."

Above all, remember that they want you to be successful. Casting director Tony Shepherd put it into perspective: "We all want you to be good, if for no other reason than once we get the role cast, we all get to go home."

After the reading

If you're unhappy with your reading, feel free to ask to do it again—*once*. Don't be negative, however. They may have thought you were terrific. When you finish, you might ask something along the lines of "Was that the general ball park?" (*not* "Was I any good?"). If you're told you went in the wrong direction, listen to their suggestions, then do it again. But don't keep asking to do the reading over and over. It's two tries and rack your cue. "When a reading is over, it's over," says producer Michael Rhodes.

Occasionally, the director will stop you and tell you what you're doing "wrong." Don't get upset. Being stopped means they think you can act; you're just going down the wrong road. They almost never stop an actor who can't act—they let him read straight through and say good-bye. Being cut off in the middle of your reading with a "Thank you" isn't a bad sign either. It probably means that they like what you're doing and don't need to hear any more. (This is decidedly different from a New York stage audition, where being cut off is almost always a bad sign.)

Every once in a while you'll be asked to read a different scene from that which you rehearsed. When this happens, ask for time to study the new sides. If feasible, leave the room. This will upset no one; in fact, it's a sign of your professionalism. Never read anything completely cold—it's the surest road to a failed audition.

After the audition, don't ask if you got the part. And make no apologies for your performance; no matter how justified, excuses always sound like excuses. Besides, you probably don't need an apology: most actors feel they did far worse than was the case. Say thanks and go.

AFTER THE AUDITION

Always call your agent, and unless you know beyond doubt that the audition was a disaster, simply say it all "went well." Don't worry your agent with a lot of unnecessary yammer about all the mistakes you think you made.

Then, if you're upset, go home and kick a door. And forget it. In fact, your reading is only a part of the casting process, the only part you have any control over. You may have read beautifully and be too tall or too short; the role may have been all but cast before you read; the producer's wife may want the part; the part may be cut; the budget may demand an actor who will work for less. "Quite often it has to do with pairings," says commercial producer Bob Wollin. "The best people aren't always cast."

In television work you often know within days if you have the part, but, in fact, that painful time span can vary from five minutes to five months, depending on the project, and it's hard to generalize. Don't expect your agent to call and tell you every time you *don't* get a part. Unless the actor is cast or is so bad as to prove an embarrassment, the casting director will not call the agent. If the role is something special, you can ask your agent to call and inquire, but don't make this request every time you read for a one-line part. If you miss this "bus," there'll be another coming down the street shortly.

CALLBACKS/SCREEN TESTS

If your reading was for the producer or director and involved only a few lines or speeches, you probably won't be called back to read again. (Callbacks are more common for commercials than for TV or movies.) You may be called back half a dozen times for a major part or a continuing role in a series.

If your reading was for a casting director, as a screening process, he'll either call you back or take you into another room to meet the producer/ director on the spot.

Regardless, the thing to remember is that you did something right, so do the second reading as close to the first as possible. Don't outsmart yourself by making major "improvements" that may move you away from what they liked about you the first time around. If you're on a callback, it's probably best even to wear the same clothes.

You'll almost never be asked to do a screen test, unless you are a new face up for a major role. If it does happen, check the material in Chapter 20, "On the Set." Again, make as few changes as possible. If the test involves you conversing, not acting, just enjoy it using your best interview technique.

Finally, we promise you'll never learn to cold-read just by studying a chapter in a book. Like it or not, you're going to have to practice: in a class, with a fellow actor, or alone in front of a mirror. And the time to start is *not* when you get your audition call.

And never forget that everyone involved in casting is on your side. "The greatest moment for us," says theatrical casting director Jane Feinberg, "is when the director says 'Him.'"

18 OFFICE SCENES

I had two people in to do one, and they set up a place setting, and candles, and real food . . . and by the time they were through setting up I was so bored . . .

Susan Glicksman, Director of Casting for the West Coast, ABC-TV

If you're not in a play, television show, or movie, and you have no videotape on yourself, an agent or casting director may ask if you've got "something he can look at." He's talking about an office scene.

An office scene is a scene (no monologues, please—they want to see you relating to your fellow actor), performed by two actors, preferably of opposite sexes, in the office of a casting director or agent.

There are certain rules of the game here, too, which you can also use as guidelines for showcases such as Performers Audition Showcase and for many theatre general auditions.

THE CARDINAL RULE

Maximum: five minutes. Strong preference: three minutes. Sound like acting for a stopwatch? When you work in TV, that's exactly what you do anyway. Don't try to cheat the time limit. We know of actors who were cut off in the middle of a scene long before, as they put it, "we even got to the good part."

It's essential that the scene fit into that three-minute time span. If it doesn't, find another scene. When you begin working on the material, read it aloud with your partner and time it. Since blocking and business will add time, when you have it ready to perform, time it again. If it's longer than four to five minutes, chop without mercy.

CHOOSING A SCENE

Your source is irrelevant. You can cull your scenes from television and movie scripts, plays and books. You can even write your own (*if* you can write and are shrewd enough to keep your authorship to yourself so your audience doesn't judge that instead). It's a good idea to keep a tape recorder near your TV set in case a good scene comes up. One of your best sources will be soap operas, which make for perfect office scenes because of their intimacy and intense actor-to-actor relationships. Beyond that . . .

Choose a scene that shows you off

Not your partner. (In a showcase production, of course, both parts will have equal weight.) Don't choose a partner who is a bad actor in hopes that he'll make you look good. He won't. On the other hand, don't choose a partner who is vastly better than you. Your partner should be serviceable, his role a kind of dramatic or comedic straight man to yours.

Cast yourself close to the grain

Forget accents, roles that call for you to be older or younger than you are, and character pieces—they're not looking for a new Dracula. Play roles you would naturally be cast in, with almost no stretching at all.

Make it self-explanatory

You don't want the viewer spending your three minutes figuring out what the heck is going on. After all, he may not have had his second cup of coffee yet. The scene should explain itself. The most you should have to say is: "This is from ___," perhaps, "By ___," and, briefly, any necessary information such as "The scene takes place on a desert island." If you feel any further explanation is necessary, you'd do better to find another scene.

Make sure it "translates" well

You're going to be doing the scene in someone's (probably cramped) office. The more activity, the bigger you have to be to make the scene work, the worse your choice. The aim of the scene, remember, is to show you relating and reacting to your fellow actor; a lot of running around defeats that. And scenes requiring emotional fireworks can be embarrassing between the typewriters at nine A.M. (You can be slightly bigger in a showcase—you'll be on stage.) The best scenes are usually two people sitting, talking, and reacting in a relatively quiet way.

Forget the "classics"

Shakespeare, Ionesco, Pinter, and the other masters may speak well of your knowledge of theatre, but they're terrible choices for office scenes. They don't tell the viewer what he wants to know: how you will come across in the typical TV fare. They also pit you against the legendary performances by the great actors. And it is possible that your viewer knows less about theatre than you do and is defensive about it.

Find something fresh

As one casting director put it, "If I see one more version of a scene from *Barefoot in the Park*, I'll scream." The best way to avoid doing a shopworn scene is to use an original piece or something from a soap opera, TV show (if the scene isn't written for a famous character like Archie Bunker), or movie (if the scene isn't too well known).

CHOOSING A PARTNER/REHEARSING

If you're not in an acting class or have no actor friends who are "right," you can tack up a notice in one of the many workshops around town. Or ask an instructor for a recommendation. Or place an ad in *Drama-Logue* or *Casting Call* and hold readings. (If you do, you'll be swamped with calls. Who wouldn't want to do a scene for an agent or casting director?) But be sure that whomever you choose understands that it is your scene, not a chance for him to upstage you.

Rehearse the scene in different locales—large room, small room, sofa, two chairs, and so forth to prevent you from being thrown by a major difference between where you've rehearsed and where you may be asked to perform the scene.

Don't have set- and prop-itis. If it takes longer than 30 seconds to set up, it's wrong. The best scenes require nothing in terms of props or set. The concentration is on the actors. And keep blocking and business to a minimum. Sit, talk, listen, and react.

OPENING MORNING

Go early, wait quietly, do what you rehearsed. Afterward, expect anything—from a compliment to a terse "Thank you" to a complete critique of you, your partner, and/or the scene itself. The reaction may have more to do with your audience than your performance. Whatever is said and whoever is saying it, be sure in your gut that the comments are true and fair, or ignore them.

V
WORKING

19   Making a Deal
20   On the Set

19 MAKING A DEAL

*Your money indicates your value. You
don't want a hungry agent who just wants
to make a deal.*

Jack Rose, President, Jack Rose Agency

With due respect to Charles Dickens, the period between your audition
and the closing of a deal really is "the best of times and the worst of times."
You know they want you, but how much? And your participation is usually
limited to saying yes or no to the deal that has been worked out between
your agent and the casting director.

Just remember that your billing is at least as important as your salary.
From the top down:

- *Star:* Name usually above the title.

- *Also Starring:* Name after the title.

- *Guest Starring:* Most often used in TV (occasionally movies). Name
  will appear before the story, after the above (it will sometimes appear
  after the story, but this is rather rare).

- *Co-Starring:* Name after the above, usually at the beginning, sometimes at the end, of the show.

- *Featured; also called "End Titles" in film:* Name only at end of story,
  in the "crawl"—the names move upward from bottom to top of
  screen.

- *Separate card:* Your name appears by itself on the screen regardless
  of type of billing. Naturally, "Star" and "Also Starring" are almost
  always separate card. "Guest Star" and "Co-Star" separate card billing may require some dickering. "Featured" almost never is put on
  separate card.

There are all sorts of variations on this basic structure ("Extra Special
Super Peachy-Keeny Guest Star," etc.), even to the size of type, whether
names are put in a special box, and so forth. Until you become a "star,"
your concern will be to move up from "Featured" to "Co-Star" to "Guest
Star." Beyond that, you no longer need this book.

As far as money is concerned, you'll be hired on a daily basis (X dollars per day—minimum $298—called "day player"); on a special three-day contract (television only; minimum $756); or on a weekly basis (called "Freelance"; minimum $1,038). Most likely, if you're working for this kind of money ("scale"), an additional 10 percent for your agent, called "scale plus ten," will be added to your paycheck. As you move up, your salary in the above categories will, of course, increase. But be careful. As theatrical casting director Ron Stephenson says, "An actor should get a raise periodically, but an agent shouldn't price an actor out of the business." And bear in mind producer William Kayden's comment: "Usually that part is budgeted. Sometimes we'll 'steal' money from another role, but generally, if you can't get one actor for your price, you get another." Sticky, isn't it?

Your employer has the right to convert you from a day player to a weekly contract player if work is progressing slowly and the producer sees you're going to have to work for, say, four days instead of the two for which you originally contracted. Two days at $298 is $596, and four days at $298 is $1,192. The producer can save money by converting your contract, since one week at scale is $1,038.

The producer will guarantee your employment for the length of time he thinks he will need you, subject to dickering by your agent. However, once you're guaranteed a certain period of employment, the producer must pay you for it regardless of whether you are needed for the full anticipated length of time or not. If you're contracted for a week and work only one day, he must still pay you the week's salary. On the other hand, your employment can, and often does, go beyond the originally contracted period of time. If it does, you are, of course, paid for the extra work.

According to SAG, you've got a firm engagement if the studio or producer gives you written acceptance; if you're given a contract signed by the producer; if you're given a script with intent to hire you; if you're fitted (other than wardrobe tests); or when you're called and agree to report.

However, once you agree to terms and your agent calls the casting director to confirm it, for all practical purposes, you've got a deal. This industry moves so quickly that a telephone conversation may be considered binding; sometimes you will be working the next day. However, as further protection if there is no time to assemble a full-fledged contract, you may have a "booking slip" sent to you along with the script, sent to your agent's office, or be waiting for you when you first appear on the set. A booking slip is a memorandum briefly outlining your length of employment, what you'll be paid, how you'll be billed, and your start date.

If you're hired but not given a specific start date, and another job offer comes along (you'll be amazed at how often jobs come in clusters; for reasons, see your local guru), you or your agent must call the producer before noon of a business day. If he gets back to you before the end of the same day and gives you a specific start date, that date and job become binding to you and the producer. If he doesn't get back to you before the end of the day, you're free to accept the other job. (If you or your agent call after noon, the producer has until noon of the next business day.)

To further clarify the process of deal making, here's what agent Jack Rose had to say about the negotiating process. Pay special attention to what he says at the end:

"There are many types of negotiations, so I'm going to give you a very simple one. . . . They call for an actor to work for a period of time to do a film. They tell us how many days they want the actor and how much they want to pay. At that point, we say, 'Well, that's not enough money.'

"They say, 'Of course that's enough money.' And then we say, 'Well, on the last film the actor got X numbers of dollars per week.' Now, some casting directors already have that information in front of them, so you can't lie to them. Once you lie to those people, forget it; forget about dealing with these people again. And you know which ones work that way, so you say, 'Yes, *but* the actor has another project that we're probably going to have to sign him for, unless you offer him more money.' Or 'You want him for a week; your film's going for three weeks, let's make it a two-week guarantee.' And you come to some kind of compromise that way.

Then you get into billing—If they're going to give billing or not and the position of the billing. Those are the simple terms of a basic negotiation. . . . Unless your agent is a good negotiator, you're going to wind up making very little money, and just working as a day player."

20 ON THE SET

Q: How much direction do actors get on a set?

A: Well, let's be honest—you're not going to get a whole lot.

Interview with Harvey Laidman, Director

Big cities, move over. There's no lonelier time or place than a first day on set. It's kind of a combination opening night/first day on a ("regular") job. If you feel a sense of alienation, you're not alone. You'll sense a curious arm's-length between you and everyone else on the set—until you work. Then suddenly you become one of the family.

PRESET DOINGS

Costumes/scripts

Once you're hired, the producer will have a complete script (assuming there is one) delivered to your door by messenger, or you'll be asked to pick one up.

Next comes the call from the costumer. When he calls depends on how soon you're working.

Now prepare yourself for an unglamorous shock: If the show is modern dress, you'll be asked to raid your closet and provide your own wardrobe. Yep—just like back in South Patooie Community Theatre. You'll be paid a fee, though. (See Appendix A.)

On the phone, the costumer and you will decide on what you will wear on the show, and you will be expected to bring your "costume(s)" with you to the first day of work. (If you don't want to drive the sound man crazy, avoid polyester. It's too noisy.)

Even if you provide your own wardrobe, however, the costumer will want to know your sizes in case the clothes you show up with aren't "right."

- *Sizes men should know:* shoe, hat, glove, shirt (small, medium, large, extra large; sleeve length, collar size), pants (waist and length), jacket, and/or coat.

- *Sizes women should know:* shoe, hat, glove, blouse, dress, pants, jacket, and/or coat.

If the show is a period piece, you'll need a fitting. After getting your sizes, the costumer will set a day and time for you to come to the studio. (You may or may not be paid for this, depending on your contract. Again, see Appendix A.)

Preparing

When rehearsing and memorizing your lines, be aware that anything can happen. It's a lead-pipe cinch your scene won't take place the way you envision it. Positive it will take place with one of the characters seated behind a desk? There won't be a desk in sight.

Know your lines, but be flexible enough to have them change drastically on the set. And don't bet on getting the cue you're expecting. Besides human error, many actors (especially the stars) take it upon themselves to "improve" the writing. They completely change their lines, leaving their fellow actors gaping stupidly, listening for cues that never come.

Rehearse the scenes in as many ways as possible; seated (looking left, then right); walking; and yes, even behind a desk. Do, however, retain your basic interpretation of the scene. You were hired at least partly because of the way you read the scene. Stay with that unless the director asks for a change on the set.

As "opening day" approaches, either your agent or the second assistant director will phone to give you your "call"—the day and time you'll be expected to arrive on the set. You'll probably get as much sleep as a rat on catnip.

ARRIVAL

Don't run up to the producer or director chirping "I'm here!" They've got other things on their minds. Report to the second assistant director. He'll show you to your dressing room (it should be private) and give you your contract or booking slip. Bear in mind it's his job to have you ready to go when the time comes, and if he's going to make a mistake, he's going to have you ready too early. There's a lot of "hurry up and wait" on movie sets.

After you've settled into your dressing room, perhaps gotten a cup of the awful coffee that's a perennial fixture on sets, it's best that you get into costume immediately, then report to the makeup artist.

Women, unless they're experienced in film-makeup application, should allow the expert to do their faces. Makeup for everyday wear is one thing, stage makeup another; a film-makeup expert knows how to make you up for *camera*, a third thing entirely.

Once you've gotten those chores squared away, sit down in your dressing room and prepare to wait . . . and wait . . . and wait. . . .

THE CONTRACT

While waiting, read over your contract. Check to be sure your name is spelled correctly, that your Social Security number, address, phone number, and salary are correct, that your billing and any other special deal is as agreed. If everything is O.K., be sure to sign all copies (usually three). Then fill out your tax forms. And then . . . more waiting.

SAVING ENERGY

We'd rather rehearse for eight solid hours than spend half that time sitting around on a set. The latter is far more exhausting, because it's not only a bore, it's a time filled with anxiety and nervousness. You'll find it very difficult to relax on your first day. Try. Don't make the mistake of running around the set. Save your energy. Lie down in your dressing room; read, if you can concentrate; do crossword puzzles. You may wait thirty minutes or eight hours before you're called; the more energy you've kept stored, the better your performance will be.

THE LINGO

Here are some terms you'll be hearing:

- *Marks:* Whenever you move, the cameraman has to know in advance where you'll stop. If he doesn't, you'll be out of focus or even out of frame (out of the picture entirely). Therefore, those stopping points are marked, and it's your job to hit those marks *dead on.* "Marks are critical," says commercial producer Bob Wollin. "You're dealing with very sophisticated lenses."

  Marks are denoted by a piece of masking tape, a chalk mark, or (for example, when you're standing on grass) a wooden *T.* They want your toes directly on the mark—in the case of the *T,* on the bar of the *T.* And they want you dead center on the mark—with the *T,* one foot on either side of the stem. This is *vital.* If you don't hit your marks, the cameraman will have to stop the shooting because he's aiming for one spot and you're in another. Keep missing your marks, and you could be fired at worst and humiliated at best. Pros hit their marks; amateurs don't—and they're not paying you to be an amateur.

  Unfortunately, if you're inexperienced at hitting marks, you'll find they can really get in the way of your acting. If you can't afford a film-technique class, practice with some masking tape at home.

- *Take Print:* If the director likes a given shot, or take, of a scene, he'll tell his assistants he wants them to print it. When you are doing the master, and you hear the director say "Print that," you know that's the take you'll need to match.

- *Matching:* You're watching a movie. The actor lights a cigarette. The camera cuts away from him for a moment. When it returns, the cigarette has disappeared. That's an extreme example of a bad match. Most matching is your responsibility. There is a script supervisor and/ or a continuity person there to check that things match from one shot to the next, but you'll be expected to match yourself.

  If you shout "Get out!" and point on the word "get" in one shot, you should point on that same word every take. You'll be asked to match all movement (when and how you rise, sit down, turn, gesture, pick something up, etc.), and you should also be certain that you look the same (costume, hair, general makeup). Be especially careful to remember if you must take a lunch break between takes. You should also match the emotional intensity of the scene from one take to the next. If you're furious in one take and merely angry in another, you're not matching.

  It's possible no one will tell you you're not matching. Except in rare cases, this goes unmentioned, but it will be spotted and dealt with in the cutting room. If you're not matching, they'll use other takes to cover. You'll lose screen time, most likely close-ups. Cinematographer Howard Wexler summed it up: "Continuity mistakes from an actor are really unforgivable."

- *Master:* The shot that sets the scene. It's always the first take of a scene and includes all actors involved in that scene. Whatever you do in the master, you must do in all other shots.

- *Two-shots/three-shots, etc.:* A two-shot has two actors in it; a three-shot, three actors, and so on.

- *Full, medium shots/close-ups, etc.:* A full shot takes in your whole body; a medium shot, your body from the waist up; a close-up, your face; an extreme close-up, anything from an eyeball to a pore.

  You can't tell by the location of the camera which is being shot. "Where are you cutting me?" is the question to ask, for two reasons. First, so that you won't make your performance too big or too small. Second, so that you will be holding important props, such as letters or books, at the right height to be seen.

- *"Action!"* That's your cue to start. Only the director may give it.

- *"Cut!"* This is when you stop acting—not a moment before. There will be times you'll feel the camera has been on you forever, but never break character until the director says "Cut." He will need this extra footage later, when editing.

- *"Roll camera"/"Turn over":* Called out by the first assistant director. Either term means the cameraman is to start running the film through the camera.

- *First/second teams:* In order not to tire the actors, stand-ins are hired. They're used to check lighting and camera positions, and may actually replace the actor in certain shots. They're called the "second team." You're on the "first team." When you hear the assistant director call "First team," they're ready for you. "Second team" means you can keep reading your *Daily Variety*. Nice to be first for a change, isn't it?

- *Wild track:* In order to prevent having to call you back another day because the sound was recorded poorly, occasionally they'll ask you to do a "wild track" on the set. You'll stand at the microphone saying your line(s) over and over as the sound man tapes them.

- *Dubbing/looping:* "Looping" is done by actors, usually in one of two ways. Let's say, because of some technical difficulty, you're looping one line: You'll hear that line on a "looped" tape that plays over and over. You listen to the way you said it and try to match the way you said it exactly, so that your words match the way your lips move.

  The other method is to have the scene projected onto a screen in front of you. You'll be wearing a headset, and when the time comes, you'll hear four "beeps." Immediately after the fourth, you start, matching your words to the movement of your mouth as you see it on the screen before you. Looping is always done in a studio; in television, often on the same day of the shoot, to save the expense of calling you back another day.

- *Key light:* The light most important to you because it's your own "spotlight." During the day, outdoors, it's the sun. If you don't know where your key light is, ask, and try to make sure you're in it when shooting.

- *"Cheating toward the camera":* Always be aware of where the camera is located, and position yourself accordingly; it's your audience. If the camera can't see it—face, prop, or whatever—it doesn't exist.

• *Overlap(ping):* Unlike theatre, where cues need to be fast and "stepping on" another actor's line occasionally can add to the excitement, in film or tape you have to be careful not to overlap lines. It makes editing the scene difficult, and, often, the take will have to be reshot. Exceptions are allowed (for example, during a "violent" argument), but in general, let your fellow actor finish his line before you speak.

• *Hot set:* When shooting is suspended because, for example, the sun is going down, the set on which you've been shooting will be labeled "hot." This means nothing is to be moved, so that everything will match when the company resumes shooting again.

• *"Wrap":* No single order is more welcomed by a tired actor or crew member. It means work's over. Never leave a set until the second assistant director tells you you're "wrapped" for the day.

THE REHEARSAL/THE SHOOT

After what will feel like (or be) an eternity, the second assistant director will come a-knocking at your dressing-room door, saying, "We're ready for you." It's rehearsal time. When you arrive on the set itself, the second a.d. (assistant director) will introduce you to your fellow actors, and you'll "remeet" the director, and if he's there, the producer

Films and films for television

The only real working difference between these two probably will lie in the number of takes you do. Film directors tend to shoot scenes over and over until they're happy with what they've got. After fifteen takes or so, it's easy to stop caring about what you're doing, but, inevitably, the take you got sloppy on will be the one they use—because the rain was just perfect.

Films for television include almost any drama made for TV except a "three-camera show" (see below). Usually, a one-hour filmed TV show is shot in a week to ten days, so you won't spend a lot of time rehearsing and filming. If at all possible, they'll want to rehearse the scene once, light it, and shoot it in *one* take. "You'd better assume you're going to do your great work on take one," says director Noel Black.

No matter what you're doing, expect very little direction. Your blocking will be vague, usually of the "play it over there" variety. Most of the time you'll be expected to come up with all the ideas. It's rare to be shown how or when to move, stand or sit, and forget any long discussions about character motivation. It won't be like the stage. Not only do film and TV directors expect you, as a professional, to be ready to perform when you arrive on the set, but many feel that giving direction to actors is "insulting." Often, the director will be a camera nut who wouldn't know how to direct an actor if his life depended on it. Above all, time is money and costs are so high; there is never enough time. For this reason, too, the director probably will say something about your performance only if he doesn't like what you're doing. As one director expressed it, "I don't have time to play school-master."

When rehearsal begins, there's a good chance that the stars of the show, or the series regulars, will apparently slough off: They may mumble their lines, read from the script, or generally act sloppily. It may be that they're husbanding their energies for the camera because of demanding roles, or it may be that they are just self-indulgent. At any rate, they can afford to do it; you can't. You, with less experience, no clout, and only a couple of speeches, are going to get only one or two rehearsals—don't "save" it. Let rehearsal be the time you blow a line because you're working too hard—not the actual shoot.

Once the scene is rehearsed, your marks will be set down. You'll then be excused and can sit down someplace while the crew lights the set.

When they're ready to shoot, you'll hear "Stand by!", then "Roll camera" (or "Turn over"), then "Speed" (called out by the sound man to let the director know his tape recorder is running). Standing a few feet away, the man with the legendary clapboard will snap it (sometimes in your face if they're doing a close-up) to synchronize sound with picture. Finally, the director calls "Action!" and you're off and running.

Bear in mind that if you're shooting a feature film, everything you do will be "blown up" about thirty-five times. Even in a film for television, stage actors will have to be careful not to be too "big" with their acting, to "step back" from the camera. Don't "show" the camera what you're thinking or doing; allow the camera to "discover" it. And stay in character as long as the camera is running. As TV newsman Dan Rather phrased it in the title of his book: The camera never blinks.

To illustrate how well trained you have to be, here's an example of what can happen to you on *one line:*

You've shot the master and they're ready to shoot your close-up. As the final seconds tick off, the cameraman says, "Listen, you're slightly off your mark, and when you say that line, cheat over a little into the light." You nod. (Now you're thinking, "Let's see: mark, cheat over, I'm angry in this scene . . .")

The sound man approaches. "Listen," he says, "try not to drop your voice so low on that line; I'm not getting you." "Right," you reply. (Now it's, "mark, cheat over, voice up, angry. . . .")

The director passes by and says, "Don't do that line quite so angry." "Gotcha," you say. ("Mark, cheat over, voice up, less intensity. . . .")

The makeup artist slips in and pads the perspiration off with a tissue as the cameraman adds, "And be sure to hold that cup up high enough so we can see it." "Uh-huh," you reply. ("Mark, cheat over, voice up, less intensity, hold up cup. . .")

The assistant director says, "Stand by."

Your costume begins to itch.

You hear "Roll camera," "Speed," a man snaps a clapboard in your face, saying "Marker," the director says "Action" . . .

And the star changes your cue.

The next time you're watching television and you think the actors are "phoning it in," remember this example. And get training. Lots of it.

Three-camera shows

We're sure you've heard an announcer say, "Taped in Hollywood before a live audience," usually at the beginning of a half-hour situation comedy such as "Three's Company." That's a three-camera show. Three cameras are used simultaneously and the show is taped in narrative sequence, almost exactly as though you were doing a one-act play. There's no stopping to change camera setups (that's why they use three), and breaks occur only if the actors must move from set to set. If you make a mistake, unless it's drastic, you keep going.

Like a play, rehearsals start with a read-through, with the cast seated at a table, and proceed to blocking and business. The rehearsal period is usually four days, followed by taping on the fifth. On the day or night of performance, you'll probably do the entire show twice, in front of two different audiences.

Stage actors will find this a delightful way to work; it's as close to doing a one-act play as you can get without actually doing one. Directors work much more with actors during the rehearsal period, and the live audience adds to the feeling of theatre. Also, the level of your performance is close to that of a comedy or musical done in a small- or medium-sized theatre.

Soap opera

These, too, are three-camera shows, but they're usually rehearsed in the morning and shot in the afternoon of the same day. Short of summer stock, there's no better training ground for learning lines, business, and delivery of a believable performance in a short period of time. "Soap operas are one of the best ways to learn your craft," says producer William Kayden. "They're marvelous training." Once again, even though there's no live audience, you only stop to move from set to set. The standard rule is: Keep going. The acting level here is extremely controlled and understated. The audience should feel as though they're observing you in your living room through a keyhole.

THE WE-HATE-TO-MENTION-IT DEPARTMENT

We wish we could promise you a grand ole time on every set, but, if the truth be known, there will be times you will think you walked into a scene out of Dante's *Inferno*—and if you're not careful, you could get burned.

Understand first of all that a caste system does exist on a set—unspoken, but there in spades. At the bottom of the heap are the extras; at the top, the stars. Extras are served last at lunch. Day players would be wise not to sit in the star's chair (at least not without permission). Stars get the best dressing rooms; other actors get smaller but still private rooms; extras of the same sex dress in one room together. "I've worked on sets where a principal comes up and we'll start talking," says one SAG actor who also does extra work, "and as soon as they find out I'm an extra there's a whole change in attitude. And they make you feel kind of . . . really crummy. And it's not just them—it's everybody." You'll see plenty of top dog/underdog manifestations of human behavior, and you'd be smart to take note of how much of it is taking place on any given set.

On some sets, this behavior is kept to a minimum, with everyone sharing in a joyful, generous camaraderie. On others, it's best to keep to yourself and not try to become "one of the boys," for you'll be at grave risk of being humiliated.

If your spouse joins you on location (there's usually no objection), be circumspect before you invite him/her to the set itself. On a good set, they'll be treated with the utmost respect and charm. On a bad set, they'll be made to feel as if they just walked in on a very private conversation.

Even on a good set, you must be discreet. Don't go running up to the star and introduce yourself or—great holy amateur night!—ask for an autograph. Have the second assistant director introduce you at the right time. Don't even start a conversation with a star; let him take the lead.

Sound like Chicken Little? A story: A *veteran* actor (one whose face you know, but whose name you probably don't) sat next to a major star on a set for hours, saying nothing. Finally, the actor turned to the star and ventured, "Hi, I'm ——. I just can't sit next to someone and not talk to them." The star slowly turned to the actor and replied, "I can."

We're not saying that your on-set experiences need be bad. Just be on your guard. As producer Michael Rhodes jokingly put it, "You already know you have to be crazy to be in this business, so, on the set, treat everybody as if they're potential ax murderers, and you'll be all right."

WRAP

If you're working the next day, the second assistant director will hand you your "call sheet." Among other things, it's a one-page list of all cast and crew needed on the set that day, their makeup calls and set calls. The former tells you when to report to work, the latter when to be on the set, made up and in costume, ready to shoot. If you're not working the next day but are still on salary, next to your name will be the word "Hold."

When you're ready to leave the set, the second assistant director will ask you to sign out. Note carefully the arrival and departure times he has recorded. This is what they will base any overtime on. Be sure the times are accurate and written in *ink*. (For more on overtime, work rules, etc., see Appendix A.)

Don't expect anyone to come rushing up to you telling you how wonderful you were, especially not the producer or director. They may have loved your work, but right now their minds are on the next scene.

Then you're on your way back to your hotel, or home. You won't be very good company that night. You'll feel as though you've just come back from another world—and you have.

VI
COMMERCIALS

21 Commercials: The Wonderful World of Happy
22 Commercial Agents
23 Composites
24 From Audition to Payoff

21 COMMERCIALS: THE WONDERFUL WORLD OF HAPPY

What do they want? What plays in Disneyland.

Pamela Campus,
Commercials Casting Director

THE COMMERCIAL TYPE

Want to know how much work you can expect to get in commercials? Or how to look? Or how you should act? Sit down in front of a TV set. With occasional exceptions, you'll see "white bread"—an industry expression describing actors with rather bland, wholesome, all-American looks. You'll see "P & G housewives with perk"—another industry expression meaning idealized midwestern-mother types oozing perkiness and cheer. (P & G stands for Procter & Gamble, but it describes a standard look.) You'll see warm, loving dads with short hair and conservative clothing, adorably cute children, teens who never saw a pimple (unless they're selling Clearasil), grandmothers still dressed as they did back in 1926. Clean streets. Musical comedy. Happy endings. Energy. Brightness. Warmth . . .

"Most calls, they want midwestern," says agent Karen DiCenzo. "You'll have to look harder for character faces, and many nights may go by between ethnic faces or actors with accents . . . unless you tune to an ethnic station, where actors of that particular group will predominate. Only a limited number of high-fashion products will use women in low-cut, sexy dresses, heavy rouge, or orange eyeshadow. Men will almost never sport mustaches or beards.

In short, you'll see what the makers of commercials want to get. And the closer you come to that look, the more you'll work. Which brings us to . . .

ARE COMMERCIALS WORTH IT?

Are they worth shaving off that beard you love so much? Are they worth changing your hairstyle and makeup from "Zoweena of Hollywood" to "Mary Smith from Peoria" just to please some faceless corporate executive who's decided (based on millions of dollars of research) that his customers relate to "Middle America"? Should you really go to all the hassle and expense of finding an agent and putting together a good composite just to work in a part of the industry that *wants the product to be the star?* (The script designation for a product is the word "Hero"!) Is spending all that money on commercial workshops, learning to convince America that it can't live without Uncle George's Better Mousetraps, worth the time of a serious actor? Three points . . .

Money

According to the Screen Actors Guild, 60 percent of the income of all actors comes directly from commercials. Put another way, commercials account for more income than all the other performing fields *combined*. When you do a commercial, you know one thing: You'll earn at least $300 and you may earn literally thousands of dollars more in residuals. Since almost all commercials are shot in one day, that's not bad wages. It beats slinging hash in a diner.

Career

We could fill these pages with the names of people who have been discovered through commercials, as commercial casting director Pamela Campus testifies: "A few years ago I walked through Columbia Pictures Studios, and I saw up on their wall all these pictures of people like Vic Tayback, Suzanne Somers . . . people I had hired five years ago. And I said to myself, 'Wait a minute, I'm training these people for sitcoms, mini-series, and television.' Let me tell you something. The top people you see in commercials today, especially if they're comedic, will be the top people you later see in series. If you stand out in a commercial, usually you'll be picked up in a series. I've seen it."

Entrée

If you're a middle-aged housewife from Peoria who's thinking of fast money or of doing commercials on a lark, we'd advise you to skip it. If you're exceedingly lucky, you'll get a commercial here and there, but the jobs will be too sparse to make it worth your while, even if you can get an agent to rep you—which won't be easy. To work in commercials on any kind of a continual basis, you need to be as well trained as any other actor in any other field. Sorry.

However, if you're a newcomer with some theatre and/or commercials training, commercials (along with industrials and low-budget films) can be the easiest way to get that first break. When it comes to casting, commercials are far more cut and dried than theatricals. By the time you're called in for an audition, the product owner, marketing department, and advertising agency have long ago mapped out on a "story board" the actions, words, and emotional message of every frame of the commercial. They know what type of actors they're looking for; fit that picture and you've got a good shot. As one agent put it, "Commercial agents sometimes sign non-SAG people because they know that if the advertising agency loves your face and loves the way you sell their product, they have enough clout—money—to get you into SAG via Taft-Hartley." (See "Unions," Chapter 7.)

Further, as theatrical agent Mary Spencer points out, "Many times, if you're new, you can get into an agency 'across the board.' If you have a great commercials look, and are salable, they'll take you on in all fields."

Just remember: newcomers yes, untrained no.

Are they worth it? If we haven't convinced you, it's probably best to stay out. If you're contemptuous of commercials, that attitude will show, and you'll only wind up making a lot of people annoyed at you, and not working anyway.

If you do want to work in commercials, get some training, make yourself look as "white bread" as possible, and find the one person you simply can't do without: a commercial agent.

22 COMMERCIAL AGENTS

You can eat your way to a fortune in this industry.

John Fisher, Commercials Agent

Two kinds of people spend their lives on the phone—telephone operators and commercial agents. Here's why.

Each commercial agency puts together a "book" (a three-ring binder containing the pictures of all the agency's clients). When casting, the commercial casting director takes these books from the shelf and looks through them. The actors deemed "right" are chosen and their agents are notified by phone. The agents then phone their clients and give them the information regarding the audition.

If the actor gets the part, the casting director phones the agent to tell him when the actor will be shooting. (Unless the actor is a celebrity, there are no salary or billing negotiations—more later). The agent then calls the actor.

Getting the idea that it's a fairly set routine? It is. In the fast, furious world of commercials, you're either right for the part or you're not. Your agent doesn't "sell" you—your pictures (and, later, you) do. "We're really order takers," says one commercials agent. Naturally, if the agent is smart, he'll go out of his way to make a friend of all commercial casting directors. He wants them to go to his "book" first. Sometimes the casting director gives casting information to the new services, one called the Breakdown Service, the other the Breakthru Service, and the agents submit your pictures for a specific part. But don't expect the kind of personal attention from your commercial agent you should be getting from your theatrical agent. Your commercial agent serves as a kind of clearing house of commercial types *before* you're cast, a messenger of information *when* you're cast, and a guardian of your financial interests (straight pay and residuals) *after* you're cast.

Then why do you need one? Besides the complex matter of residuals, there's little opportunity to submit yourself directly for a commercial. In Los Angeles, most casting directors free-lance; besides, commercial casting is a speedy business, often going from first audition to the end of shooting within a week. You can search the trades from now till Elsie the Cow comes home and never know what's casting.

Voice-over agent Don Pitts: "In New York you can make the rounds to the ad agencies and production houses. Out here, if you start making the rounds to the production houses, there's nobody there to talk to, and at the ad agencies, nobody wants to talk to you. You really have to rely on your agent."

SEEKING/CHOOSING AN AGENT

. . . And the larger the better. Big agencies are the ones that receive the bulk of the calls. "The others get the crumbs," as one commercial casting director put it. Since you won't need the personal attention that you do in theatricals, there's nothing wrong with your commercial agency having a client list that numbers in the hundreds. In fact, it helps. Generally, the larger the commercial agency, the more the casting director trusts that agency and knows the agents within it, and consequently the more calls they get. Some of the best-known commercial agencies are

Abrams-Rubaloff & Associates
Nina Blanchard Enterprises, Ltd.
Sonjia W. Brandon's Commercials Unlimited
Carey-Phelps-Colvin
William Cunningham & Associates
Flaire Agency
Tylor Kjar Agency
Jack Rose/Dorothy Day Otis Agency
Charles H. Stern Agency
Sutton, Barth & Vanneri
Herb Tannen & Associates
Wormser, Helfond & Joseph
Ann Wright Associates

There are others; they are indicated with a capital "C" on our list or on the list you pick up from SAG.

Many theatrical agencies also have commercial departments. If you sign with one of these, make sure the agent who handles commercials doesn't also handle theatricals. A single individual really can't do justice to both.

How do you interest a commercial agent? By sending them a *good* commercial headshot (with résumé). Recommendations always help, but one good picture along with a covering letter will do the trick if the agency is looking for your type. Compared to the usual search for a theatrical agent, it's often a refreshingly simple process.

When you do get called in, use all the techniques found in "The General Interview/Look-See" (Chapter 16) and add a good helping of "perk."

(And for information about commercial-agency contracts, see Appendix A.)

DEALING WITH/MOTIVATING THE COMMERCIALS AGENT

It's a given that you should take your agent to lunch and try to make a friend of him, even in the area of commercials. Beyond that . . .

What he'll expect of you

He won't expect you to get work on your own, for the reasons we discussed earlier. He won't care that much if you do plays and showcases except as a way for you to keep fresh and promote your general value as an actor; they don't usually play a direct part in casting. And he won't expect you to be calling him with ideas and suggestions regarding the best way to submit you for a part.

He will expect you: to be a fantastic auditioner; to be on time and not to miss interviews; to keep your *Academy Players Directory* listing current (one of your two alloted pictures should be your commercial headshot); to pay him his commission; and to keep track of your residuals and, especially, your conflicts (see Chapter 24). He'll also want you to put together a composite (see next chapter) and to supply him with enough copies so that he'll have plenty to put in the books as well as for those occasional direct submissions. Some commercial agents give new clients a list of commercial casting directors and production houses and ask them to drop off a photo to each for their agency books. The stated idea is to give you an opportunity to make personal contacts. It's a bit of an imposition, and much of it is a waste of time because of the widespread free-lancing, but for the sake of interoffice public relations and that occasional lucky shot, do it anyway.

Above all, be reachable! You're away from home. You call your commercial agent at eleven A.M. You're "clear." Ten minutes later, he gets a call from a commercial casting director, telling him they need you *now*. You don't call back until three P.M. You have just lost out on a commercial interview. Although this can occasionally occur in theatricals, it's far more common in the fast-moving world of commercials. Do all in your power to be sure your agent can reach you on a moment's notice.

He may not mention it, but he'll probably want you to take as many workshops taught by commercial casting directors as you can afford. The reason? Again, because they don't often grant general interviews and are not that easy to meet.

What you should expect of him

Assuming you've given him good pictures and that you're "white bread," you should go out on commercial auditions far more often than you do those for movies and TV shows. It may take you a little while to get rolling, but once you do, expect to go out at least twice a week.

"The most I ever went out on," says one good commercials-type actor, "was ten in two days." Those numbers will be lower if you are not "white bread," if your agency is not one of the largest, if you haven't got good pictures, or if you suddenly "cool off" for a while (when that happens, hang in there; things will pick up again eventually).

Beyond this, your agent's most important function is to keep track of your residuals and conflicts.

And to help you put together an excellent composite.

23 COMPOSITES

*I look for salability, sparkle, and an
expressive 'grabber'-type shot.*

Tracey Jacobs, Commercials Agent

Commercials are a picture-oriented business. . . .

The owner of a bakery, along with a commercial casting director, is thumbing through photos of actors. He comes across a headshot of a man in a business suit. Next he sees a composite including a shot of a friendly fellow in a chef's hat, holding a tray of rolls. Which actor gets called in to audition?

Don't hock your wedding ring. Have your agent use your commercial headshot(s) until you can afford a composite, are sure you're happy with your agent, and are convinced that you're enough of a commercial type to warrant the investment.

Then remember that while a smiling headshot will do, a composite will do better.

SPECIFICATIONS

A composite consists of one large close-up on the front and from three to six other photos on the back. (Four are best.) Measuring eight-and-a-half-by-eleven inches, it's slightly larger than an eight-by-ten headshot. It is usually printed in a matte finish, with three holes punched out on the left for easy insertion in agency books. Unlike headshots, in addition to your name, your stats are included, as is your agent's logo, address, and phone number (see illustration).

PLANNING THE SESSION

The average composite session lasts about three to four hours. Presumably you will have chosen a photographer who is familiar with the area of commercial composites and is good at it, who has ideas to contribute but won't take umbrage at your own, who will work with a child or dog if you want them in a shot, who will go "on location" to a park, a supermarket, etc. You will decide between the two of you when to do the session (avoid high noon, when lighting is harshest), who provides the props (bring at least some of your own—his have already turned up in other actors' composites), what costumes you'll need to bring. All this will require some planning, starting with . . .

Talking with your agent

First, ask him to show you some good composites. You'll very quickly get the idea of how they should look. Next, ask him for suggestions. What kinds of pictures does he think will best sell you? Are you the classic "P&G housewife with perk"? Should you have a "loving daddy" shot or are you still too young? Do you look like you belong in an office? A supermarket? A kitchen? A baseball diamond? Would you look silly holding a monkey wrench? If so, you might be convincing in a bookkeeper's shade. Remember, this is a business of cliché and stereotype, and the better the fit the more you'll work. Does your agent see you selling dishwasher detergent or shampoo? Cadillacs or Fords? Toothpaste or computers? In commercials, there's not a lot of room for disagreement between you and your agent as to how you should be utilized.

The agency may specify how many photos you should use. In any case, determine the "must" photos (a young mom type will be at a disadvantage without one shot of her relating to a child).

The agent may direct you to a particular printer who is familiar with his composite specifications and already has a negative of the agency logo at his shop. There's nothing wrong with that, assuming the printer's rates are reasonable, or with the agent suggesting a couple of photographers but don't let him insist on any one person; sad to say, he may be getting a kickback. Go with the photographer you like.

How you'll appear

A good composite includes:

• At least one close-up for the front of the composite.

• One shot of you from head to foot.

• Probably, one shot of you in a business suit, jacket, or dress.

• At least one shot in casual dress (can be most shots).

• At least one "costume" shot (meaning anything from a pair of glasses, whether you wear them or not, to an apron and chef's hat, a football uniform, tennis togs, nurse's uniform, etc.).

• For women, at least one variation on hairstyle, if possible.

- One shot in full or three-quarters profile.

You can then mix and match the above with a variety of your own ideas and the following suggestions:

- *The "consumer shot"* of you about to chomp into a hamburger or sipping a shake, or pushing a cart full of groceries, pumping gas into your car, etc. Be sure the brand names of products you use as props don't show. It won't help your chances if you're up for a Coke commercial and your composite shows you drinking Pepsi.

- *The "loving mommy/daddy shot":* It's rent-a-child time. The photo should show you relating warmly to a child, but be sure the focus of the picture is on you. The most we should see of the child is his profile. You don't want the little bugger stealing the scene. . . .

- *"At-work shot,"* white- or blue-collar, and including housework. Make these shots active and full of fun. For example, if you look like you might work in a supermarket, you can deck yourself out in cap and apron and appear to be rescuing a stack of apples from falling over.

- *"Outdoorsy/sports shot":* You're shown jogging, camping, fishing, playing baseball, jumping over the net with a racket in your hand, and

FRONT (ABOVE) AND BACK OF A TYPICAL COMPOSITE...

so forth. Your entire composite could be outdoorsy if you're that kind of person. One important note, though: don't photograph yourself doing any activity you're not actually able to do.

Be sure to reread our chapter on résumé shots. Actually, doing a composite can be fun . . . but don't shortchange the planning. If you depend on the photographer for ideas, you will get recycled poses and props . . . try to think of fresh variations on the standard themes.

Again, it's crucially important to know your type and play to it, no matter what photos you may use on your composite. Take as an example of this the composite of one actor who has an upper-class air and a slight English accent. His composite consists of five photos: on the front, he is pictured in a jacket and turtleneck, hair neatly in place, a warm smile on his face: your basic commercial headshot.

Picture two, on the back, is a full body shot of the actor in a suit, a small briefcase in his hand, leaning against a Rolls-Royce with a mansion in the background (his "work" shot).

Picture three is the actor in an expensive tux, menu in hand, warmly beckoning the viewer to sit down. In the foreground, an expensive-looking bottle of wine is barely discernible (a mixture of "costume/work" shot).

Picture four shows him in a shirt and hat suggesting an African safari guide, looking very handsome and elegant (a mixture of "costume/outdoorsy" shot).

Picture five features him on a boat, wearing a casual jacket and open-necked shirt. Yachts are seen in the background ("outdoorsy" shot).

Each picture, everything you see, proclaims "upper class," "expensive," "cultured," exactly the aura the actor exudes when he walks into a room. Now that's a composite!

24 FROM AUDITION TO PAYOFF

We actors often tend to overanalyze things . . . I don't want to complicate it. When it comes to commercials, it's selling. There's no other way to put it. It's selling the product.

John Edwards, Actor

If you're depressed, skip the pills and go out on a commercial audition. There you'll find a roomful of people who are up, bright, and happy. (If they want to work, they'd better be.) Just being around all that enthusiasm will have to brighten your day.

BEFORE THE INTERVIEW

When your agent calls, get the usual information (when, where, for whom), and press the agent to be as specific as he can regarding the part. Unlike movie/TV auditions, where your clothes merely suggest the part, in commercials you'll want to dress as close to the part as you can without visiting a costumer. For example, cowboy hats, jeans, and boots are the order of the day if you're up for a Western commercial, but not six-shooters and spurs—you don't want to look *too* eager. As one commercial actor put it, "I once went up for a commercial in which there was a writer. I've never seen such a profusion of pipes in one room in all my life."

Commercial agent Kathy Smith advises, "Always have at least one casual and one 'upscale' outfit in your closet. When the call comes in, that's no time to try to run to the dry cleaners." Many commercial actors keep these "audition clothes" in their car, along with a box of probable props (boots, sneakers, eyeglasses, and—yes—pipes, etc.), just in case they're out of the house when they check with their agents and discover a call has come in. Their portable equipment also includes photos, résumés, and a clipboard (you'll learn why later). And they keep their cars gassed up.

Once again, arrive early to the audition with composite in hand. Then find the table with the "sign-in" sheet. On it, you'll be asked for your name, Social Security number, agent, what time you were told to be there (called "Player's Actual Call"), and the time you arrived. Leave blank, for the moment, the next box that says "Player's Time Out"; put your initials in the next box, and circle the number that corresponds with whether it is your first, second, third, or fourth audition for that commercial. This is very important, as these sheets are sent to SAG or AFTRA. You'll really be inconveniencing the casting director if you forget to sign in or out.

Often, in addition to your composite/headshot, they'll want to take a photo of you with an instant camera.

What you do next will depend on the kind of audition you'll be doing, but at any rate the audition will almost always be videotaped. After screening out the obviously inappropriate candidates, the casting director sends these tapes to the advertiser, often in another city, for him to choose what actors he wants to cast or call back.

PREPARATION

Preparing for the general interview audition

You'll rarely do a general interview with a commercial casting director to size you up for unspecified future work. Your "general interviews" in commercials will be a form of audition for specific assignments. If this is the kind of interview you'll be doing, you'll need to be proficient in the techniques described in our chapter on "The General Interview/Look-See," especially regarding the art of choosing a topic. And be upbeat as all get out.

The improvisation audition

There's really nothing to prepare. Just relax and save your energy. When it comes time for the taping of your audition, you'll be given a "situation" and asked to improvise it. There won't be a script. The best approach is to be alert and alive, have fun, not to stand there like a lump, thinking. Here's where classes in improvisation and pantomime can be of immense help.

If you're asked to do this kind of audition, SAG says you should be paid a fee (what's to prevent the advertiser from stealing your great line or idea?). Please note, however, that if you do ask for the fee, the advertisers will just say never mind, send you home, and proceed to audition the actors who'll do it for free . . . and for much bigger bucks if they're hired.

The scene audition

As you read the script, ask yourself: What's the tone of the scene? Intimate? Yahoo? Slice of life? If the script itself isn't in storyboard form (a shot-by-shot illustration of the commercial), ask the casting director if there's a storyboard nearby that you can look at. The more you know about how to approach the commercial, the better.

If you're going to audition with a partner, ask who the actor will be and work with him on it. You may find yourself one of a "family unit" that includes a child or even one of a group of actors. Try not to be swamped by them, especially the young-un'. Make a friend of the little bugger, then control him.

If you've got only a line or two in the scene, go ahead and memorize. Otherwise, it's not necessary.

As you work on it, bear in mind that even the most realistic slice-of-life commercial should be kept relatively light. If you're doing a commercial for Dr. Zhivago's Wonder Elixir and your character has a headache, be mildly in pain—not all-out agony.

You will probably find the dialogue horrendously stilted. After all, it's a sales pitch, not a play. It's your job to make those words sound as if you just thought of them, and as if you naturally say, "Man, that's coffee!"

At the same time, your acting will usually be broader than for most movie/TV work. A good approximation is sitcom level.

The spokesman audition

These are the most difficult. It's just you and the camera. You'd better be a well-trained actor before you go out on one of these. And be vocally trained, and know how to enunciate ("comin'" and "goin'" will not get you workin').

You'll be given twenty-three seconds of copy and, if hired, will need to withstand the pressure of being asked to take tenths of a second off your reading, stretch a word here, emphasize a word there, while at the same time looking into the camera and appearing absolutely warm and genuine. Without solid training, we doubt you'll be able to hold up to the stress. Be ready or pass.

Spokesman commercials—indeed, all commercials—present a *problem,* followed by a *solution,* followed by a *resolution.* Mentally or, preferably, in pencil (so you can erase it after the audition), break down the copy into these three sections. Your approach to each will be slightly different. You *present* the problem, *emphasize* the solution, *sum up* with the resolution.

Often, these sections are preceded by "transition words": "so," "but," etc. Punch these words slightly harder, take a beat, then continue—so as to let the viewer in on the fact that the solution/resolution is coming.

Also look for "billboard words"—words to be emphasized. These can include "only," "delicious," "bigger," "better," "safer," "new," "superb," as well as any price included in the copy (if the price is there, the advertiser thinks it's a selling point). Ask yourself, "If I owned this product, what part of the copy would I want to stress?"

Next, as you say the speech—out loud—work to create the "golden triangle" of spokesman commercials: you to the viewer to the product. One of the most common errors beginners make is to treat the copy like a speech to an audience. It isn't. It's a *conversation* between you and one other person, seated in his living room. Your job is to talk to him about the product. If you can, imagine that person sitting right in the middle of the camera lens.

Don't try to memorize lines—just the first and last lines for maximum effect. Give some authority to your voice; make the viewer feel that you know what you're talking about. But don't be a bully. And don't point. Make all gestures, even facial gestures, "soft" and restrained. Do it standing. *And love your product.*

Finally, find a way to "tag" your reading: That's a gesture that winds up your "act" and gives them a little something to remember you by. Acting schtick is to be deplored generally, but it has its place here (and in all kinds of commercial auditions). We saw an actress wink at the end of her reading—*wink*, for Pete's sake!—and it worked just fine. Smile, nod knowingly, do something that puts an ending on the ending.

Because of the close parallels in breaking down copy for voice-overs and for on-camera spokesman commercials, you'll do well to heed voice-over agent Don Pitts's excellent summary:

"Don't make them feel that you're trying to sell something. Rather, make them feel that you're sharing some information with a friend." He adds, "The successful performer will go through the copy sentence by sentence and look for the key words—look for the 'hooks' in the copy. That's what separates the successful performer from the one who's just good." (For more on voice-overs, see Chapter 25, "Stocking Stuffers.")

THE AUDITION

When you walk in, you may see one lone person standing behind a videotape camera or any combination of producer, director, advertising-agency representative, product rep, or casting director. Try to remember names, if that won't throw you, and remember to jot them down later for your files.

The first thing you'll be shown is where to stand or sit (if possible, stand—it's easier to be energetic). Next, they'll probably ask you to "slate"—give your name—into the lens, take a beat, and start. (Some casting directors will want you to include the name of your agency; others won't. Ask for their preference.) Treat the "slate" as part of your scene; first impressions, you know . . .

You may see an "idiot card" next to, above, or immediately beneath the camera lens. Try not to use it. If you do, you'll look as if you're reading the commercial. If you have a lot of lines, put the copy on that clipboard we mentioned and hold it up at eye level, just out of camera range. Glance at the copy as needed. Naturally, you could hold the copy itself without the clipboard, but even the slightest case of nerves will cause the paper to shake, rattle, and roll.

If anyone says anything, listen very carefully. Casting director Pamela Campus says, "Listen for the key word whenever you're given direction. For example, someone says to you 'You're looking out the window. It's raining. It's a Sunday afternoon and it's cozy and intimate with your spouse.' 'Cozy' and 'intimate' are your key words." The common complaint in commercials (as well as theatricals) is that actors don't listen. "You don't have a lot to say. More important is to listen to what's said to you," says commercials producer Bob Wollin.

If you don't like your reading, you can ask to do it again. But don't be surprised if they say no. In commercials, they're often seeing more than one hundred people for a part. Also, don't assume a "no" answer means that they didn't like what you did—they may have loved it. Whatever you do, don't make negative comments on your reading—especially while the tape is running. We've seen actors finish their reading with lovely smiles . . . then, before anyone says "cut," the actors say *"Aaaargh,"* with accompanying grimaces. That's the last thing anyone watching those tapes will see—the actor with a contorted, ugly face, being negative. *Aaaargh.*

AFTER THE AUDITION

Be sure to sign out. The Screen Actors Guild says if the commercial makers have kept you longer than an hour, they must pay you ($18.75 for every half hour). But as one commercial casting director says, "If it's only five or ten minutes, to keep good relations with the casting director, I'd advise you to be kind and sign out under that one hour." It's that old penny-wise, pound-foolish thing again.

Then go home, feed your goldfish, and don't give the audition another thought. The advertiser and the producer are back at a studio, arguing over the length of your eyebrows.

After screening the original tape, the advertiser will want to call back (often several times) some of the best auditioners before making his decision. If that happens, remember you didn't get there by doing something wrong. Not only should you match your original reading as close as memory allows—unless instructed otherwise—but you should wear exactly what you wore the first time.

A FINAL WORD ABOUT AUDITIONING

It's one thing to read about doing commercial auditions, another to do them. There's also the added problem of dealing with the camera. We've seen that little collection of wires intimidate even the most experienced of actors.

If you want to do commercials, take a workshop on the subject. Be sure the class uses videotape, that you get plenty of turns on camera, and that it's taught by someone (usually a casting director) who works in the field. Such a person will be best equipped to teach you how to be a "P & G housewife with perk." "Every one of my clients has taken at least one commercial workshop with a commercial casting director," says agent Kathy Smith. "Schools can teach, but commercial casting directors can relate experiences."

And watch commercials—lots of them. Notice the "spokesman" style; what trends are current, how various products are advertised. Those "messages from our sponsor" are your own personal school bells

THE DEAL

If you get the job, you'll be paid $300 for the day (called your "session fee"). This is called a "scale" commercial—and makes up the bulk of all commercials produced. Unless you're a star, celebrity, stuntman, or established model, you'll never get paid more than $300 (an "overscale" commercial).

All other factors governing the shoot—length of workday, overtime, meal penalties, transportation and expenses, wardrobe fees, etc.—are (basically) the same as those governing the day player earning $600 or less (see Appendix A).

WAITING TO SHOOT

You'll get a wardrobe call, and most likely have to go to a fitting. Since most commercials are shot off the lots, you'll also be given a map to the location. And don't change a thing about your appearance. That groovy suntan can wait.

ON THE SET

The only real difference will probably be the number of takes and the number of possible "advisers" hovering around the director.

Anyone from the account executive to the product owner himself may be watching intently. You'll see numerous huddles after each take. Everybody worries a lot. Somebody doesn't like the way your hair looks. Somebody notices the product was at the wrong angle. Somebody thinks the direction is getting too serious. And, yes, somebody doesn't like the way you said, "Golly Martha, this stuff is great." Try not to let all this throw you or to take any of it personally. Even if some joker says something incredibly tactless, it could be that he's not a show-biz type and isn't used to working with actors. Throughout the day, your best bet is to have a "Hey, no sweat" attitude.

Since they've got you for eight hours and have only 30 seconds of film to put together, you'll probably say "So eat Munchies!" enough times to dream about those little crackers for weeks. As commercials producer Bob Wollin said, "Even if the very first take is good, they may pick at it for hours."

Afterward, go home and, again, forget it. Don't hold your breath waiting for all those residuals to come rolling in. Even if everything went beautifully, they may never use the commercial.

EXCLUSIVITY/CONFLICTS

What is the advertiser buying for his $300, besides your services as an actor on the day of shooting?

As your contract states, he's buying the right to keep you "exclusive" to his product—regardless of whether or not he puts that commercial on the air.

Do a commercial for, say, Maxwell House Coffee, and you can't turn right around and do another for a competing product such as Yuban. That's called a "conflict."

If you do the second commercial, both companies will become perturbed—but Yuban can become perturbed enough to sue your agent *and* you, and force the two of you to rob your piggy banks to pay for a new commercial sans your presence. Figure, oh, about $60,000 or so. Plus the loss of your agent. Plus trouble with the unions.

Never try to get away with doing a conflicting commercial, not even if the one you've got running is only being shown in Dry Prong. Keep careful records. Remind your agent if he calls with an audition for a conflicting commercial. Voice-over agent Don Pitts says, "It's very important to keep records of conflicts and not to assume it's only the agent's responsibility." How long does this exclusivity last? As long as the advertiser sends you a payment of $300 every 13 weeks, it can continue for 21 months—called the "maximum-use period." Again, the advertiser doesn't have to air the commercial. (We go into details concerning exclusivity, as well as use fees—"residuals"—in Appendix A.)

USE FEES (COMMONLY CALLED RESIDUALS)

"Don't ask me about residuals," says a commercial agent. "I've been in the business for thirteen years and I still don't understand them."

Yep, they're complicated. Mighty. In this book we have space only for a very summary look at the basics.

First, don't confuse use fees ("residuals") with holding fees. "Use fees" are paid when the commercial is aired. "Holding fees" are paid to keep you exclusive regardless of whether or not a commercial is aired. (However, the advertiser will deduct what holding fees he's paid you from what he owes you if the commercial does air.)

Basically, what you're paid for the use of a commercial depends on how the advertiser intends to use it and how it's used.

Network commercials

Technically, these are called "Program Usage Commercials." Here's where a down payment on that Porsche potentially lies. You're paid every time this kind of commercial airs, based on a preestablished fee scale involving the number of cities, and the populations of those cities, in which the commercial airs. Anyway, it can mean big bucks.

Wild spots

Ever watch Witch Women of Azusa on your local late show, and in between evil spells keep seeing the same commercial (an evil spell in itself)? That's probably a "wild spot." This kind of commercial can't air on a network show (unless they cut to a local station). You're paid a flat fee, again based on the number of cities and their populations. For that flat fee, the advertiser can show the commercial as many times as he likes, without paying you anything more. (Of course, he has to pay that fee every 13 weeks.) It wouldn't be an overstatement to say that there's a bit of controversy over these commercials, specifically because the advertiser can air them time and time again without additional compensation to you. As it stands, however, dem's da rules.

Dealer commercials

A local Toyota dealer, say, wants to run a national Toyota commercial at his own expense. In this case you'll get a flat fee and he'll get unlimited use of the commercial for six months. Don't be too distressed, since few dealers can afford to run a commercial over and over again. But remember that you do remain exclusive to him for a relatively small amount of money.

Seasonal commercials

When you see Santa Claus selling "Ralph's Reindeer Vitamin Supplements," that's a "seasonal." Again, you'll be paid a flat fee, but the advertiser can use the commercial only for 13 to 15 weeks. (Santa Claus in May wouldn't work anyway.) The advertiser can, however, bring back that commercial for another run a year later. You are *not* exclusive when you do a seasonal. You may do a commercial for a competing product, but you'll need to notify the second advertiser that you've got a seasonal.

Test commercials

Sometimes an advertiser wants to see if a given commercial will work, so he airs it only in a limited market in order to see what reaction it gets. That's a "test." Some of these have guaranteed sums paid to you; others don't, paying you use fees only when it airs. Since by definition the commercial will run only in a few cities, there's obviously very little money in test commercials—yet, as in other commercials, you're forced to remain exclusive to the advertiser. The only real benefit you might derive from it is if the advertiser gets great response and decides to go national with it. Then the commercial is converted to "program usage." (This is called a "rollout," perhaps because, as far as you're concerned, it means "roll out the money.") Nice—if it ever happens.

Ultimately, you have to look at commercials not only as income producers but as possible blocks to future income. Do a test, for example, and you're cut off from auditioning for all other competing products for as long as you remain exclusive to the advertiser who makes that test. Maybe no national commercials will come along during that time for which you would be "right"—but especially if you're a good commercial type, you'll need to be circumspect before you do any commercial that cuts you off from the potential high earnings of a national commercial.

Agents' commissions

Your agent gets 10 percent of every dime you make, regardless of the kind of commercial you do, what use fees you are paid, and including your session and holding fees, for the first 21 months. After that, he'll have to renegotiate for at least scale-plus-10 if he wants to make any more money on that commercial.

For more details on agents' commissions, use fees, holding fees, and work regulations, see Appendix A.

KEEPING TRACK

How does anyone know if your commercial runs at 4:30 P.M. in Padooka? Do the unions hire little gnomes to sit in front of TV sets all over the country to be sure you get all your residuals? Who keeps track of all this?

Believe it or not, the very people who pay you. Specifically, the advertising agency, on a more or less "honor system." And it works. *Almost* all the time. (Since the agency gets a commission from the advertiser every time his commercial is run, it's to the agency's benefit to keep accurate records.)

Still, foul-ups do occur. It wouldn't hurt to contact your friends around the country and ask them to keep a watchful eye out. (It's not all that much of an imposition; people love to spot friends when they appear on the tube. It's exciting to know somebody's who's actually "making it" in Hollywood.)

You might even keep a "commercial notification file" of your friends around the USA, and whenever you do a commercial, send them self-addressed postcards asking them to fill in:

"I saw you on a __PRODUCT__ commercial on __DAY__, __DATE__, at the approximate time of __TIME__."

If you find you haven't been paid for that "run," you or your agent can contact the advertiser or SAG. Once you've got a starting point—that is, a date and city—it can be checked. Every station, by federal law, must keep a log book of everything they show on that station from sign-on to sign-off.

The cost of the stamps and postcards could ultimately net you some very decent "found" money—use payments you didn't even know were owed you. It's happened before.

If it does, you owe your buddy a dozen roses or a six-pack.

VII
OTHER KINDS OF WORK

25   Stocking Stuffers
26   Theatre
27   Acting Classes

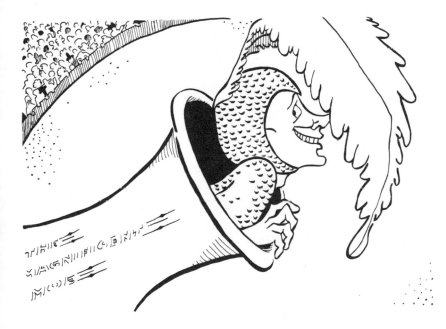

25 STOCKING STUFFERS

*It's not something you'll want to plan to
pay the bills on.*

Karen DiCenzo, Agent

Ms. DiCenzo was talking specifically about modeling in Los Angeles, but
that line could fit every type of peripheral endeavor we'll be discussing in
this chapter. Hence the title. Understand, we have as much respect for
someone expert in these fields as we do for an expert actor. It's just that for
the average Hollywood actor, they will be sidelines at best—and not often
rent payers.

INDUSTRIALS/LOW-BUDGET FILMS

Along with commercials, here's the way to get that first break, and, possibly, a SAG card (see "The Unions," chapter 7). And on-the-job training
("You're polishing your craft at somebody else's expense," says industrial
film producer Don Ciminelli). And a way to get film on yourself.
Industrial films break down into three types:

- *Documentaries:* You've seen these on TV. The only "actor" is the
  narrator.

- *Educational material:* Remember falling asleep in class during that
  film called *How the Dewey Decimal System Can Change Your Life?*
  Remember staring fascinated at that dramatization of the life and
  times of Émile Zola on PBS? These are just two examples of educational films.

- *Corporate image:* General Motors, say, puts out a new line of cars
  and wants to excite its salesmen about it. They make a film extolling
  the virtues of the cars, directed to the salesmen. The film is not
  intended for, and probably will never be seen by, the general public.

By their very nature, documentaries usually don't use performers, and
their narrators are often "name" actors. But opportunities for newcomers
are excellent in educational and corporate-image films. Why? Because they
want "low-profile" people. They don't want the actress playing that dentist's
receptionist to be Raquel Welch. Too distracting. And that's where you
come in.

You can attack industrials on two fronts. Happily, here is one area where you truly can make the rounds. Try to get your picture and résumé to as many industrial film houses as you can find in the *Producers Guide, Studio Blu-Book, Studio Directory,* etc. Some have in-house casting directors; others don't. But try to wangle appointments with someone at each, and keep in touch with them periodically.

If you want to really make contacts and find people and places (such as General Telephone, hospitals, etc.) who hire actors to do industrials, even slide shows—places many actors don't know about—your best bet is the Informational Film Producers Association (IFPA) and the Association of Multi-Image/Southern California (see "Lists" section). Their memberships are comprised of people working in all areas of industrials, including acting. For your $60 (each) membership fee, you'll get a list of production houses and others who hire actors. Then you can seek work many actors don't even know exists. At any rate, their meetings are open to the public—call to find out when and where.

Also check *Drama-Logue* for ads for industrial film acting jobs.

In addition to being a good way to get experience, film on yourself, and a SAG card, your industrial film contacts may well move up into major films or TV. "The advancement is extremely rapid," says industrial producer Marsha Jeffer.

- *Union industrials/low-budget films:* Here, depending upon the length of the film and its basic purpose, you'll be paid somewhere in the neighborhood of $225 to $250 a day, $787 to $875 a week. To fully understand all the ins and outs, go down to SAG and ask for the "Industrial-Educational Contract Provisions." Also, part of the agreement the producer of a typical low-budget film such as *The Mad Moppet of Motown* signs with SAG is to inform you of a special meeting to discuss all the rules. These meetings are held at SAG, and the producer may not be present.

- *Nonunion industrial/low-budget films:* If you're a member of any union, you're not supposed to do these films. You're not protected. The producer can promise you the moon and deliver a vacuum. He can sign a contract made of iron, but as industrial producer Don Ciminelli says, "All the paper in the world isn't going to get you paid if the guy doesn't intend to pay you." If you're going to do one of these anyway, check up on the producer if you can. Certainly you should ask him politely what he's done in the past, how you'll get paid, and *especially* if you're going out of town, he should provide you with a prepaid plane ticket *in both directions* before you set foot on the plane. It should also be clearly understood how much per diem he's going to be giving you and whether that includes hotel rooms. You don't want to arrive in Oshkosh only to have him say, "Well, have you got your room yet?" We've heard of cases where actors came out of these deals happy as milk-fed cats. We've also heard a lot of horror stories. Be very, very careful.

STUDENT FILMS

Here's another way to get experience in front of a camera, to get film on yourself (albeit unpaid), and to make contacts for the future. George Lucas, Steven Spielberg, and Francis Ford Coppola—just to name a few—were once student filmmakers.

Your best source of casting information for these is *Drama-Logue*. Students, most often from the University of Southern California (USC), the University of California, Los Angeles (UCLA), and Columbia College, often advertise for actors. It's another good idea to nose around the bulletin boards of college film and drama departments, acting schools, and the unions.

You'll find competition for parts keen, so don't audition thinking that you can slough off. If you're cast, you may be asked to be available during the day (especially on weekends), and during the shoot, don't be surprised if you're asked to tote a light or move a prop. The whole film will be a learning process for all concerned. It'll take a little patience (or a lot), and it won't be very unusual if your director doesn't know camera right from camera wrong.

Since you'll be working for free, part of the "deal" should be your own copy of the film (or at least the student's willingness to let you make a copy). Also, ask to watch the editing, looping, and final presentation of the film to the student's class. You'll learn plenty.

SAG/AFI films

The Screen Actors Guild has a program for its members called the "SAG Conservatory," part of which is permitting SAG actors to participate in the making of student films out of the prestigious American Film Institute, where filmmakers—called "fellows"—come to study from all over the world. Not only is doing a student film there an excellent learning experience, but an AFI film is to student films what a Mercedes is to automobiles. And it can be a real asset on your résumé.

To be eligible for these films, you'll have to join the conservatory itself. It'll cost $10. For your money, you'll be eligible not only for SAG/AFI casting but for a host of other conservatory programs that make joining worthwhile (see "Miscellaneous" in the Lists section of Appendix B).

Applications are available at the SAG office or in the September edition of the *Hollywood Actor's Newsletter,* SAG's local "newspaper" for its members. You may join the conservatory anytime between August and March. Bring your application and fee along with two headshots/composites, two résumés, and a self-addressed, stamped envelope to SAG (*not* AFI).

Once you've joined, your pictures will be placed in a book of photographs. When an AFI fellow is casting (usually a 30-minute tape or a 16mm film), he goes to those books and chooses the actors he wants to have in for an audition. You'll need to update your photos at least once a year, since they soon become dog-eared from handling.

To increase your chances of being auditioned, bear in mind that student directors are like anyone else in this business—they like to work with people they know. Since the fellows are constantly in and out of the SAG/AFI office (located at AFI, 2021 N. Western Avenue, Los Angeles 90027), it wouldn't hurt to volunteer to work in the SAG/AFI office once or twice a week. It's open from ten A.M. to four P.M. Monday through Friday (ten A.M. to one P.M. in summer). Call 856-7736 for information on volunteering.

VOICE-OVERS

Of all the performing fields, this is the toughest to break in to. It's a highly competitive, extremely lucrative area of the business—for about a dozen or so already entrenched people.

If you keep hearing that you've got a great voice, however, and you want to take a crack at it, first get yourself into a good voice-over workshop. Regardless of how talented or generally how well trained you are as an actor, you'll absolutely have to have some specific training in voice-over technique. Next stop probably will be a recording studio (though many V/O teachers have their own equipment) to put together a good demo tape. On your tape (reel-to-reel, seven-and-a-half speed), you'll want to put about three or four "commercials," using anything from magazine copy to TV or radio ads and gearing your choices to the impression your voice gives the listener (called how you "come in"). Can you come in "motherly"? How about doing a baby-powder commercial? Can you sound sexy? Try a perfume spot. Is your voice light and bright? Soda pop might be a good choice.

We didn't mention character voices (old man, wicked witch, etc.) for this reason: Agents mainly want to hear how well you vary your own voice. They'll only want to hear any different voices you may have at the end of your tape. If you include these, be certain you have what the industry calls "good separation" of voices: clear distinctions among characters. If you think you can do twenty characters, choose six, write a few lines of dialogue for each, and place them at the end of the tape. Just be certain the entire tape is not longer than three minutes, with the first two-and-a-half minutes or so demonstrating variations in *your* voice. "The people who make the most money in this business are those with one voice but are able to have thirteen variations of that voice (intimate, bright, etc.)," says voice-over agent Don Pitts.

And be sure that not only is your tape professionally done but that *you* are a pro. If you need more training in voice-overs, get it before you start sending out anything. Arlin Miller, voice-over teacher, sums it up: "You're only going to get one shot in this town. Make it your best shot. Don't rush it. Wait until you can give them something dynamite to hear, because that's what it's going to take. It's going to really have to blow them away. *Good's not good enough.*"

Send a copy of your tape to the voice-over agents at those agencies that handle the area (look for a "V" on our list or AFTRA's). If he likes what he hears, he'll call you in and have you read some copy to him so he knows it didn't take you six months to put together a decent tape.

Once you are signed, your agent will call you in periodically (along with other voice-over clients who have the required sound) to tape an audition, which he will send for consideration to the ad agency doing the commercial in question. He'll probably also give you a list of production companies, etc.—not only in Los Angeles but all over the country—and ask you to drop off or mail your tape to them. (These can number in the hundreds.)

If hired, you'll do a session ($225.60 for television, $110 for radio) and will be paid residuals according to the SAG or AFTRA rules covering off-camera and/or radio announcers and actors.

"Walla," "sync," "looping," "foley," etc.

These are all forms of putting additional sound to a movie or television show. "Sync" is the same as "looping" (see Chapter 20). "Walla" is "atmosphere noise"—nonscripted background dialogue, grunts, laughs, etc. "Foley" means sound effects—people walking, matches being struck, etc. All of these can provide additional income (usually $298 per day).

- *Walla:*   Once you are fairly well known in the voice-over community, you can join any one of a dozen different "walla" groups that have sprung up around town, such as the Glee Club, the Talk Shop, Rolls-Voice, the Walla Walla Company, etc. You can find them through your voice-over coach, and while they're not big on publicizing themselves or in a hurry to get more members, once they know you, you'll certainly have a shot. You'll need to be a good improvisor as well as a good actor.

- *Sync, looping:* You're hired to deliver a specific line. Mickie McGowan of "Lip-Shtick" (who handles casting for looping) says the same criterion is used—get known in the voice-over community. "It's all based on trust," she says. Pay scale is basically the same ($298 per day).

- *Foley:* Sound effects is an extremely closed area. Your best shot is to try to attach yourself to experienced people, called "walkers," and become an "assistant walker." To find them, check the sound people at the various studios. Then, good luck.

"The Voicecaster"

Specifically, Bob Lloyd. As of this writing, he's the only established voice-over casting director in L.A. we know of. Getting him to give you a listen involves no more than bringing him a professionally recorded tape. You can use your standard V/O tape. In *this* case, however, it's irrelevant how long your tape is. You'll want to put every different kind of voice you can do on it—as long as those voices are, as Mr. Lloyd put it, "competitive"—that is, if they can compete with the already established pros.

If he likes what he hears, Mr. Lloyd will retain your tape and put your name in his computer with a description of all the good voices you do. When people (from all over the country) call him asking for specific types of voices, he pulls those names for possible consideration.

For the address and phone number of his office, check "Miscellaneous" in the "Lists" section (Appendix B).

MODELING

Basically, the kinds of modeling work available are

- *High-fashion/runway:* You'll need to be beautiful or handsome, and very photogenic. Women are in their prime between the ages of sixteen to twenty-one; men, eighteen to twenty-two. If you haven't started by age twenty-five, it's best to forget it completely. Women also need to be at least five seven and wear a size 6, 7, or 8 dress. Men must be about six feet and wear a size 40 regular suit.

- *Print:* This includes anything printed for advertising purposes—billboards, magazine ads, etc. The bulk of the work goes to high-fashion models, but you can possibly make a few dollars regardless of your "look," size, weight, or age.

- *Commercial:* In this case, we mean nonspeaking modeling "roles" on commercials. You can be anything from cute to pretty. Even older and more "real" types occasionally get work.

- *Parts of the body:* Got luscious legs? Handsome hands? Fantastic feet? Totally titillating teeth? Lush, lascivious lips?

- *Industrial:* This includes demonstrating products at trade shows, fairs, department stores, supermarkets, and so forth. If you can be cheery, perky, and get along well with people, you'll have a shot. If you're a young, beautiful, sexy lady to boot, your chances are better. There's little work for men. None for grumps.

If you really want to pursue any of these fields seriously, go to New York. That's where most commercials are shot: Manhattan is the fashion and communications capital of the USA.

Wherever you are, the way to start is to send your headshot or composite—even a snapshot will do in this case—to agencies that also do modeling (indicated with an *M* in SAG's list and ours). In addition, the Joan Mangum Agency, 8831 Sunset Boulevard, is a well-known agency specializing in print work.

While all models have "books" (portfolios of photos), there's no need to throw money at photographers to get one. As agent Karen DiCenzo says, "I don't think it's right for a person who wants to be a model to go out and spend five hundred dollars on a book, because they might not be the right material to be a model. Maybe one hundred dollars' worth of pictures, but even that's not necessary." If the agent thinks you're promising, he'll send you to various "test photographers" he knows, and they'll shoot you for free. Then you can complete your book gradually, from your assignments.

Enrolling in a modeling school isn't a requirement either. If you're model-material, you'll get a lot of on-the-job training.

Obviously, the kind of money you'll make will depend on the kind of work you do and how well known you become. For example, a beginning high-fashion model may earn about $75 an hour. For a "star model," the sky's the limit.

In the end, modeling is a young person's game. And as Karen DiCenzo puts it, "In most cases, models turn into actors. Actors rarely turn into models."

EXTRA WORK

"Anyone who says 'Don't do extra work' is crazy," says one casting director. We agree—up to a point.

Never been on a set? Need a SAG card? It's worth it. (Check our chapter on unions for the reason why.) But pursue extra work on a continual basis? Not if you want to be an actor. It's just too time-consuming. All the time you'll spend registering with the casting agencies, calling them (at least every half hour), etc., is time taken away from your acting career. Even the time you spend on the set is wasted except for obtaining general knowledge. You can't really use it to make contacts. Why? Because in Los Angeles (not necessarily in New York, where extras are handled by SAG), if you're known as an extra, you're in danger of being labeled as such.

"When you do extra work, stay in the background," suggests one actor who knows the scene. "Don't be in too much of a hurry to get your face on the screen or to meet the director. If so, they'll think, 'Why should I hire him as an actor for three hundred dollars a day and up if I can get him for seventy-nine fifty? And if he's a serious actor, why isn't he pursuing his acting career?' "

Finally, if you're thinking extra work is an easy way to make a living, listen to what Roy Wallack, Screen Extras Guild president, has to say: "Working as an extra is very tough. Actors have agents, but extras don't. It's work getting work. I would say, of one hundred people who start out doing extra work, at the end of a year you'll probably have ten or fifteen left. It's really a rough, *rough* type of business."

NIGHTCLUB WORK (AND RELATED)

You'll do far better getting your feet wet in an out-of-the-way bar in Podunk than beginning this part of your career in Hollywood.

There are places, however, where a performer can hone his skills in front of an audience, such as the Comedy Store, the Improvisation, and Herman's Cabaret (formerly the Last Stop). Each has its own particular rules as to how you go about getting onto its stage, but, basically, you first perform on an "off night" such as Monday or Tuesday, and if you're good, you move up to a more desirable night and time. Depending on the particular place, you'll then be paid somewhere in the neighborhood of fifteen to thirty-five dollars per "set."

Certainly these places afford performers—especially stand-up comics—showcases for their talents. And certainly performers have been discovered there. And mostly they are democratic, in that the best people move up and on. However, you'll most likely be performing either for free or for a very small salary.

Yer don't get yer money and yer makes yer choice.

For paying work, such places as Disneyland and Knott's Berry Farm often advertise open calls for talent in the trades.

For versatile performers, a good variety agent or personal manager wouldn't hurt. Or consider that besides health insurance and other benefits, union membership in AGVA means that there's at least one place a person looking for someone with your abilities can call. While we were at the AGVA offices, the phones were ringing off the wall, and some of the calls came from the studios—looking for this person or that talent.

STUNT WORK

"I don't try to act—don't you try to do stunts," said a stuntman to us a long time ago. If you're ever on a set and the director or producer asks you to do a stunt, should you refuse?

"If you're concerned with your safety, take a stand," says theatrical casting director Mike Fenton. "No one will get upset at that." Offered an additional thousand dollars to do a stunt? I errific. It will make a great down payment on a wheelchair.

Actors considering stunts as a career may be discouraged to learn that not only is it at least as difficult to become a "star" stuntman (in the sense of earning big money) as it is to become a "star" actor, but there are additional "dues" to be paid in the form of broken bones, bruises, and cuts—and that's if you're lucky. While the pros take all sorts of safety precautions—often to the extent you'd swear they were planning a space flight—accidents do happen. Stuntmen have died.

Still, if you want to become one of these brave, creative craftsmen, you'll first need to get your SAG card (all stuntmen must be SAG). Then put together a composite and a résumé with all the physically oriented things you can do. "Have a good background in sports—everything from scuba diving to horseback riding," suggests Judy Lowry of the Stuntmen's Association.

And then make the rounds of the studios, production houses, and especially any producers, directors, and stunt coordinators you get to meet, and hope that they're willing to take a shot on a newcomer when they've got plenty of old-timers they can use.

You could take a stunt workshop, but it isn't vital.

If you're hired, you'll be paid the standard SAG wages for stunt players, plus a sum for the particular stunt you're asked to do. This usually is negotiated by you and the producer or director right there on the set, and you're paid each time you do it, whether the camera jams or the director "just wants another one." "Stunts such as high falls are often negotiated by the foot," says agent Karen DiCenzo.

And two last words of caution. First, carry insurance—lots of it. Second, as an ad recently run by a group of stuntmen in the trades said, "No shot is worth a life."

PORNOGRAPHY

Questions of morality aside, if the film is "hard core," it's a career killer. As soon as you become known for grunting your way through the hard stuff, you'll become virtually unhirable for legit films, TV, and commercials. Even if you should do one only in a moment of desperation, that film will later cause you more career grief than ten times the $100 or so you'll be paid. (We know of a rare established star who did one, and now would kill to get the negative.) Even "soft core" is iffy.

Pass.

26 THEATRE

I believe in about four or five years Los Angeles will be a major theatre capital.

Larry Fonseca, Legitimate/Theatrical
Agent

Hollywood is still Hollywood—not Broadway West. Yes, the town still has its eye focused mainly into the lens of the camera. Yes, there still are showcase productions by actors who don't know upstage from down. Yes, some audiences still emerge from theatres raving about plays that move like sludge on a dirt road.

But that picture has changed significantly, is changing now, and where it stops, nobody knows. Los Angeles is becoming more sophisticated about theatre—actors, audiences, film and TV industry employees, everybody. "Anything that is sloppily put together goes down very quickly now," says David Ralphe, Executive Director of the Los Angeles Theatre Alliance.

The decade from 1971 to 1981 saw the emergence of the 99-seat Equity Waiver system, the Los Angeles Theatre Alliance, the importance of regional theatre in general and Los Angeles theatre in particular (through such major award-winning plays as *The Gin Game, The Shadow Box,* and *Children of a Lesser God*).

Not long ago, much of the TV/film industry regarded L.A. theatre condescendingly as the supposed province of the would-be and the has-been. But the seventies also saw a great influx of stage-trained actors who brought with them their love of, and skills in, live theatre. At the same time, grants to the arts boomed. The result has been a significant increase in quality smaller theatres and, in turn, of audience-building hit shows. The theatre scene is developing structure and prestige.

Where do things go from here? LATA's David Ralphe says the association looks to London, a theatre/film/TV center, for a growth model, but he acknowledges that "We will always be an industry [film] town." There are problems: Those grants are now hard to come by. There is a shortage of mid-size houses into which Equity Waiver hits can evolve and prosper, though some building plans have been announced.

And cable TV? It's both a promise and a specter. When the corporate, legal, and union problems iron themselves out, will its need for product cause the boom in theatre some predict, or will it be just another false hope of actors who are looking for a sellers' market that never comes? And if cable does marry the girl, will the players profit or only the producers? And if more and more rules are needed to protect actors from exploitation, what will become of Equity Waiver, which has flourished under the unions' hands-off policy?

In view of all of the above, bear in mind that, as we go to press, the Los Angeles theatre scene is about as stable as the San Andreas Fault.

EQUITY WORK

The pickings are slim. There are four LORT (League of Resident Theatres) in town, and no Equity dinner theatre at all (though they flourish in neighboring Orange County, for actors who don't mind the commute).

Still, what there is, is worth an effort, so a good first stop for the newly arrived actor are the Equity offices in Hollywood. For 25 cents each, he can pick up lists of Equity-franchised agents, LORT theatres, Equity dinner theatres, and Equity Stock (also see "Lists" section). The Equity hotline, 462-8505, disseminates casting information, updated daily.

Major touring companies journeying to or from New York head for large theatres such as the Ahmanson or the Dorothy Chandler Pavilion (two-thirds of the tri-theatre Music Center complex downtown), the Schubert in Century City, or the Pantages or Huntington Hartford in Hollywood. Often, opportunities for local actors are limited to chorus work, though occasionally second parts—or even a lead—opens up. Actors with legit agents have an edge.

The Mark Taper Forum/Center Theatre Group (last third of the Music Center theatres) is the premiere LORT theatre in town, and one of the best in the country. The Taper holds auditions on the first Monday of every month. On that day, active members of Equity can call 972-7374 between the hours of ten a.m. and one p.m. to schedule an audition a week or so later. The audition consists of one or two monologues, a maximum of four minutes in either case. Non-Equity actors don't phone; instead they come in person to the Music Center Annex (601 W. Temple Street) between the same hours for a brief interview, with pictures and résumés in hand.

The other LORT theatres are the Long Beach Civic Light Opera, just changed from community to professional theatre status; the Los Angeles Public Theatre, formerly the Los Angeles Shakespeare Festival, now doing contemporary plays at the Coronet Theatre near Beverly Hills; and the promising new Los Angeles Stage Company in Hollywood. These theatres cast through agents and open calls advertised in the trades.

It is also a good idea to write the theatres with pictures and résumé, requesting an interview. If you don't mind going out of town, do the same for the dinner theatres and for other LORT theatres in the state, such as the blossoming South Coast Repertory in nearby Costa Mesa, the newly rebuilt and expanded Old Globe Theatre in San Diego, and, up north, the Berkeley Repertory Theatre and the famed American Conservatory Theatre (ACT). The latter holds auditions in Los Angeles for its acting company, around April of each year, and for its conservatory's advanced training program, generally in March.

EQUITY WAIVER THEATRE

It started because actors needed to showcase their talents to the film industry. It continued to grow because actors needed and wanted to hone their abilities in front of an audience. ("One of the best ways to overcome frustration is to do ninety-nine-seat Equity Waiver theatre," says actress Viola Kates Stimpson.) It became an "institution" in 1972 when, after much debate, Equity ruled:

Actors Equity Association will waive all Equity rules in theatres not capable of or never having had, seating facilities for more than 99 people in the Los Angeles and San Francisco areas, covered by the Hollywood Area/Bay Area Theatre Contract. This will not include any theatre operating as a Cafe, Dinner, or Children's Theatre.

Here's a quick thumbnail sketch of life among the Waiver theatres:

A 1980 study showed that 70 percent of the theatres surveyed reported 50 percent of their members belonging to one or more of the four performing unions (AEA, SAG, AFTRA, SEG).

More than half reported in the same study that they voluntarily paid their performers *something* (although 12 claimed that their actors earned $100 or more per run, the 99-seat house-size dictates that compensation almost always has to be carfare or pin money—so, in lieu of cash, theatres commonly offer services such as workshops or use of the theatre for personal projects). Some theatres charge dues, a perhaps necessary evil to keep their doors open—but one not unlike asking your dentist to pay for the privilege of working in your mouth.

Some theatres open-cast all productions; some cast from set memberships and look outside only when necessary.

And (a point to be pondered if you don't think free/near-free Waiver work is worth your time) six theatres surveyed by LATA in the same year replied that from 30 percent to 95 percent of their members got agents and/or film and TV work from their Waiver appearances.

Choosing a theatre

Rather than depend on a theatre's reputation, which waxes and wanes as people come and go, attend a production and decide if the quality and kind of work they do is right for you. You can get a lot of information about the policies of various theatres from the annual *Drama-Logue Guide to Southern California Theatre* and *Los Angeles Actors Guide*, and from LATA (as we discussed in our chapter "Arriving in L.A."). There is another theatre publication, *California Theatre Annual*, but it is expensive—$15 in 1981. *Drama-Logue* is an excellent source of weekly casting information.

Getting in

Whatever the theatre's policies on getting in and working, bear in mind that there's a certain amount of politicking at any theatre. The best way to get involved with that group you're just dying to work with is to *volunteer for tech work*. "Actors I can get, but good tech people are hard to find," says one director.

Once you're an established presence, you can start to mumble things about wanting to act. They'll be a lot more receptive to your audition once they know and trust you than they will be to the equally talented stranger who walks in cold. One hint, however: Be good at tech but not *too* good. You don't want them refusing to cast you because they don't want to lose a good technician!

Rules of the game

Before you commit yourself to a theatre, check the list of questions Equity suggests you ask at the outset. (You can pick up the list at the Equity offices.) Among key areas to check out are: What are the dues and/or initiation fees? What work other than acting are you expected to do? Are you insured for injury in performance and/or rehearsal? What is their policy on complimentary tickets?

You can learn a lot about how often, how prominently, and how favorably theatres are reviewed by regularly reading the critics in the daily, weekly, and trade newspapers.

Further, the very nature of the Equity Waiver agreement places no obligation on you to stick it out if you're unhappy. As David Westberg of Actors Equity says, "The actors have control. That's one of the beautiful things about the Equity Waiver situation. If you don't like the play, if you don't like what's going on, if you don't like who you're acting with, if you don't like the way the theatre's being run—leave."

Nobody is advocating irresponsibility—but bear in mind that whenever you do a play in Los Angeles, you put your career on the line. Agents, casting directors, producers, and directors all have very long memories— not only for what's good but for what's awful. As producer Buddy Bregman says, "If it's a bad production, it'll permeate the person's psyche, and the fallout will drop on your head—even if you were brilliant."

If you are interested in maximum industry exposure, as opposed to the shows you do for the sheer joy of the doing, here's the "play shopping" criteria ABC TV's West Coast casting director Susan Glicksman outlines for herself: "I look for something new. I don't want to see any more *Barefoot in the Parks* or *Lovers and Other Strangers*. I look for something local, prefer- ably a large cast, twelve to fifteen people—I don't want to see a two-person show. No Shakespeare."

The Los Angeles Theatre Alliance

In addition to the services LATA provides for actors, it helps Waiver and other not-for-profit member theatres with management assistance and re- ferrals, low-cost rental of storage, rehearsal and work space, rental of cos- tumes and lighting equipment, reduced-rate advertising, fund raising, and other cooperative services. And its newsletter and quarterly magazine help to spread the word.

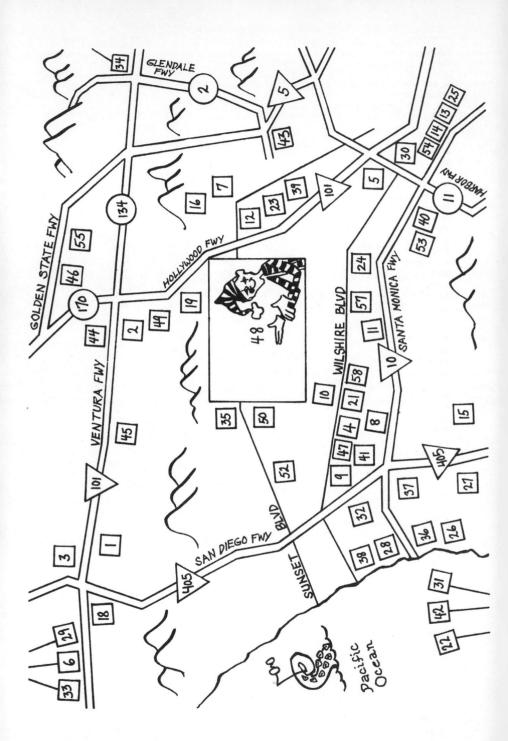

Los Angeles Area Theatre Map Key

A sampling of Los Angeles area theatre. Equity Waiver theatres are indicated by (EW), members of the Los Angeles Theatre Alliance by*. (*Map not drawn to scale.*)

1. Actors Alley, 4334 Van Nuys Blvd., Sherman Oaks 91403, 986-7440 (EW)*
2. Actors Forum, 3365½ Cahuenga Blvd. West, Los Angeles 90068, 876-9101 (EW)*
3. Back Alley Theatre, 15231 Burbank Blvd., Van Nuys 91401, 780-2240 (EW)*
4. Beverly Hills Playhouse, 254 S. Robertson Blvd., Beverly Hills 90211, 652-6483 (EW)
5. Bob Baker Marionette Theater, 1345 W. First St., Los Angeles 90026, 624-3973
6. California Arts Theatre (California Institute of the Arts), 24700 McBean Pkwy., Valencia 91355, (805) 255-1050*
7. Cast-at-the-Hyperion Theatre, 1835 Hyperion Ave., Los Angeles 90027, 661-9188 (EW)*
8. Century City Playhouse (Burbaqe Theatre Ensemble), 10508 W. Pico Blvd., Los Angeles 90064, 839-3322 (EW)*
9. Comedy Store West, 1627 Westwood Blvd., Los Angeles 90024, 477-4751
10. Coronet Theatre (L.A. Public Theatre), 368 N. La Cienega Blvd., Los Angeles 90048, 652-4241
11. Ebony Showcase Theater, 4720 Washington Blvd., Los Angeles 90016, 936 1107
12. East-West Players, 4424 Santa Monica Blvd., Los Angeles 90029, 660-0366 (EW)*
13. Embassy Auditorium, 847 S. Grand Ave., Los Angeles 90017, 622-4530
14. Ensemble Studio Theatre, 839 S. Grand Ave., Los Angeles 90017, 656-0470 (EW)*
15. Forum, Manchester and Prairie Aves., Inglewood 90306, 673-1300
16. Greek Theater, 2700 N. Vermont Ave., Los Angeles 90027, 660-8400
17. Group Repertory Theatre, 11043 Magnolia Blvd., N. Hollywood 91601, 241-8886 (EW)*
18. Herman's Cabaret, 17271 Ventura Blvd., Encino 91316, 501-3737
19. Hollywood Bowl, 2301 N. Highland Ave., Los Angeles 90068, 876-8742
20. Inglewood Playhouse, 400 W. Beach Ave., Inglewood 90302, 649-7451 (EW)
21. Laurence Playhouse (Company Theatre), 1653 S. La Cienega Blvd., Los Angeles 90035, 274-5153 (EW)*
22. Long Beach Civic Light Opera, Terrace Theatre, 518 E. 4th St., Long Beach 90801, 435-7605
23. Los Angeles City College, 855 N. Vermont Ave., Los Angeles 90029, 669-4000
24. Los Angeles Cultural Center, 1308 S. New Hampshire Ave., Los Angeles 90006, 387-1161 (EW)*
25. Los Angeles Philharmonic Auditorium (Offices, Pasadena Playhouse), 427 W. 5th St. #627, Los Angeles 90013, 629-1394 (EW)*
26. Los Angeles Theatre Works, 681 Venice Blvd., Venice 90291/Box 49605, Los Angeles 90049 (EW)*
27. Loyola Marymount, Loyola Bl. at W. 80th St., Los Angeles 90045, 642-2700
28. Mayfair Music Hall, 214 Santa Monica Blvd., Santa Monica 90401, 451-0621
29. The Megaw Theatre, 17601 Saticoy St., Northridge 91325, 881-8166 (EW)*
30. Music Center (Ahmanson Theatre, 972-7401; Dorothy Chandler Pavilion, 972-7550; Mark Taper Forum/Center Theatre Group, 972-7353*), 135 N. Grand Ave., Los Angeles 90012
31. Old Globe Theatre, Balboa Park, P.O. Box 2171, San Diego 92112, (714) 231-1941
32. Odyssey Theatre Ensemble, 12111 Ohio Ave., Los Angeles 90025, 826-1626 (EW)*
33. Pacific Conservatory of the Performing Arts/Solvang, P.O. Box 1700, Santa Maria 93456, (805) 925-4009
34. Pasadena Playhouse, 39 S. El Molino Ave., Pasadena, 792-8672 (EW)* (See L.A. Philharmonic Aud.)
35. The Roxy, 9009 Sunset Blvd.; W. Hollywood, Los Angeles 90069, 878-2222
36. Santa Monica Civic Auditorium, 1855 Main St., Santa Monica 90401, 393-9961
37. Santa Monica College, 1815 Pearl St., Santa Monica 90406, 450-5150
38. Santa Monica Playhouse, 1211 4th St., Santa Monica 90401, 394-9779 (EW)*
39. Scorpio Repertory Theatre, 426 N. Hoover St., Los Angeles 90004, 660-9981 (EW)*
40. Shrine Auditorium, 3228 Royal St., Los Angeles 90007, 749-5123
41. Shubert Theatre, 2020 Ave. of the Stars, Los Angeles 90067, 553-9000
42. South Coast Repertory Theatre, 655 Town Center Dr. (P.O. Box 2197), Costa Mesa 92626/1197 (714) 957-2602
43. Studio Theatre Playhouse (The Colony), 1944 Riverside Dr., Los Angeles 90039, 665-3011 (FW)
44. Synthaxis Theatre Foundation, 4319 Lankershim Blvd., N. Hollywood 91602, 877-4671 (EW)*
45. Theatre East, 12655 Ventura Blvd., Studio City 91604, 769-8373 (EW)*
46. Theatre Exchange, 11855 Hart St., N. Hollywood 91605, 765-9005 (EW)*
47. Theatre Forty, 241 Moreno Dr., Beverly Hills 90212, 277-4221 (EW)*
48. Theatre Row and vicinity (see Theatre Row map)
49. Theatre West, 3333 Cahuenga Blvd. West, Los Angeles 90068, 851-4839 (EW Special Contract)*
50. The Troubador, 9081 Santa Monica Blvd., Los Angeles 90069, 276-6168
51. Universal Ampitheatre, Hollywood Freeway at Lankershim, Universal City 91608, 980-9421
52. University of California, Los Angeles (UCLA), 308 Westwood Blvd., Los Angeles 90024, 825-4321
53. University of Southern California (USC), University Park (between Vermont Ave. and Figueroa St.), Los Angeles 90007, 743-2703
54. Variety Arts Theatre, 940 S. Figueroa St., Los Angeles 90015, 623-9100*
55. Victory Theatre, 3326 W. Victory Blvd., Burbank 91505, 843-9253 (EW)*
56. Westwood Playhouse, 10866 Le Conte Ave., Los Angeles 90024, 479-6502
57. Wilshire-Ebell Theatre, 4401 W. 8th St., Los Angeles 90005, 939-1128
58. Wilshire Theatre, 8440 Wilshire Blvd., Beverly Hills 90211, 653-4490

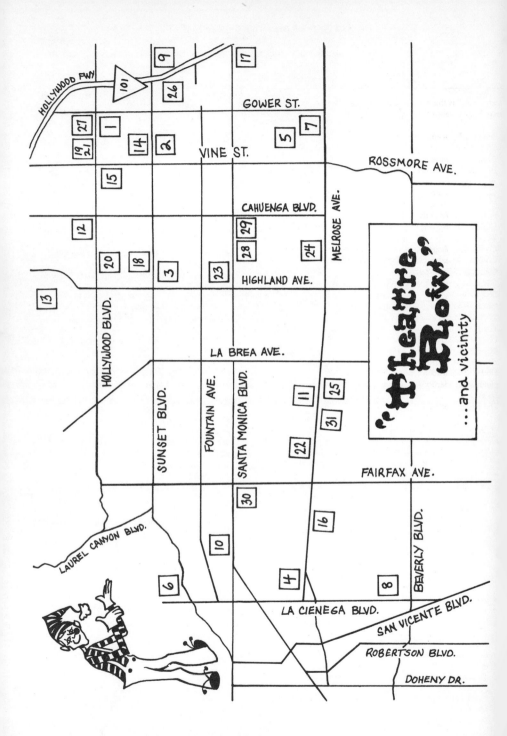

Theatre Row Map Key

"Theatre Row" is the nickname for Melrose Avenue, along which a number of the better-known Equity Waiver theatres are located. Equity Waiver theatres are indicated by (EW), Los Angeles Theatre Alliance members by *. *(Map not drawn to scale.)*

American Theatre Arts, 6240 Hollywood Blvd., 466-2462 (EW)*

Aquarius Theatre, 6230 Sunset Blvd., 466-2161

Bullring Theatre (Actors Center), 1445 N. Las Palmas Ave., 462-2961

Callboard Theatre, 8451 Melrose Pl., 852-9205 (EW)*

Cast Theatre/Cast-at-the-Circle, 804/800 N. El Centro Ave., 462-9872/462-0265 (EW)*

Comedy Store, 8431 Sunset Blvd., 656-6225 or 275-7641

Company of Angels, 5846 Waring Ave., 464-9674 (EW)*

Coronet Theatre (L.A. Public Theatre), 368 N. La Cienega Blvd., 652-4241

Gene Dynarski Theatre, 5600 W. Sunset Blvd., 465-5600 (EW)

Globe Playhouse (Shakespeare Society of America), 1107 N. Kings Rd., 654-5623 (EW)*

The Groundlings, 7307 Melrose Ave., 934-4747 (EW)*

Hollywood Actors Theatre, 1715 N. Cahuenga Blvd., 464-0300 (EW)

The Hollywood Bowl, 2301 N. Highland Ave., 876-8742

Hollywood Palladium, 6215 W. Sunset Blvd., 466-4311

Huntington Hartford Theatre, 1615 N. Vine St., 462-6666

The Improvisation, 8162 Melrose Ave., 651-2583

17. Los Angeles Actors Theatre, 1089 N. Oxford Ave., 464-5500 (EW Special Contract)*

18. The L.A. Connection, 6671 Sunset Blvd., 467-5399 (EW)

19. L.A. Public Theatre (offices), 6253 Hollywood Blvd., Suite 222, 469-3974*

20. L.A. Stage Company, 1642 N. Las Palmas Ave., 461-2755*

21. L.A. Theatre Alliance, 6253 Hollywood Blvd., Suite 312, Los Angeles 90028, 467-6690

22. Matrix Theatre (Actors for Themselves), 7657 Melrose Ave., 852-1445 (EW)*

23. McCadden Place Theatre, 1157 N. McCadden Pl., 462-9070 (EW)*

24. Melrose Theatre, 733 N. Seward St., 465-1885 (EW)*

25. The Met Theatre, 649 N. Poinsettia Pl., 932-8614 (EW)*

26. Nosotros, 1314 N. Wilton Pl., 465-4167 (EW)*

27. Pantages Theatre, 6233 Hollywood Blvd., 462-3104

28. Pilot Theatres (I & II), 6600 Santa Monica Blvd., 469-6600 (EW)*

29. Shepard Theatre Workshop (mime), 6468 Santa Monica Blvd., 462-9033 (EW)

30. Lee Strasberg Theatre Institute, 7936 Santa Monica Blvd., 650-7777 (EW)

31. Zephyr Theatre, 7458 Melrose Blvd., 653-4667 (EW)

27 ACTING CLASSES

It doesn't get any better not doing it.

Michael Rhodes, Producer

Producer-director Buddy Bregman says, "The only way you can 'stretch' is in a class. You can't 'stretch' on a commercial." Or on a beach.

Maybe it's the air. Or the lack of pulsating, shoulder-to-shoulder humanity. Whatever, as one producer put it, "It never ceases to amaze me how lazy the actors are in L.A."

In New York, you'll often find actors hurrying to a different class every night—and apologizing for taking Sundays off. Don't let "ole laid-back L.A." affect your drive. "Keep active," advises theatrical agent Colee Viedelle. "Our finest surgeons continue to study."

That sentiment was echoed by every single person we interviewed. It's a rare actor, no matter how well trained, who doesn't go stale if he doesn't work at his craft. And somehow that audition call will always come when you're at your stalest.

The absolute best training and way of keeping sharp is on a stage in front of a live theatre audience. You'll learn more doing one show than you can learn in six months of intensive training at even the best acting schools. The audience is the best teacher.

However, theatre alone isn't the answer. You can't learn cold reading, film technique, commercial technique, etc., on a stage. The specialized arts—dance, singing, dialects, mime—also require teachers. "Acting is like being a doctor or a lawyer or anything else; it takes an investment of time and money," says theatrical agent Mary Spencer.

And, perhaps most important of all, in a company town such as Los Angeles, where you will be performing under the critical eyes and long memories of film industry personnel, *classes are the only safe places where you can go to be bad*—where you can take chances, experiment, stretch your talents, and fall on your face—in privacy.

That brings us to . . .

USING CLASSES PROPERLY

One of the hardest lessons for actors to learn is that there's nothing wrong with "bombing out" in a class. You learn by being bad at least as much as you do by always being the Alec Guinness of Acting 101.

Many classes in Los Angeles offer "industry nights" where agents, casting directors, producers, and the like are invited to see what you can do. Show-cases of any sort are valuable and hard to come by, but the practice can negate the key reason for being there in the first place. Certainly the scene you do for "industry night" should be something you can do well without stretching. If you take such a class, make it an adjunct to, not a substitute for, the class you take to learn.

It's not necessarily wise to put an arbitrary time limit, such as one year, on a particular class, because you may find a teacher with whom you'll want to study for the rest of your life. Instead of asking "How long?", ask "Why am I still here?"

If the answer involves friendships with your fellow students, the fact that everyone thinks you're sooooo good, or your fear of moving on—move on. You're nesting, and that will hold you back. In general, though, it's best to move around to various teachers. You'll learn different approaches to act-ing, acting with a more varied group of people, and, probably, keep your classes more in perspective.

That's a very important point. No class is the end-all and be-all of your career. Nobody ever made a dime in an acting class. And remember, your acting teacher, no matter how good or how bad, is *not* your daddy or mommy.

WHICH ONE FIRST?

What a toughie! The answer is so relative to your circumstances that we can give you only very generalized advice.

If you're new to Los Angeles, first find yourself a class that will orient you to the business of the film business.

If you're new to acting itself, get yourself into a good beginning acting class. All other classes pale in significance until you've learned the career realities and good acting technique.

And, no matter where you are as an actor, you should make a point of attending a good cold-reading workshop, if you haven't yet got that skill down. If you're a good commercials type, a commercials workshop is a priority.

Beyond that, if you already have some training, play to your weaknesses. If you've done a lot of stage, make a beeline to that film-technique class. Done nothing but commercials? A general acting class that emphasizes truthfulness in acting and that forces you to abandon your "shtick" and bag of tricks, will prepare you for film, TV, and stage drama. Bombed in that one comedy you did a few years ago? Look for a comedy workshop. Are you a character actor or ethnic type? A repertoire of dialects and accents will be invaluable. Used to relying on a lot of very exacting directors? Improvisation will loosen you up for working with directors whose only instructions are "Play it over there."

FINDING A CLASS

That's easy. Besides the teachers we list (see "Lists" section) there are plenty of fine, legitimate teachers out there. All the trades can be of help, as can the *Los Angeles Actors Guide* and *Drama-Logue*'s annual *Southern California Legitimate Theatre Guide* (which also lists workshops, teachers, and specialty coaches), the Los Angeles Theatre Alliance, agents, casting directors, and your fellow actors. (The unions, however, will not get involved in suggesting classes or teachers.)

There are two organizations of professional teachers: the Acting Coaches and Teachers Association (ACTA) and the Organization of Professional Acting Coaches and Theatres (OPACT), another source of leads. They include *some* of the reputable teachers in town—but not all, not by a long shot. There are many fine teachers who just aren't joiners. Membership in these or any other groups can help assure you that their members are on the up-and-up; but it doesn't guarantee that the teachers are good, or good for you in particular; nor does it tell you that a nonmember teacher is bad. You're still going to have to know how to go about . . .

CHOOSING A CLASS

Don't get too caught up in the "reputation game." A large, famous Hollywood acting school isn't by definition any better than an obscure teacher in Van Nuys—or vice versa. By the time a school has become famous, it's possible that the people who made it famous are no longer there.

And don't base your decision on how expensive a school or teacher may be. Someone who charges you three times what others do isn't necessarily three times better. Fancy brochures and pamphlets only tell you that the teacher/school knows his public relations.

Some suggestions . . .

Does the teacher make promises?

The only promise a teacher should make is to do his best to train you as an actor. Teachers have indeed found agents and jobs for talented students on occasion, but someone who promises this to a stranger is proffering bait; bite and you're the fish.

What's the teacher's background?

"The only teachers you should study with are people who have been or are in the industry," says agent Doris Ross. Be sure the teacher knows his stuff. Find out what he's done; where he's gotten *his* knowledge.

Will he let you audit?

There are perfectly reputable teachers who won't. "You either want to study with me or not," says one. However, our thinking is that you shouldn't buy *anything* without looking it over, much less an acting class. By their very nature, these can get pretty darn personal. If the teacher won't let you audit, he should at least be willing to give you an easy out if you're not happy with him. His refund policy should be very clear and flexible.

How large are the classes?

The maximum size is fifteen to eighteen. You're not paying to sit around all the time watching others work. You should get individualized instruction at least three out of every four classes.

What's the general level of the class?

You'll want to be working with students who are basically at your level, perhaps a little better. "I've got a B.A. in drama," says one actress, "and I got into this class filled with beginners. Talk about frustrating; it drove me crazy to act next to them."

Is videotape employed?

Many excellent classes don't use videotape, but it is enormously helpful for you to see for yourself what you are doing. You'll pick up on some good things and some mistakes the teacher doesn't notice or doesn't take the time to mention. Also, Hollywood is film-oriented; you should know how you come across on camera.

What goes on in the class?

Either while auditing or while in the actual class, ask yourself:

- Is this training practical, or is it artsy-craftsy? Here's what one actor said about his class: "They teach you to be very self-indulgent . . . and a lot of psychotic behavior comes out." Also, an acting teacher is not a psychologist. It's not his job to pick at your psyche.

- Is the class too sloppy? A good laugh can be refreshing, but the class shouldn't be a barrelful of monkeys either.

- Is the class too disciplined? Can the students question the teacher? Do they question him too much? If the teacher turns bright red with anger because a student disagrees, you're dealing with a bush-league Hitler. If there are constant challenges, either the teacher can't control the class or there is an underlying lack of respect for him.

- Does the teacher flatter or criticize too much? The teacher's job is to critique work but not to tear the students apart. We've seen some pretty rotten actors tell us how their instructors thought they were just marvy, dahling. We've also seen competent actors seriously damaged by withering attacks and other "head games" played on them by their teachers. Some teachers, unfortunately, will do or tell you anything to keep you paying them money. Listen to your gut. If a vague little voice tells you something's wrong, it probably is.

- Does the teacher care? Does he give you the feeling he's more interested in the tuition than the students? Do you get the feeling he's improvising what to do next because he hasn't prepared for class? Does he constantly talk about himself and how good he is? (Who cares? You're there to act.) Is he fully aware of the delicacy of his position, dealing with people's emotions, needs, and hopes? How does he phrase things? "I don't think that worked because . . ." or "That stinks"? Is he out to show you how rough the business can be? (You know that already. You don't need his "help.") Is he straightforward? Nonmanipulative? Bored or involved? Kind?

MOVING ON

At the end of each "semester," you should ask yourself two questions: Are you better off for having studied with that person? Can you learn more from him or is it time to move on?

Notice we didn't say "stop." As theatrical casting director Mike Fenton says, "Do not vegetate . . . if all you're going to do is sit on your butt, then continue to be a waiter because that is all you will ever do. You must eat, you must be employed . . . drive a cab—but leave yourself time to study."

Think you're well trained? How about a seminar or two on film production or the emergence of the cable industry? A class on fencing? Dance? Horseback riding? Business? Directing?

Sounds like a lot of time and money? You got it. Sounds like an actor never stops learning? You got it again.

VIII
MERRILY YOU ROLL ALONG

28 Publicizing Yourself
29 Your Management Team
30 General Financial
31 Miscellaneous
32 Assessing Your Career
33 Conclusion

28 PUBLICIZING YOURSELF

*Good manners never offended any critic,
but, more than that, a thank you note is
one more pass of the actor's name
before his eyes.*

John C. Mahoney, Drama Critic, *Los
Angeles Times*

Since you won't need or be able to afford a publicist until you really get rolling, you're going to have to be your own publicist. Your main concern will be to become known within the industry—in a positive way. Before you publicize anything, ask yourself, "What am I calling attention to? How will it affect others' perception of me and/or my career?"

GETTING INTO THE TRADES

There are several columns in the *Daily Variety* and the *Hollywood Reporter* that are fertile ground for a little "planting" of your name. It will take only a minimum of effort and a postage stamp.

The important thing is to make your submissions properly. And that starts with your agent. Ideally, he is the one who should submit news of your casting to the trades. The business letterhead on his stationary talls the paper that the information is probably true. However, if your agent refuses or just doesn't get around to it, there's nothing wrong with doing it yourself. It's done every day. Just be sure not only that the information is correct but also that you aren't jumping the gun on a producer or publicity department before they're ready to issue casting information. If your part is small—say, one or two scenes on a TV show—you needn't concern yourself about this. But if the role is of any size, you'd do well to check with the producer and/or publicity department. Second, be sure your agent isn't making these submissions—the papers don't appreciate duplicate submissions.

Start by reading the columns. Each has its own style, and if you're smart, you'll follow it closely—down to the paper's preferred punctuation.

Keep the copy short—about one sentence—and type it, double-spaced, on a piece of paper separate from your covering letter. As Ruth Robinson, Associate Editor of the *Hollywood Reporter*, says, "Make it as easy to put in the paper as you can." Next, write a brief covering letter along the lines of "Dear Sir: Enclosed, information for your ____ column. Thank you."

It might help if your covering letter has a letterhead on it. "Become a company," suggests a person who deals with the trades all the time. "Is your name Steve Mayfield? Become 'The Steve Company' or 'The Mayfield Company.' Wouldn't hurt." The less devious can settle for decent personal stationery.

Finally, include the name of the column on the envelope. Cumulative time: about ten minutes. Cumulative effect: your name (possibly) in the trades.

Where to submit what

- Cast in a film? "Film Castings" or "Pix, People, Pickups," *Daily Variety;* and "Feature Casting," *Hollywood Reporter.*

- Cast in a TV show? "Telecastings," *Daily Variety;* and "Briefs," *Hollywood Reporter.*

- Cast in a stage production? Be sure the theatre sends a cast list to "Legit Bits," *Daily Variety;* and "Stage Notes," *Hollywood Reporter.*

- Traveling? "Who's Where," *Daily Variety;* and "Travel Log," *Hollywood Reporter.* A word of warning: There's nothing to stop a burglar from reading these to find out who's out of town.

- Just signed with a new agent or personal manager? "Agents Alley," *Daily Variety;* and "Artists/Agents," *Hollywood Reporter.*

Until you're well known or until you are doing something really special, you probably won't have a lot of success "planting" your name in the trade/social columns by Hank Grant ("Rambling Reporter," the *Hollywood Reporter*), George Christy ("The Great Life," *Hollywood Reporter*), and Army Archerd ("Just for Variety," *Daily Variety*). Still, charm and a genuinely novel or amusing anecdote can produce the occasional exception. Unlike the other columns we've listed, however, submissions to these three should be exclusive (go to one columnist only).

This may sound like a lot of self-involved silliness to you, but it most definitely isn't. An actor is his own business, and *every* business must advertise to flourish.

"It really doesn't matter all that much *why* your name appears in the trades," says publicist Barbara Best. "Most people forget that. They just remember *that* they saw your name."

ADS IN THE TRADES

Are trade ads worth it? It depends on what you're advertising and the impact of the ad itself. Obviously, getting your name before the industry is valuable, but ads in the trades are expensive investments to struggling actors.

A one-fourth-page ad (about as small as you should get) will cost $270 in *Daily Variety;* $266 in the *Hollywood Reporter.* A one-half-page ad will cost $480 and $463 respectively; a full-page ad, $755 and $775. (Full-page ads on certain "special" pages can add a couple of hundred dollars more to the tab.)

Advertising is not the solution to all problems. Not only is "Joe Idle, seeking representation" a waste of money, but it calls attention to the fact that you haven't been able to get an agent to sign you.

Ads announcing "Ginger Peachy signs with Super-Keeny Agency" (almost always paid for by the actor, by the way) may flatter the agency, and they do have some news value to casting directors, but, on the whole, "So what?", as one producer put it.

Ads asking you to "See Prudence Krapotnik in *Alaska One-Oh*" might be of real value if you're calling attention to a decent part. "Don't take out an ad for a one-line part, *please,*" says theatrical casting director Ron Stephenson.

A tacky or amateurish-looking ad is probably worse than none in an industry where style and status are important. The ad should have a certain size (at least one-fourth the page), although enough graphics savvy can beat the drawback of small size. It should look uncluttered; contain your photo, name, and agency representation; and sport copy that is not negative, silly, needful, or excessively braggadocious.

You may be tempted to include review after review until nobody will read it. Don't. Keep the copy short and to the point.

If you can't afford to have your ad done professionally by a graphics house, the graphics pros in the ad departments of *Variety* and the *Reporter* will lay out your ad for you at no extra charge, as long as it doesn't involve major artwork.

"If I wanted to have my face seen, I'd put it in the Thursday/Friday editions of the trades," advises Ruth Robinson. The TV and film production charts are included on those days, so readership is high. Call the paper for deadlines. While the ad salesman can't guarantee where your ad will appear, he might be able to get you on the same page as the charts or on the page opposite—prime space for an advertiser. Other good spots include placement opposite any major column; on the right-hand side of any page (even, in the case of *Variety*, near the crossword puzzle). In any case, it won't hurt to ask.

GROUP ADS

- If you're in a successful play, it might be a good idea to take out an ad for the production. The cast can split the cost. Include a quote or two from reviews that might excite people about the play (just don't clutter the ad with them).

- Your commercial agent may ask you to put up a portion of the cost of an ad in a monthly periodical such as *Entertainment Monthly* (formerly *Commercials Monthly*). These ads usually include photos of a dozen or more clients. While this is a perfectly acceptable practice, we wonder if the agency doesn't benefit more from this kind of ad than the client, who becomes a face in the crowd.

USING THE BREAKDOWN SERVICE

The same Breakdown Service that provides casting breakdowns and the casting directors guide offers other services as well. For particulars, call 658-5684. Some of their services are

- *The "Go-Between":* For $50, they'll hand-deliver your invitations and announcements to all casting directors; for $80, they'll deliver to producers. It's a bit expensive, and you might want to opt for their cheaper alternative of label sets as mentioned in the·budget (Chapter 4).

- *Delivery service for shows/theatres:* If you're in a show, and your group prints up an eight-and-a-half-by-eleven flyer that includes the names of *all* cast members, the Breakdown Service will hand-deliver the flyer to all agents and personal managers for *free*.

- *Theatre line/label sets:* Among their services for theatre groups are preparation of press announcements, mailing of press releases, and other publicity aids. If your theatre group doesn't have a publicity person or department working on this vital area, they might want to know about this service.

WRITING THE CRITICS

If you're in an Equity Waiver play, it's vital for the producer to understand the importance of getting someone who knows what he's doing to work on publicity, especially in regard to the critics.

"I try to tell people *we don't know they're opening*," says Bill Edwards, drama critic for *Daily Variety*. "Usually an actor is assigned to do publicity who doesn't know a thing about it. . . . Very often I'll get a call on Thursday night saying, 'Are you coming to our show tonight?' and I answer, '*What show?*' "

All notices should go out two weeks before you open, followed by phone calls a day or so in advance. If a critic likes your performance, a brief thank-you note might be nice. "That's no more than reasonable public relations," says Sylvie Drake, a drama critic for the *Los Angeles Times*. "My usual answer to thank-you notes is to tell the actors they have only to thank themselves . . . and the next time, if they get a bad review, they have only to thank themselves too."

MAILING SERVICES

Ostensibly, these services send photos of selected clients as direct submissions for particular roles. Certainly, the services vary in quality, but casting directors tell tales of photographs arriving by the pile. Even if you're not represented by an agent, you can do a lot of this work yourself for the cost of stamps and envelopes, and your photo will arrive by itself.

IN GENERAL

Throughout this book, we've mentioned the importance of letting people know what you're doing through use of letters, postcards, news releases, ads, and even phone calls. Strangely enough, the entire area of publicity is often neglected by actors. Take advantage of their foolishness by filling the void with positive, upbeat, and continuous mention of your name. Show business is synonymous with publicity.

29 YOUR MANAGEMENT TEAM

Everyone should plan for success.

A. Morgan Maree, Business Manager

Your management team is divided into:

- The people you need to obtain immediately.
- The people you need to obtain later.

IMMEDIATELY

Certified Public Accountant (CPA)

His services per se may cost you a little more than a guy seated at one of 33 desks in a storefront operation, but we're fairly sure that no matter how little you earn in any given year, ultimately he'll save you money. Not only can he help you preplan your tax deductions, but you'll want someone in your corner who knows your tax background in case you should suddenly get "hot" and have a financial windfall. Be sure he's entertainment-oriented and that he can and will take a power of attorney and go with you (or in your place) in case of an audit.

To find a CPA, ask the bright show-biz people you meet for recommendations. Ask your agent; if the CPA is doing a good job on his returns, he'll probably do well by yours.

Attorney

Eventually, someone's going to hand you a contract, a letter of agreement, something with a lot of wherefores and whereases that will be such gobbledy-gook you'll have no idea what you're being asked to sign. And the worst time to go hunting for an attorney is when you need one. There's no need to pay him a retainer. Just establish a basic relationship with him for the future. Once again, you'll want him to be entertainment-oriented. A nonspecialist can't possibly understand all the ins and outs of this peculiar industry.

Banker

A banker?!? You, who earned only $3,000 last year, need a banker?!? Yes. You're planning for success, remember? Put on a coat and tie, go down to your bank, and introduce yourself to the manager or assistant manager. Afterward, every once in a while, drop by and say hello. If you establish a good relationship with him—along with good credit—you'll be amazed at how he can grease the corporate wheels if you need a loan, even for "small" things such as changing accounts, check-guarantee cards, credit cards, and so forth. A "connection" can save you a lot of time and bother and can spare you dealings with rule-bound bank clerks.

Insurance agent

As an actor, you're what is known in the insurance industry as a "target risk." If your car slams into someone and he recognizes your face from a TV show, he will be more inclined to start shouting "Whiplash! Whiplash!" (Don't you know all actors are rich?) As your career progresses, you'll need to have higher limits on your car, house, even personal insurance. Getting a good insurance agent now—one who doesn't try to sell you every kind of "benefit" he can think of to make a commission—can make life a lot easier for you in the future. Again, ask your friends, banker, and lawyer for recommendations.

LATER

Personal managers

"I know an actor who has done sixty films and you still don't know his name," says personal manager Cathryn Jaymes.

Not all agents concern themselves with your *career*. Some can be very long on their 10 percent, very short on your future. Even the most conscientious of agents can't give you the kind of personalized attention you ought to have . . .

. . . Enter the personal manager, who can be anything from a godsend to the guy you pay 15 percent to wreck your career.

Ostensibly, he's your own personal career guidance counselor, the foreman of a ranch that includes you, your agent, and all your talents. Done a lot of theatre? He makes sure you have an agent in New York. Sing? He gets you on the nightclub circuit. Been offered a part at a theatre in Missouri? He makes sure you're happy with your dressing room. Been offered a role on an episodic television show? He advises you whether or not to take it, based on how it may affect your career game plan. Not sure your agent is submitting, or even thinking of you? Your "PM" checks over his copy of the Breakdown Service and calls your agent to nudge him a little. Need an agent with more clout? He helps you get one.

And on top of all that, he introduces you to important people. He opens doors that might be locked to you and your agent. There have been cases where a personal manager has introduced a total newcomer to the right producer, and *zooom!*

Indeed, there would be those who would question our putting personal managers under the catagory of people to obtain "later." Their (very legitimate) argument would be to get yourself a good personal manager *first* and have *him* get you your agent.

However, for every person who believes in personal managers, there are others who have mixed opinions or downright hate them. "I don't think they're very valuable, unless they have access to packaging," says one producer. "They're only helpful if you're a star and they also can provide business advice," says another. "They're nothing more than ambulance chasers," says still another.

Ask an agent what he thinks of personal managers, and don't be surprised to see smoke come out of his ears. Many agents have as much love for personal managers as they have for root-canal work.

Why this divergence of opinion?

First of all, you can put down this book, pick up a piece of wood, paint your name on it, followed by the words "Personal Manager," and you're in business. You don't have to have any idea of what you're doing. You don't have to be franchised with any union. You don't have to be licensed by the state. And you can charge anyone dumb enough to sign with you any percentage you want. Then you can get on the phone and start making ridiculous demands of agents, casting directors, even producers and directors. The mere fact that you're destroying your client's career may never enter your mind.

Second, the going rate for personal managers is 15 percent (and upward) of your gross income. Since he's not franchised or licensed, he can't negotiate a legal contract. With or without him, you're still going to have to have an agent. Add the agent's commission to his and you are paying out 25 percent—one-quarter—of your income so that you can meet people and ensure that a lot of things get done that, if you think about it, you could do yourself.

Third, even if the personal manager is top-notch, he's not always going to be right. And his mistakes can be dillies. Maybe his demand for that fancy dressing-room in Missouri is just enough to make the producer say, "Look, let's just skip it." Maybe he "nudges" your agent once too often and destroys a relationship you've been working on for years. Maybe he counsels you not to take a part, and you don't work for another year. Maybe he "manages" you right out of the business.

If a personal manager has expressed interest in you, check him over very, very carefully. He should have been in business for at least a few years or, at any rate, have solid show-business connections; he should charge you no more than 15 percent of your gross; and he should demand *no* money up front. Most agents and casting directors should know and respect him. His clients should look sharp and have good pictures and résumés. He should have no more than about 10 to 15 clients, if that. And, most important, he should have solid well-informed judgment—that's really what you hire a personal manager for.

If you want to look for one, check the *Studio Blu-Book,* the *Academy Players Directory* (actors often list their managers), or the trades, and use the same methods we discussed in "Seeking an Agent."

If you're a newcomer, your best chance will be if you have the potential to become a teen heartthrob, glamour girl, or handsome hunk. Less rarefied beings must often wait until they have reached a certain level in their careers—if, indeed, they need a personal manager at all. That's why we put personal managers in the "Later" category—with reservations.

If you're multitalented (sing, dance, direct, etc.) and feel you need someone to organize and flesh out all those possibilities, a personal manager might be of help once you've got some credit. If you're earning more than $100,000 a year, a personal manager could be just the ticket to catapult you into superstardom.

There's just no clear-cut answer to the question "Is a personal manager worth it?" That depends on the manager, your circumstances, and how the industry views you both. It's just a pity that in today's Hollywood it may take two people to get one job done.

"I do all the things agents used to do when they had the time," says personal manager Jerry Cohn. "Unfortunately," says business manager A. Morgan Maree, "today you get for twenty-five percent what you used to get for ten."

Business Manager

You won't need a business manager until you're making upward of $100,000 a year. By that point, you should have developed a good relationship with a CPA who can offer you business advice, act as your business manager, or refer you to one. Some personal management firms also offer business management services.

A business manager's title tells you what he does—he manages your business, helps you preplan tax deductions, suggests possible investments, arranges loans, puts together your portfolio and annual financial statement, etc. If he's good, he'll help you make and save money.

The usual contract calls for him to get from 5 to 6 percent of your salary as an actor, but there are variations on this.

Regardless of whether you've got a business manager or not, the more knowledge you have of business the better. A lot of stars have lost their shirts through either their own bad investments or those of a bad/shyster business manager. Are you in college and thinking of becoming an actor? A major or minor in business will not only give you something to fall back on if it doesn't work out but will provide you with the proper background to make the most of your earnings if it does. Out of school? There are plenty of community college business courses and seminars available.

Publicist

"Until you're famous, you can probably do the same things for yourself as any publicist," says Ruth Robinson, Associate Editor for the *Hollywood Reporter*. No publicist can help if you're not doing anything worth publicizing. And a community-theatre production in Pasadena doesn't qualify.

However, once you're starting to get hot, a publicist can be invaluable. Through strategic planning, he can keep your name before the public, and, more important, the industry, for weeks, months, and even years ahead. He can keep everybody convinced that you just never stop working and are in constant demand. And when he does that, he's earned the $1,000 (and upward) per month he'll charge you. As publicist Barbara Best puts it, "You'll know your publicist is doing a good job when people come up to you and tell *you* how well you're doing."

30 GENERAL FINANCIAL

I know it's not very exciting or glamorous,
but if you want my best advice, keep records.

David Perren, Certified Public Accountant
with the firm of Barkin, Blank, Perren &
Elam

TAXES

W-2, W-4 Forms, etc.

Withholding taxes are a problem for actors. Whenever you work, your employer follows a tax table that "assumes" you make that kind of money week in and week out. Bang! There goes a substantial portion of your paycheck.

Obviously, you may get that money back in your tax refund, but don't you need the money now? And why should you "rent" that money to the federal government for free?

Until the IRS clamped down, many actors would fill out a form saying they were "exempt" from withholding, or they would claim ninety-nine exemptions. Using this, the employer withheld nothing.

Well, that's gone. Oh, you can still do it, but if you claim you're "exempt," or if you claim more than fourteen exemptions, your employer is required to send a copy of that form to the IRS. The IRS can take that form and match it against your tax return. If your tax return shows you don't qualify for the number of exemptions you've claimed, they will then send you a letter asking you to substantiate those exemptions. If you can't, or don't respond to that letter, they will write your employer and ask him to withhold your taxes as if you were single, claiming zero exemptions. We don't think we have to tell you what that will do to your paycheck.

There is, however, one thing you can do. For every $1,000 of deductions you took last year (not only your business expenses but others, such as alimony payments, losses from business investments, etc.), you may claim *one* additional exemption. If you had $7,000 worth of deductions, you get an additional seven exemptions. Add those to your standard exemptions (Single = 1, Married = 2, etc.) and that's the number of exemptions you may legitimately claim on your W-4 form. It won't get you all of your money, but it can cut down on that withholding "bite" and give you more cash when you need it—now.

What's your line?

When can you put the word "actor" on your tax return? That's a bit of a gray area. Certainly you can call yourself an actor if that's your chief source of income. But if the amount of money you make in any given year as an actor was to be the sole criterion, we don't have to tell you that most actors simply wouldn't qualify. Therefore, the best answer seems to be: *how much time did you spend trying to make money as an actor?*

Keeping records

Way back, we mentioned the importance of a daily diary when it comes time to file your income tax. At least once a week, it's a good idea to enter into your diary all the expenses you incurred as an actor. Did you have lunch with your agent on Thursday? Enter it. Did you buy a theatre book on Friday? Write it in. Not only will that diary serve you well in case of an audit, but often it will remind you of expenses you simply might have forgotten.

Next, keep receipts—even for the items you buy by check or credit card. Without receipts, you're leaving yourself open to having your deductions disallowed, no matter how legitimate. Why should the IRS believe you spent $150 on résumé shots on March 16 if all you have to show them is a penciled-in entry in your diary?

Some actors like to attach receipts directly onto their daily diary (next to the expense entry for that day). It's a darn good idea. "It gives the diary more substance," says certified public accountant Mel Blank.

And, speaking of accountants, once again, get yourself a good entertainment-oriented CPA.

In Appendix A, we give a list of "typical" tax deductions for the professional actor.

A word about per diems

As we note in Appendix A, when you go on location you get a minimum per diem of $42 a day for expenses. You'll need to keep careful records of these expenses too, even though you don't report them to your employer. He must file a 1099 form with the IRS, telling them you were paid the expense money. Therefore, you'll have to report that expense money as income. If your expenses equal the per diem, obviously they'll ultimately cancel each other out. If your expenses were greater, that's an additional deduction. If they were less, that's taxable income.

In case of an audit

Don't jump off a bridge. Nobody's going to send you to jail (unless you're defrauding the government, which has nothing to do with this book). All they'll do is check your return and ask you to substantiate your deductions. When you get the letter, call your CPA or tax adviser. He'll advise you what to do, perhaps even take a power of attorney from you and go to the audit with your records in hand, all by himself. Then either they'll declare a "no change" (your return is accepted as filed); they'll disallow certain deductions (for which you have the right to be billed at a later time); or you may even get a refund.

INVESTING

Sooner or later, you're going to have either a small or a giant windfall. What do you do with the money? First, it would help to understand the concept of "paying yourself first." Each month, if you're like most people, you pay your bills, saying, "Well, I'll just use whatever's left over on myself." If you're smart, you'll reverse that. Pay yourself *first*. Before you pay any bill, put a ten spot in a savings account. Drop a fiver in a piggy bank.

And when you get that windfall, extend that concept. Before you invest in that diamond mine in New Guinea, *invest in yourself*. New pictures, an ad in *Variety*, and/or a good presentation tape will do you better in the long run. A. Morgan Maree, business manager, suggests this order of investment:

1. Invest in yourself
2. Invest in insurance (especially if you have dependents).
3. Invest in a place in which you'd be comfortable living.
4. Other investments (and seek competent investment counseling).

UNEMPLOYMENT COMPENSATION

We don't have the space to go into all the rules and regulations governing this. Just don't view it as charity—you earned the money. As one actor remarked: "I think of unemployment compensation as the national endowments for the arts."

Basically, if you earn $900 or more, you go down to any branch office listed in the telephone directory. You'll be given an appointment and lots of forms to fill out. You'll return, be interviewed, and two weeks later, based on your records, you'll be sent a statement telling you your "award"—how much money you'll be getting each week. This will be based on the most amount of money you earned in any three-month period. Every two weeks you'll fill out another form and you'll be mailed a check. You'll also occasionally be asked to go in person for another interview.

Whenever you apply for unemployment compensation, you're given a little booklet containing all their rules and regulations. Read it.

Especially bear in mind that when you're receiving unemployment compensation, you must report any work and any income you get. *That includes residuals.* Don't fail to report a single dime. If you do, you may think you've gotten away with it. Then, six months later, you'll get a letter. It can mean big trouble.

31 MISCELLANEOUS

Doing the job ain't that tough—it's getting it.

Bob Lloyd, "The Voicecaster"

SAG CONSERVATORY

Like bargains? Here's a lulu. A $10 membership in the conservatory entitles you to participate in a host of programs, all at no additional charge (for how to join, see the "Student Films" section of our "Stocking Stuffers" chapter).

Some of the programs are

Conservatory workshops

A nifty way to get some feedback on your audition technique—for free. Each Monday, about ten conservatory members are invited to participate in a videotaped "cold reading" of a typical spokesman commercial. Alone with the "instructor," each member of the group tapes his audition once, has it played back to him with advice on how to improve it, then tapes it again. Later, when everyone has had his chance, both tapings are shown again, in front of the entire group, and are further critiqued.

The following Wednesday you return to do a mock general interview and theatrical cold reading. Both are critiqued afterward.

The instructors are always fellow actors, generally very kind, and what they tell you will be based on the accumulated knowledge from previous sessions.

We wouldn't advise doing this as a substitute for a good commercials workshop or cold-reading workshop (you're only permitted to go once, hardly enough training if your technique needs work), but it can be a good backup if you know what you're doing and a revelation if you don't.

Summer seminars

Once a year the conservatory puts together an all-day series of interviews, lectures, and "Q-and-A" sessions with casting directors, agents, fellow actors, etc. Once a psychologist came to talk about handling rejection. This program too is free to conservatory members, and besides the knowledge you'll gain, there's a general feeling of warmth to the day, which will make you feel good about yourself and your fellow actors. Just bring your lunch and enjoy.

Agents seminars

Off and on, the conservatory invites an agent to a "Q-and-A" session. It's a great way to meet an agent or to gain some insights, and, once again, you can't beat the price: free to conservatory members.

General seminars

These are "Q-and-A" sessions with various industry people. We've seen Martin Sheen talking about the making of *Apocalypse Now*, a genuinely witty Neil Simon and Marsha Mason, etc. Often these seminars are of the general-interest variety. Don't expect to get a lot of hard information about how to go about your career. Also, often the questions from the audience (actors who are conservatory members) are surprisingly close to the "fan club" variety. Still, it's interesting and free.

AFTRA/SAG CREDIT UNION

This is "the actor's savings and loan." To open an account, you'll need to be a member of SAG or AFTRA. Offices are at 1717 N. Highland Avenue, Suite 320, in Hollywood (461-3041). You'll need to make an initial deposit of at least $25. Among the benefits are: higher rates of interest on savings accounts; interest checking; and a lower rate of interest on any loans you take out. (All funds are federally insured through FDIC.)

Perhaps its most important benefit is that by banking with an institution run solely for the benefit of its actor members, you'll find a lot more understanding when you need a loan. For example, how many other places can you think of that will consider a portion of your unemployment compensation as part of your income when you apply for a loan?

We'd suggest using the credit union for this purpose and for a medium-range savings account. There's only one office, making the continual withdrawals and deposits of a checking account rather inconvenient.

(Through the credit union, you can also get discounts on auto parts, and even a visit to an amusement park or two.)

SAG FILM SOCIETY

Open only to paid-up members of SAG, its cost last year was $45. Your membership entitles you and a guest to see a first-run film every other Friday or Saturday at no additional charge. That's the equivalent of fifty-two admissions to films such as *Star Wars*, etc.—sometimes even before they're actually released to the general public. We're sure you see why the film society sells out every year.

Other benefits include not having to wait in line. You walk right in, present your ticket, take a seat and, wonder of wonders, they even start the films on time. When was the last time that happened at your local Bijou?

The only real drawbacks are that you don't get to select the films, and you have to go on the day and time assigned (unless you want to take a chance in the "off-time" line, and hope the house doesn't fill up before you get in). But even if you don't want to see half the films chosen, you're still saving $85 from what you'd normally pay for twenty-six admissions to thirteen films.

Contact SAG and/or watch for the ad that appears in the SAG magazine. Join quickly; it sells out fast.

Oh, yes, there's one other drawback. No popcorn.

SAG "RAP"

Once a month, usually on a weekday afternoon, you can go to SAG and air your grievances and/or solicit advice. It's free to union members. Check your newsletter or call SAG for further information.

TWOFERS

If you're thinking of going to the theatre and your Los Angeles Theatre Alliance benefits don't apply (see "Arrival in L.A."), give the Twofer L.A. Company a buzz and find out if you can get two tickets for the price of one. (Or pay them a visit at one of their two locations; they're based in the Theatrix theatre and dance shops at 1093¼ Broxton Ave., Westwood, 824-4773, and the Galleria shopping center in Sherman Oaks, 783-2220). Hours are from twelve to eight P.M., Tuesday through Sunday. There's a small service charge ($2), and you must buy tickets with cash or by traveler's check, day of show only.

"FREE" PHOTOS

If you're broke but really need new pictures, consider contacting a school for photographers, such as the Hamilton School of Photography (820-7565), for a swap of services instead of cash. Hamilton's policy is to require 30 hours of posing from you (no nudity) and then they'll do a session consisting of 48 shots and throw in six eight-by-ten prints. Since the average headshot session costs about $85, in essence you're being paid about $3 per hour for all that posing. That's far from a king's ransom, but it can get you new photos without any money changing hands.

COLLEGE SEMINARS

Many colleges in the city offer noncredit "extension" or "continuing education" courses, open to the general public. They're a great way to fill in those gaps in your knowledge. One typical semester at UCLA, for example, includes "Cable Television Today" and "Producing the Television Commercial," among others; across town, USC counters with offerings like "How Networks Work" and "Preparing to Meet the Press." Costs vary from under $50 to a few hundred dollars. Call the schools and have them put you on their mailing lists.

L.A. INTERNATIONAL FILM EXPOSITION (FILMEX)

This is to film buffs what roast beef was to Henry VIII. For 16 days, usually in March, you can trek down to the ABC Entertainment Center in Century City (west L.A.) and see a couple of hundred movies from all over the world that might not otherwise have seen the dark of a Los Angeles theatre. You can purchase tickets per movie, or (for true believers) in series of 6, 20, 40, or 60. The local papers and media always give FILMEX publicity, so you aren't likely to miss it.

ACADEMY OF MOTION PICTURE ARTS AND SCIENCES

Besides handing out those little gold statuettes you may have heard something about and publishing the *Academy Players Directory,* they also have a research library on the film industry and hold seminars, interviews, retrospectives, etc., many open to the public. If you don't want to miss out on these, send a three-dollar check to: Academy Foundation, 8949 Wilshire Boulevard, Beverly Hills 90211. That will put your name on their mailing list for one year.

WOMEN IN THEATRE

Here's a chance to learn the theatre scene and do a little "networking" in a business where contacts are worth their weight in gold. Membership is open and costs $20. Among their activities are readings, seminars, and a resource file of members' abilities. You can write them at P.O. Box 3718, Los Angeles 90028.

WOMEN IN FILM

Another "old-girl network," this one aimed at career women in the film industry. Includes newsletters, guest speakers, workshops, and the like. If interested, you'll need three years' craft, guild, or professional experience and two WIF members as sponsors. Initiation fee is $10, dues $76. Write WIF, 8489 Third Street, Suite 49, Los Angeles 90048.

WESTWOOD CLINIC PREVENTATIVE MEDICINE

This clinic has made an agreement with certain unions to give their members preferred rates on complete physical exams. They run just about every test you can think of and include a consultation between you and a doctor. Their usual charge is $200, but with a SAG, Equity, or SEG card, you pay $150. They're located in Westwood at 10850 Westwood Boulevard, Suite 370. Phone: 475-5841.

STARTING YOUR OWN NETWORK

A few years ago, two enterprising women, Tani Guthrie and Dran Hamilton, started a small group they called Actors Helping Actors (AHA). Meeting once a week, the group discussed careers, evaluated one another's résumés and résumé shots, etc., and, once they got rolling, invited guest speakers (casting directors, agents, etc.) to "Q-and-A" sessions.

Great ideas, like strong flowers, are hard to keep underground. Today, there are many such groups, and they keep popping up all the time.

Another group of actors got tired of paying eighty bucks to the various showcases around town and formed their own showcase—Out to Lunch. It, too, is working.

Still another group of actors formed Actors for Themselves and produced one of the most successful Equity Waiver theatre hits ever, *Are You Now or Have You Ever Been*. In fact, many of the now-established Equity Waiver theatre groups began with a few actors who just got tired of waiting around for roles at other people's theatres and formed their own.

Since getting into established groups may be difficult for you, the new kid on the block (even finding them may be a chore), there's nothing, absolutely nothing, stopping you from forming your own. All you need is a place to meet (many savings and loans associations have "community rooms" that they'll let your group use rent free, provided you don't charge admittance to your meetings), and a group of willing, eager actors.

In any case, all it takes is a little ingenuity, a willingness to do a little extra work, and a dash of panache. And brother, can it pay off.

32 ASSESSING YOUR CAREER

Q: What advice would you give actors?

A: Self-examination on a steady basis.

Interview with Ruth Robinson, Associate
Editor, *Hollywood Reporter*

We don't believe in arbitrary time limits on your acting career, but at some point you're going to have to examine what's been happening. New Year's is as good a time as any for reflection, so we'll assume that between toasts or kickoffs, you wandered away to do a little thinking. If so, you probably found one of the following to be true:

- You've gotten a good amount of work.
- You've gotten some work.
- You were getting work, but somehow your career has stopped.
- You've gotten nothing.

A GOOD AMOUNT OF WORK

Congratulations. If you earned $10,000 or more during the year, you're in the upper 10 percent of the Screen Actors Guild. Think over what you've been doing right and plan to keep doing it. Then go back and toast yourself.

SOME WORK

Before you climb all over your own back, bear in mind that if you earned more than $2,500 during the year, you're in the top 30 percent of your class. Make that a pat on the back instead.

Now: How to get more work? Look at the jobs you did get. How did they come about? What did you do right? Next, make a list of obvious weak points in your game plan. Is it your agent? Your pictures? Are you showcasing yourself enough—especially in Equity Waiver theatre? Have you kept in touch with those for whom you've worked? How many new contacts did you make? Did you nurture those contacts? Do you think you tend to blow auditions? Maybe a cold reading workshop would help. Or a commercial workshop. How about a class in improvisation? Did you lose a role because you can't ride a horse? Or dance? Or do a French accent? . . .

You might make a monthly plan to cover your weak areas, then break down that plan into weekly and daily goals.

Actress Cindy Randall says, "I write out, 'til my hand gets tired, what it is I want to happen and, eventually, it happens."

YOU WERE GETTING WORK, BUT YOUR CAREER HAS JUST "STOPPED"

We can't think of a more frustrating turn of events. If it helps at all, this is a phase most actors go through periodically. Everything is going swimmingly, then bam! When you weren't looking, somebody pulled the plug out of the pool.

First, see if you can figure out what's happened—unemotionally. Has your agent gone cold on you? Have you been sitting back, waiting for him to do it all? Was your type just "out" this season? Were there union strikes? Have you priced yourself out of the market? Maybe you need new pictures. Maybe you need to do an Equity Waiver play. And maybe, just maybe, you've become, through no fault of your own . . .

Yesterday's mashed potatoes

Hollywood never seems to lose its insatiable appetite for the "new." We know you've heard of producers who went everywhere from East Boohoboora to South Wales looking for a "new face" to put in their movie—while all the time there were thousands of faces sitting idle in Hollywood—probably, we might add, with a heck of a lot more training.

Somehow it seems that you're given an indeterminate amount of time to become a "hot item." Exceed it, or "merely" become a yeoman actor who consistently does good work, and you may wake up to find out you're passé. You're old news. "Out." And you may be typed to boot.

If this is the case, you'll need to do one of two things:

- Double your efforts: Especially in meeting new people. You're not passé to them. Try to find a play that shows you off in a new light. Done nothing on TV but scroungy villains? Play a judge or a doctor reeking with distinction. Been typed as a bookish accountant? Buckle a swash or two. Tired of playing Miss Goody Two-Shoes? A musical comedy in which you play a vamp might juice up your career again. In essence, you're trying to get yourself "discovered" by those who don't know you and "rediscovered" by those who do. It's a pain in the neck, we know, for an established actor to have to go back to work-getting work. But there it is, and you have to do something if you don't want to really become past tense.

● *Turn bicoastal:* "The place to go is New York," says legitimate/theatrical agent Larry Fonseca. "There, they'll take shots on people. The talent is what counts. Out here, they'll go for a name, or the (casting) precedent has been set." If you're starting to sense that casting directors say "Oh, *him,*" when your agent submits you, it might not be a bad idea to pack up and head east. There, you'll be dealing with an entire city that looks on you as "new." Even better, with film credits under your belt, you'll find it a lot easier to interest agents.

Naturally, that's too expensive a decision to enter into lightly, but it's one to consider. If you're good, have credits, can hold your own on stage, and can audition, you'll have a genuine shot at breaking away from playing nothing but law clerks . . .

. . . And then some Hollywood producer will see you in a play, bring you out to L.A. for his next picture, and everyone will ask, "Where have you been hiding all this time?"

IF YOU'VE GOTTEN NOTHING

We don't have to tell you something's wrong. You're probably hurting inside. Should you quit? Give it six more months? Keep going indefinitely? Here's what producer/director Buddy Bregman has to say: "After you've been at it a year or so, if you find it's totally negative and your ambition is metza-metza, it's time to think about whether you should carry on or not. Because sometimes persevering against a brick wall is a waste of time. But if you really think you've got the talent, and this is all you want, then don't stop; it would be wrong to stop."

If you decide to quit, try to do it happily. You're not a failure. This just wasn't the profession for you. There's nothing wrong with racking your cue if all you're doing is scratching; it just wasn't your game. So what?

Besides, you took your shot. The rest of your life will be free from that torturous question "What if?" That alone is an enormous gift to yourself— ask those who didn't try.

And remember, you're being relieved of all the problems, all the nonsense, all those receivers being hung up in your ear. And if you return home to another state, you'll be relieved of all the smog, traffic, and gold chains. And you'll never again have to hear someone say, "Let's *take* a meeting Tuesday."

And one other thing. Leaving the acting profession doesn't have to mean leaving the film industry. You tried playing second base; how about catcher or shortstop? How about becoming an agent, casting director, a gaffer, a makeup artist, a producer, a director, a stage manager, a writer, a personal manager, a continuity person, an editor, a lighting technician . . . there are hundreds of industry jobs to choose from, and although none is easy to get, all are going to be filled by somebody. Ultimately, you may find far greater satisfaction helping other actors to look good or to "make it."

The industry can always use more happy set decorators and fewer miserable actors.

33 CONCLUSION

> *Concentrate on your career, but have a*
> *personally enriched life along with it,*
> *which means dating . . . marriage . . . and*
> *having some fun.*
>
> Viola Kates Stimpson, Actress

It's 1977. He lives in the South, working a typical nine-to-five job. He's a true fan of a famous actress. He even sent her a dozen roses once when she won an Academy Award.

While he's talented and enjoys acting in community theatre, he has no intention of pursuing a career as a professional actor. He's a rather shy person, reticent around strangers, so his interview technique needs some work. His cold-reading technique, however, is nonexistent. He'll admit if he doesn't get the script long enough to memorize it, he doesn't have a chance.

He's nonunion. He doesn't have any résumé shots or résumés—after all, what does he need them for? He *never* goes to L.A. or New York seeking work.

And, on top of all that, he's partially handicapped.

One day, a local director asks him if he'd like to appear in a show he's putting together in that city. . . .

Cut to: the present. He's appeared on stage in a hit New York show for two years. His face has appeared on the front page of the *New York Times*'s theatre section, and he's gotten excellent reviews.

He's been on a European tour, including performing for and meeting the Prince of Wales.

And one night his favorite actress happens to be in the audience. After the show, she goes backstage, tells him how much she enjoyed his performance . . .

And then she gives him a kiss.

Sound like the script for a B movie?

It's all true. We know; it happened to a friend. Call it Fate, the Karmic Kosmos, or more things than are dreamt of by us Horatios. The point is that this business is just plain magically nutsy.

You can stand at a corner with a comic book in your hand, turn left, and bump into a guy with his shirt open to his navel who says, "You! You're perfect!" And zoooom.

Or you can be at the same corner with this book under your arm, turn right, and wind up struggling for twenty years.

Well, that's the job-getting business. At least you know the game a little better, which will cut the odds a bit.

In any case, whether you have that unlikely instant luck or the usual period of struggle, we hope you'll never forget the sheer joy of: a mustard-slavered hot dog at the ball park, kissing your loved one for no good reason whatsoever, or just plain having a hearty laugh.

We also hope your acting coach never asks why you secretly hate your little brother. We hope your agent calls you once a month desperate for more pictures. We hope the receptionists you run up against don't give you terminal frostbite. We hope casting directors sensitively understand why your hands are so clammy. We hope producers pay you all your meal penalties and directors shoot you in close-up.

And, finally, we hope that blowhard who told you you'll "never make it" is backstage when your favorite actress walks up to you and tells you how wonderful you were . . .

And gives you a kiss.

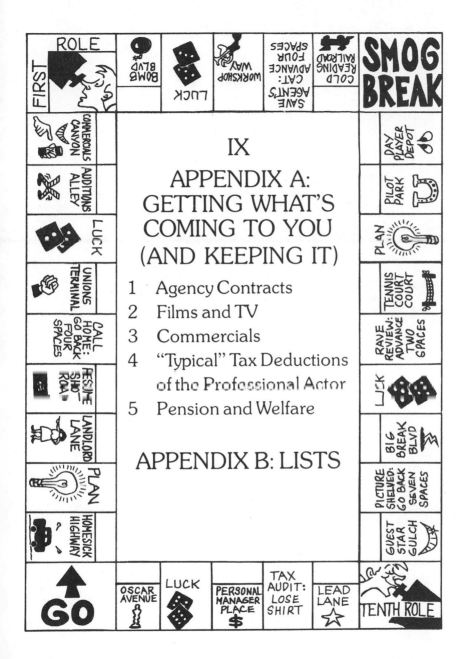

IX
APPENDIX A:
GETTING WHAT'S COMING TO YOU (AND KEEPING IT)

1 Agency Contracts
2 Films and TV
3 Commercials
4 "Typical" Tax Deductions of the Professional Actor
5 Pension and Welfare

APPENDIX B: LISTS

APPENDIX A

Getting What's Coming to You (and Keeping It)

1 AGENCY CONTRACTS

THEATRICAL AGENCY CONTRACTS

When your theatrical agent is ready to sign you, he'll hand you three different contracts (three copies of each):

1. *Television Motion Picture Talent Agency Contract:* Eight pages, on blue paper. Sent to the Screen Actors Guild, it covers the agent's representation of you in films made for television. (We'll call this SAG-TV.)

2. *Theatrical Motion Picture Artists Manager Contract (Agency Contract):* Seven pages, white paper. Also sent to SAG, covers his representation of you in movies. (We'll call this SAG-Film.)

3. *Standard AFTRA Exclusive Agency Contract Under Rule 12-B:* Four pages, white paper. Sent to the American Federation of Television and Radio Artists, it covers his representation of you for taped television productions and radio (not commercials). (We'll call this AFTRA.)

These three contracts have been hammered out by the respective unions in conjunction with agents. There's no hidden fine print, and you can feel safe signing them, since they are meant for your protection as well as the agent's. Furthermore, the provisions found in one contract are often similar to provisions found in the other two, although they may be found in different places in the different contracts.

Nonetheless, always read any contract carefully. We're not attorneys, and we haven't the space to go into each contract point by point. We'll discuss major terms, but, in all cases, you're signing the *whole* contract. Also, as we mentioned, there is movement toward a possible merger between SAG and AFTRA, and even SEG (the Screen Extras Guild).

So these provisions may change. If you have any questions about your contracts, the unions will help you.

TOP OF THE CONTRACTS

At the very beginning of all three contracts, you'll find the following. We've filled in the blanks in capital letters with the variables you should see there:

> This Agreement, made and entered at __(LOS ANGELES)__
> by and between __(NAME OF THE AGENCY)__, hereinafter
> called the "AGENT" and __(YOUR NAME)__, Social
> Security No. __(YOUR SS#)__ . . . .

TERM OF CONTRACT:

Also on the first page of all three contracts—Paragraph (2), SAG-TV and SAG-Film; Paragraph (3), AFTRA—you'll see:

> The term of this contract shall be for a period
> of __(ONE YEAR)__, commencing the __(DAY OF MONTH)__
> day of __(MONTH)__, 19 __(YEAR)__.

The first time you sign, your agent can't ask you to sign for longer than a year. Later, he may want you to sign a three-year contract.

10 PERCENT PROVISION

Still on the first page of all three contracts—Paragraph (3), SAG-TV and SAG-Film; Paragraph (4), AFTRA—you should see the number ten typed in. That's what you'll be paying the agent as his commission. No other number should be there.

Immediately after this, you'll see a number of paragraphs labeled alphabetically, (a) through (j) on SAG-TV; (a) through (h) on SAG-Film; (a) through (g) on AFTRA. These provisions include: certain instances when a commission is not payable (wardrobe fees, meal penalties, etc.); the fact that the agent gets no money if you don't; the information that, should you fire an agent, you must still pay him his commission on any work he had obtained for you; and so on.

To avoid getting into problems, read these provisions—and if there's something you don't understand, ask the union.

91-15 PROVISION

Obviously, you can fire your agent when your contract runs out. But what if you're unhappy with him and you've still got months to go? This is probably the most important provision found in these contracts. It's the "out" we talked about earlier, Paragraph (6) on all three contracts. Edited, it reads: ". . . If during any period of 91 days . . . the actor fails to be employed . . . for fifteen (15) days . . . the actor or agent may terminate . . . employment . . . of the agent . . . by written notice to the other party. . . . "

In other words, if you don't work, or at least get paid to work, for 15 days during any 91-day period, you can fire your agent (or he can fire you). In the SAG contracts, Saturdays and Sundays are specifically included in the counting days (Paragraph (6)(e), SAG-TV; Paragraph (6)(d), SAG-Film).

Immediately following, you'll find exceptions and additions to this provision (Paragraphs (a) through (m) on SAG-TV; Paragraphs (a) through (o) on SAG-Film; Paragraphs (a) through (j) on AFTRA). These include but are not limited to:

- If you take a leave of absence, those days don't count (Paragraph (g), SAG-TV; Paragraph (l), SAG-Film; Paragraph (g), AFTRA).

- You'll still owe your agent commissions on any work he helped you obtain (Paragraph (f), SAG-TV; Paragraph (m), SAG-Film; Paragraph (d), AFTRA).

- If you turn down a job while signed with your "old" agent, and later (within a time limit) accept it while signed with your "new" agent, you owe your "old" agent the commission. The time limitation on both SAG contracts is 60 days later (Paragraph (k), SAG-TV; Paragraph (n), SAG-Film). However, on the AFTRA contract, the time limit is 90 days, and is written as a separate provision, Paragraph (5).

- If you turn down a job at your "usual salary," and the job offer comes "from an employer commensurate with the actor's prestige," as all three contracts put it, the days you would have worked are counted as days you actually worked (Paragraph (c), SAG-TV; Paragraph (k), SAG-Film; Paragraph (c), AFTRA).

- On both SAG contracts (Paragraph (l), SAG-TV; Paragraph (m), SAG-Film), it's ruled that, if you haven't worked or turned down work and you've reached the 77th day, you may dismiss your agent. (The rationale is that even if you got a 15-day job on the 77th day, it would equal 15 days' work in 92 days.) This provision is not in the AFTRA contact.

PARAGRAPH (8)

On all three contracts, you'll find a blank space where your agent will ask you to write in the name of the agent or agents actually representing you.

LAST PAGE

On the last page of all three contracts, you'll find the place to date and sign the contract. Your agent will also have a place to sign (or stamp) it. Immediately beneath this, look for the following information:

1. Your agent is licensed by the Labor Commissioner of California.
2. Your agency is franchised with SAG (or AFTRA).
3. The contract has been approved by the Labor Commissioner.
4. The contract has been approved by SAG (or AFTRA).

DIFFERENCES

It should be obvious that there are differences between SAG and AFTRA contracts. We've touched on some, but there are many others—even including the way your "usual salary" is computed (see Paragraph (6)(a), (b), (c) on SAG-Film as an example).

One major difference is . . .

ONE-YEAR ANNIVERSARY

You'll find this in Paragraph (10) on both SAG contracts. If you've signed a multi-year contract (usually three years), you may fire your agent on the anniversary of the day you signed by giving him 30 days' notice in writing—*regardless of whether or not you are working.* However, this provision does *not* appear in the AFTRA contract. Its significance is this: If you are in a hit series under SAG's jurisdiction, you can replace your agent on the yearly anniversary date in favor of an agent better suited to take advantage of your sudden celebrity. If the show is under AFTRA's jurisdiction, you can't.

Another difference . . .

BOX ON PAGE 1

You'll find this only on Page 1 of the SAG-TV contract. It has to do with commercials. If you're signing only with a theatrical agent, *leave the box alone.*

PRODUCERS RELEASE FORM

In order to prevent you from "forgetting" to pay commissions, your agent may ask you to sign one more form. It authorizes a producer to send your checks directly to your agent, and releases the producer from any responsibility if the check is mishandled. The agent then deposits your check into a special "Client Account" and writes two checks against it—his check for 10 percent of what you've earned and a check for you for the balance. He mails you this second check, along with your pay stub.

There's nothing wrong with an agent asking you to sign this form. And you can always check his figures against your pay stub. Do you have to sign it? Well, no . . . and yes. As one agent put it, "If you refuse to sign it, as far as I'm concerned, you don't trust me. And if you don't trust me, I don't want you for a client."

COMMERCIAL AGENCY CONTRACTS

Exactly what you'll be asked to sign depends on whether you're signing with an agent *only* for commercials, or whether you're signing for representation in TV and films as well.

COMMERCIAL REPRESENTATION ONLY

You'll sign the standard AFTRA contract and the standard SAG television contract. You won't sign the SAG film contract. You'll also be given a "commercial rider" to initial; you'll find it attached to the back of the standard SAG television contract. It's one page (front and back) on blue paper. Most of the rider concerns the agent's duties regarding "exclusivity" (see Appendix A, III; see also "From Audition to Payoff," Chapter 24). However, there's one provision that's very important: Paragraph (C) makes it slightly tougher for you to leave your agent. Instead of requiring that you get 15 days' work in any 91-day period, it requires that you make $2,000 in 151 days. If you want to fire your agent, you'll have to wait five months and earn less than $2,000 in those five months.

COMMERCIALS, TV, AND FILM REPRESENTATION

You'll sign the three contracts discussed previously. Then you'll be asked to initial one of two things: You'll initial *either* the rider mentioned above *or* the box found on the first page of the SAG-TV contract (the box says the contract also covers commercials representation). You won't initial both.

If you put your initials in the box, the agent is still bound by the 91-15 provision; if you initial the rider, the $2,000 in 151 days takes precedence. Which you will be asked to sign depends on the agent and how difficult he wants to make it for you to leave.

2 FILMS AND TV

Note: All information in this section is based on the current contract, which expires July 1, 1983.

WARDROBE FITTINGS

1. *Day player, $600 or less:* If you are called in for a fitting on a day other than the day you actually work, you are guaranteed one-hour minimum payment.

If you stay beyond that first hour, you are compensated on a basis of each additional 15-minute period.

If your fitting is on the same day you work, you won't receive any additional compensation, but the hour(s) you spend in a fitting count toward your regular workday.

Be sure the costumer hands you a voucher indicating time in and time out, which you will sign.

2. *Day player, more than $600 per day:* If you're making more than $600 per day, you receive no additional compensation for separate fitting calls.

3. *Three-day contract, television only:* If you're guaranteed three days' work, you must supply the producer with two hours' "free" fitting time on one day. If the fitting takes place on the day you work, it too counts toward your regular workday.

4. *Free-lance weekly:* If you're on a weekly contract, you must supply the producer four hours' "free" fitting time on two days if it's a film and three hours' time on two days if it's a TV show. (Again, if the fitting takes place on a workday, the time spent counts toward your day.)

Your agent gets 10 percent of anything you're paid for wardrobe fittings, provided you're making more than scale.

WARDROBE ALLOWANCE

For supplying your own wardrobe, you're paid a fee of $10 per outfit ($15 for formal wear).

Your agent gets no commission on this.

MEAL PENALTIES

These rules are the same for all actors. If you're working in a studio, you must get your first meal break five-and-a-half hours from the time you were called. If you're on location, it's six hours later. (A second meal break must be given within six hours of the time you returned to work following the first meal break.)

Meal-period violations are payable as follows: $25 for the first half hour; $35 for the second half hour; $50 for each half hour thereafter.

Your agent gets no commission on meal-period violations. Also, you should know that meal periods do not count as time worked. The producer deducts that time, up to one hour.

LOCATION/STUDIO WORK

Before you can compute overtime, you must first know the differences between:

STUDIO WORK

If you're working on the lot, naturally, that's studio work. You get no money for getting yourself there—time spent or mileage used.

NEARBY LOCATION

SAG defines a "nearby location" as "one to which a player is transported from the studio and returned on the same day. . . ."

If you're working on a nearby location, either you'll report to the studio and be transported by car or bus to the location, or if it is within 30 miles of what is called the Hollywood Studio Zone (any place within a 30-mile radius of Beverly and La Cienega boulevards) you may be asked to report directly to it. In that case, you'll be paid 30 cents per mile, based on the mileage from the studio to the nearby location. If you happen to live 30 miles away from the studio and they're shooting next door to you, you still must be paid as though you had first driven to the studio, then to the location.

Any mileage owed you can be paid in cash on the set or be included in your check. Your agent gets no commission on mileage.

Any time spent in traveling to or back from a nearby location, if you do not do the driving, is a part of your day. If the traveling time takes you into overtime, it's paid at time-and-a-half.

OVERNIGHT LOCATION

First, the producer must pay your transportation and your expenses, which we'll talk more about later. Whether you get paid additional money for time spent traveling depends on your contract:

1. *Day player:* You get paid a full day's pay for traveling to the location and a full day's pay for returning.

2. *Three-day contract, $2,100 or less, TV only:* You go on salary the day you leave and remain on salary till the day you return.

3. *Weekly player, $3,500 or less:* Same as 2, above.

4. *Weekly players, over $3,500:* If you can get to the location within 24 hours, you'll go on salary when put "on call," but you can't go on salary any later than 24 hours after reaching the location.

COMPUTING OVERTIME

All overtime is computed from the time you were first called to the time you were excused, excluding meal breaks. Whether or not you're due overtime depends on what kind of contract you are under and, in some cases, whether you're at a studio or on an overnight location. Your agent gets 10 percent of any overtime you earn.

1. *Day player, $900 or less:* Overtime begins at the ninth hour, at time and a half for the ninth and tenth hours. Thereafter, it's double time.
Overtime is paid in hourly units. If you work 15 minutes overtime, you're paid for an entire hour.

2. *Day player, more than $900:* Overtime begins at the ninth hour, as above, but there is no double time. All overtime is paid in hourly units at time-and-a-half, based on $900, regardless of how much more per day your salary might be. (That's $168.75 per hour.)

3. *Three-day player, $2,100 or less:* Overtime starts after the tenth hour at double time, in hourly units. Also, if you work more than 24 hours straight time over the three-day period, you get overtime at time-and-a-half, computed in six-minute units.

4. *Three-day player, more than $2,100:* Overtime starts after ten hours in hourly units at double time based on $2,100 (that's $175 per hour).

5. *Weekly and series players earning $3,500 or less, TV only:*

- *Studio week:* If you're working at the studio or are on a nearby location, you will have a five-day workweek consisting of 44 hours. First, any work that exceeds ten hours on a given day is payable in hourly units at double time. Second, for two days of the week, you may work up to ten hours without any additional compensation. However, you do get overtime if you work more than eight hours on a third, fourth, and/or fifth day. That overtime is paid at time-and-a-half, in half-hour units, for the ninth and tenth hours. Past ten hours is still double time, in hourly units.

- *Overnight location:* If you're on an overnight location, you will have a six-day workweek consisting of 48 hours. (Your daily overtime is the same as for a studio week. The longer location week, however, requires the producer to pay you a bonus four hours' overtime, whether you work those four hours or not. So you have the equivalent of a 44-hour week plus four hours' automatic overtime. And it applies whether you work the full week or only part of it. This is called "location premium.")

6.   *Weekly players, $3,500 or less, movie work:* Work on any day beyond ten hours is paid in hourly units at double time. Work beyond 44 hours in five days is paid in six-minute units at time-and-a-half. If you're on an overnight-location work-week (six days), the producer is required to pay you four hours overtime, whether you work or not.

7.   *Weekly players, more than $3,500, films and TV:* Daily overtime is paid after ten hours, in hourly units, at double time figured on the basis of $3,500 (that's $159.10).

Simply figure out the number of hours you worked overtime, then check the list below.

Note: "Pro-rata"—"daily" or "studio"—simply means what the producer is actually paying you per day if you're on a three-day or weekly contract. By the way, he will use this figure to pay you if you work a day or more beyond what you've actually been contracted for.

*Location Premium** is the four hours he must pay you regardless of whether or not you worked the full week and whether or not you worked overtime. It is arrived at by dividing your weekly salary by 44 hours, them multiplying that figure by four.

Straight time is what you're being paid per hour before you reach overtime.

---

* Determined by whether you were on location on *Saturday* of that week.

DAY PLAYER
OVERTIME BREAKDOWN

Base Salary	Straight Time	Time-and a-Half	Double Time
$298.00*	$ 37.25	$ 55.88	$ 74.50
300.00	37.50	56.25	75.00
325.00	40.63	60.94	81.26
327.80†	40.98	61.47	81.95
350.00	43.75	65.62	87.50
375.00	46.88	70.31	93.76
400.00	50.00	75.00	100.00
425.00	53.13	79.69	106.26
450.00	56.25	84.38	112.50
475.00	59.38	89.06	118.76
500.00	62.50	93.75	125.00
525.00	65.63	98.44	131.26
550.00	68.75	103.13	137.50
575.00	71.88	107.81	143.76
600.00	75.00	112.50	150.00
625.00	78.13	117.19	156.26
675.00	84.38	126.57	168.76
700.00	87.50	131.25	175.00
725.00	90.63	135.94	181.26
750.00	93.75	140.63	187.50
800.00	100.00	150.00	200.00
825.00	103.13	154.59	206.25
850.00	106.25	159.38	212.50
900.00	112.50	168.75	225.00

* Scale
† Scale plus 10 percent (10 percent agent's fee)
Note: Players receiving more than $900 per day are paid at time-and-a-half for all work beyond eight hours.

THREE-DAY TELEVISION

| | | Overtime Rates | | |
Base Salary	Pro-Rata Studio	Straight Time	Time-and a-Half	Double Time
$ 450.00	$150.00	$18.75	$ 28.13	$ 37.50
500.00	166.67	20.83	31.25	41.67
550.00	183.33	22.92	34.38	45.83
600.00	200.00	25.00	37.50	50.00
650.00	216.67	27.08	40.62	54.16
700.00	233.33	29.17	43.75	58.33
750.00	250.00	31.25	46.88	62.50
756.00*	252.00	31.50	47.25	63.00
800.00	266.67	33.33	50.00	66.67
831.60†	277.20	34.65	51.98	69.30
850.00	283.33	35.42	53.13	70.83
890.00‡	296.67	37.08	55.62	74.16
900.00	300.00	37.50	56.25	75.00
950.00	316.67	39.58	59.37	79.16
979.00§	326.33	40.79	61.19	81.58
1,000.00	333.33	41.67	62.51	83.34
1,050.00	350.00	43.75	65.63	87.50
1,100.00	366.67	45.83	68.75	91.66
1,150.00	383.33	47.92	71.88	95.84
1,200.00	400.00	50.00	75.00	100.00
1,250.00	416.67	52.08	78.12	104.16
1,300.00	433.33	54.17	81.26	108.34
1,350.00	450.00	56.25	84.38	112.50
1,400.00	466.67	58.33	87.50	116.66
1,450.00	483.33	60.42	90.63	120.84
1,500.00	500.00	62.50	93.75	125.00
1,550.00	516.67	64.58	96.87	129.16
1,600.00	533.33	66.67	100.00	133.34
1,650.00	550.00	68.75	103.13	137.50
1,700.00	566.67	70.83	106.25	141.66
1,750.00	583.33	72.92	109.38	145.84
1,800.00	600.00	75.00	112.50	150.00
1,850.00	616.67	77.08	115.62	154.16
1,900.00	633.33	79.17	118.76	158.34
1,950.00	650.00	81.25	121.88	162.50
2,000.00	666.67	83.33	125.00	166.66
2,100.00	700.00	87.50	131.25	175.00

* Scale, ½–1 hr. program   ‡ Scale, 1½–2 hrs. program
† Scale plus 10 percent for above   § Scale plus 10 percent
Note: Players receiving more than $2,100 are paid overtime on the base of $2,100.

FREE-LANCE WEEKLY

			Overtime Rates		
Base Salary	Daily Pro-Rata 1/5ths	Location Premium 4/44ths	Straight Time	Time-and a-Half	Double Time
$1,038.00*	$207.60	$ 94.36	$23.59	$ 35.39	$ 47.18
1,050.00	210.00	95.45	23.86	35.79	47.72
1,100.00	220.00	100.00	25.00	37.50	50.00
1,141.80†	228.36	103.80	25.95	38.93	51.90
1,150.00	230.00	104.55	26.14	39.21	52.28
1,200.00	240.00	109.09	27.27	40.91	54.54
1,250.00	250.00	113.64	28.41	42.62	56.82
1,300.00	260.00	118.18	29.55	44.33	59.10
1,350.00	270.00	122.73	30.68	46.02	61.36
1,400.00	280.00	127.27	31.82	47.73	63.64
1,450.00	290.00	131.82	32.95	49.43	65.90
1,500.00	300.00	136.36	34.09	51.14	68.18
1,550.00	310.00	140.91	35.23	52.85	70.46
1,600.00	320.00	145.45	36.36	54.54	72.72
1,650.00	330.00	150.00	37.50	56.25	75.00
1,700.00	340.00	154.55	38.64	57.96	77.28
1,750.00	350.00	159.09	39.77	59.66	79.54
1,800.00	360.00	163.64	40.91	61.37	81.82
1,850.00	370.00	168.18	42.05	63.08	84.10
1,900.00	380.00	172.73	43.18	64.77	86.36
1,950.00	390.00	177.27	44.32	66.48	88.64
2,000.00	400.00	181.82	45.45	68.18	90.90
2,050.00	410.00	186.36	46.59	69.89	93.18
2,100.00	420.00	190.91	47.73	71.60	95.46
2,150.00	430.00	195.45	48.86	73.29	97.72
2,200.00	440.00	200.00	50.00	75.00	100.00
2,250.00	450.00	204.55	51.14	76.71	102.28
2,300.00	460.00	209.09	52.27	78.41	104.54
2,350.00	470.00	213.64	53.41	80.12	106.82
2,400.00	480.00	218.18	54.55	81.83	109.10
2,450.00	490.00	222.73	55.68	83.52	111.36
2,500.00	500.00	227.27	56.82	85.23	113.64
2,750.00	550.00	250.00	62.50	93.75	125.00
3,000.00	600.00	272.73	68.18	102.27	136.36
3,250.00	650.00	295.45	73.86	110.79	147.72
3,500.00	700.00	318.18	79.55	119.33	159.10

* Scale
† Scale plus 10 percent
Note: Players receiving more than $3,500 a week and guaranteed less than $35,000 per picture are paid overtime on the base of $3,500

DROP AND PICK UP (DAY-PLAYER CONTRACT ONLY)

The producer and director of a motion picture are planning the production and notice that they will need you on March 21, but they won't need you again until May 24. In order to avoid keeping you on the payroll all that time for doing nothing, they'll employ "drop and pick up," or what the contract calls "consecutive employment." They'll pay you for the March 21 and "drop" you until May 24. They must give you an exact date on which you'll be picked up; there must be at least 10 days intervening; and they must start paying you again on that date, regardless of whether they use you or not.

They may pick you up on either a daily or a weekly contract. This option may be used only once by the producer. If you are originally placed on a weekly free-lance contract, your employment is continuous from the first day you work through the last day. You cannot be dropped and picked up.

REST PERIODS

- *Daily:* With only one exception, you must be given 12 hours of rest between workdays. The exception: If you're working outdoors ("exterior photography"), your rest period may be reduced to ten hours once every fourth consecutive day. No reduction is allowed on the first day of employment, however.

- *Weekly:* On a five-day week, you must be given one rest period of 58 hours. One exception: shooting at night, primarily exterior, rest period can be reduced to 56 hours as long as your call is not earlier than three P.M. and you're dismissed before midnight Friday.

On a six-day location week, your weekly rest period is 36 hours.

Violation of the daily or weekly rest period is called a "forced call," and the penalty is one day's pay or $950, whichever is less. Your agent gets no commission on rest-period violations.

When you sign out, check the time under "Time Dismissed Studio" against your next call on your call sheet. That will tell you if you're under a "forced call" or not.

TRANSPORTATION EXPENSES

If you're traveling to an overnight location, the producer must provide you with:

- First-class transportation (when you fly, it's first class).

- A private single room.

- A per diem (meal allowances): $8 for breakfast, $12 for lunch, $22 for dinner. Total: $42. If the producer supplies a meal, he may deduct that from your per diem. Also, these are the *least*-amount figures. If you're going to a place that's expensive (Tokyo or London, for example), then the producer must adjust these figures upward. Your agent gets no commission on transportation and expenses.

- $100,000 travel insurance, if you travel by plane.

- $250,000 travel insurance, if you travel by helicopter.

SIGNING OUT

When you're wrapped, the second assistant director will hand you either a time card or a production time report, with times written in under the following headings:

- Date Worked

- First Time Call

- Time Arrived Location

- Lunch

- Dinner

- Time Dismissed Location

- Time Dismissed Studio

Be sure that all times are entered in ink and are correct. If it's a nearby location, be especially watchful that he's given you enough traveling time from location to studio.

GETTING PAID

1. *Day player:* You're supposed to get your check within three days after your last day of work.

2. *All others (weekly players, players under three-day contract, etc.):* You get your check no later than the studio payroll date (usually Thursday) of the week following the week you worked.

If you don't get your money on time, the producer is supposed to pay you $10 a day late-payment damages up to 15 days. Beyond that, SAG will send him a letter. If he fails to respond in five days, damages will continue to accrue at $2.50 per day. Your agent gets no commission on late penalties.

However, be sensible about this. If a producer is one day late, don't run to him screaming, "I want my ten dollars in damages!" He'll have to pay it, but he doesn't have to hire you again. At the same time, don't sit around for days or weeks on end. . . .

GO GET YOUR MONEY . . .

If you discover your check is "light," don't sit around grumbling—go after what's legitimately coming to you. First, call your agent, explain the problem, and have him call the accounting office or producer. Often, it's just an honest mistake on someone's part; only occasionally is there deliberate evasion in paying you your due.

If your agent is reluctant to do this, make the call yourself (and give consideration to changing your agent). If your claim is disputed, don't try to do battle with a producer by yourself—that's what the unions are there for.

One more thing. We've barely scratched the surface of union regulations that can affect you and your pocketbook. We chose the rules you'll most often come up against, but there are a myriad of others. Go to SAG, AFTRA, and Equity and ask them for their digests of rules and regulations. Read them carefully. You and your banker will be glad you did.

. . . BUT USE COMMON SENSE

We can't leave this topic without mentioning that you don't live in a vacuum. Union men may bridle at this, but the simple fact is that there may be times when you'd ultimately do better not to press too hard for what is legitimately coming to you. Sound awful? It is. But consider the following:

An actor we know received his check only to find that it was missing a one-hour fitting fee ($37.50) and a 45-minute meal-period violation ($60). To be certain he was correct, he first called SAG and explained the circumstances. SAG assured him that he was due the money in both cases. Then the actor called his agent and told him to go get his money. When the agent called the actor back, the agent said, "Look, they say the wardrobe fee was an 'oversight,' but they're getting very uptight about the meal penalty. If you want me to, I'll go after the meal penalty, but it just may make the producer angry enough never to hire you again." The actor swallowed hard and said, "Skip it."

Was the actor wrong? A damn fool? The unions would shout, "Yes!" The actor's agent would shout, "No!" We'll say he definitely wasn't a fool. As to whether he was wrong? Well, maybe . . . maybe not.

Yes, go after your due—but use your head.

RESIDUALS

Your initial salary entitles the producer to one run of the show. After that, you're into "subsequent runs" (reruns). That's where residuals come in. What you're paid depends.

TELEVISION PICTURES

These include:

- *Network Prime Time:* Whenever your television picture is rerun on network television between the hours of eight and eleven P.M., you're paid 100 percent of your *actual salary,* subject to the following "ceilings" (the most you can be paid):

Length of Show	Ceiling
½ hour	$1,600
1 hour	2,200
1½ hours	2,400
2 hours	2,600
2 hours +	3,000

- *Network Nonprime Time:* When your television picture is rerun on a network, outside of the times mentioned above, you're paid a percentage of the *union scale* prevailing at the time you first did the work, regardless of what you actually may have been paid. For example, if you worked one week in 1982 and were paid $5,000 per week, you'll get a percentage (see below) of $1,038—*not* the $5,000. ($1,038 was the prevailing union scale for a week's work in 1982.)

- *Syndication:* When your show goes into syndication, it's usually shown on independent stations. You'll also be paid a percentage of the prevailing union scale at the time you worked, but the percentages are slightly smaller (see below).

Run	Network Nonprime Time (Percent of Scale)	Syndication (Percent of Scale)
2	50	40
3	40	30
4–6	25	25
7–10	15	15
11–12	10	10
13th and each succeeding run:	5	5

FEATURE FILMS TO TV, CABLE TV

You want complicated? Boy, do we got complicated! The essential thing to remember is pointed out by Mark Locher, associate editor of SAG's *Screen Actor*

Publications: "A lot of actors believe every time their film is shown on television, they'll get a payment. Not necessarily."

In other words, in this case, residuals are *not* paid on a per-play basis. According to an extremely complicated formula, you're paid a percentage of your salary when the producer's gross hits certain plateaus. It's extremely difficult for you to keep track of what and/or when you're supposed to get a payment. You could call SAG and get their latest figures on the producer's worldwide grosses, but then you'd have to know and understand the formula for figuring out how much of the 3.6 percent allotted to the entire cast is to be allotted to you. It's just best to rely on SAG to get you your money.

FOREIGN TELECASTS

Every once in a while, you'll get relatively small residual checks from that episode of "Baretta" you did nine years ago that's now running in South Zanzibar. The method of computing what you should get is the same for *Feature Films to TV, Cable TV* (see page 258). Again, it's far too complicated to go into here. Suffice it to say, you won't get rich.

AGENTS' COMMISSIONS AND RESIDUALS

Your theatrical agent gets a commission only on *prime-time network residuals of television shows.* He gets no commission on feature films, nonprime-time TV, syndication residuals, etc.

WHEN YOU'LL GET THEM/HOW THEY'RE PAID

Residuals are first sent to the unions. They record them and, later, send them to you. If the show was on a network, the producer's got thirty days from the day of airing to get the check to the unions. If the show is in syndication, the producer has up to four months. If it is a foreign telecast, he's got up to six months. Add at least a two-week delay for the unions to handle them, and you can see that you'll have to hold off on that party you were planning.

We've only skimmed the surface on all of these areas. It wouldn't hurt to get the digests of agreements from your unions and read them. Also, the unions occasionally hold special seminars on these agreements, which can be a great help, as can the general membership meetings. In the latter case, you're notified by mail; in the former, see your newsletters.

A NOTE ABOUT AFTRA SHOWS

If the program is run on network prime time ("All in the Family," "Three's Company," etc.), the pay rates are exactly the same ($298/day, $1,038/week minimums, etc.), and the work rules are almost exactly the same.

However, daytime soap operas, variety shows, game shows—anything not shown on network prime time—have different rules and pay scales for each type of show. Call AFTRA for further information.

Finally, as we've mentioned, there is a strong movement toward merger with SAG, which would make things even more uniform. Already, AFTRA and SAG jointly negotiated the commercials agreement, and the rules we'll discuss in the next section hold true for both unions.

3 COMMERCIALS

(All the material below is based on the current contract, which expires February 6, 1985.)

WORKDAY AND OTHER RULES

The rules governing your workday in commercials are almost exactly the same as those governing a day player earning $900 or less (see "Films and TV" in Appendix A). There's one major difference, however: Should the advertiser shoot more than one commercial on your workday, you must be paid an additional "session fee" for each additional commercial shot.

Some of the minor differences:

- *Wardrobe allowance:* Nonformal wear (per outfit): $10
  Formal wear (per outfit): $20

- *Meal-period violations:* First and second half hours: $25
  Third and each additional
  half hour: $50

EXCLUSIVITY

You're held exclusive to the advertiser for a period of twenty-one months (called the "maximum use period"). This starts as of the date of the shooting of the commercial. You may not do a commercial for a competing product as long as you are held exclusive.

The twenty-one-month period is divided up into seven thirteen-week periods. Each thirteen-week period is called a "fixed cycle." Your session date is the start of the *first* fixed cycle; the thirteen-week anniversary of that date starts your *second* fixed cycle; thirteen weeks later starts the third, and so on.

If the advertiser sends you (or your agent) a "holding fee" at the beginning of each fixed cycle, he holds you exclusive to him, provided he sends that fee within twelve working days.

If he fails to do this, you're automatically released; his right of exclusivity is canceled. (If you've heard you have to have a release letter from the advertiser, that's not true. However, it's still best to have your agent call the advertiser for you, just to be sure there haven't been any foul-ups.)

Should the advertiser want to reinstate the commercial, that's up to you, provided, of course, that in the meantime you haven't done a commercial for a competing company. In that case, you, of course, are then exclusive to *them.*

If you allow the advertiser to reinstate, he'll have to pay you a one-time double holding fee for the privilege.

261

In any case, as each thirteen-week cycle goes by, you'll get closer to that twenty-one-month maximum. Sometime between one hundred twenty and sixty days before the end of those twenty-one months, you or your agent must inform the advertiser that your commercial is coming up for renegotiation. If you or your agent fail to do this at the end of the first twenty-one-month period, a brand-new twenty-one-month period will start up *automatically*. Once again, you'll be exclusive to the advertisers, and there will be only a 10 percent increase in what you're paid, which for the second twenty-one-month period will serve as your agent's commission.

- *Use cycle:* A "use cycle" begins when the commercial is actually aired. Each use cycle also lasts for thirteen weeks and is the determining factor on when you're paid your "use fees" (commonly called "residuals"). Use cycles run within "fixed cycles." The former pays you for use; the latter keeps you exclusive.

- *Holding fees/use fees:* The advertiser will credit any holding fees he pays you against any use fees he may owe. However, he may credit only one holding fee against any use fees in any fixed cycle.

USE FEES/("RESIDUALS")

What you're paid for the use of a commercial depends on the type of commercial. . . .

PROGRAM-USAGE COMMERCIALS

These are usually network commercials, the official ruling being that the commercial is shown on "interconnecting stations." You're paid each time the commercial airs. The payments must be sent to you or your agent within 15 working days of the end of each week the commercial runs. What you're paid depends on whether the commercial is a Class A, B, or C commercial.

Class A: If the commercial airs in more than twenty cities.
Class B: If the commercial airs in six to twenty cities.
Class C: If the commercial airs in one to five cities.

Since Class B and C commercials are fairly rare, we include here only what you'll be paid for a Class A commercial. (These rates are for *on*-camera performers. Off-camera, Class B and C rates, etc., can be obtained from SAG.)

CLASS A COMMERCIAL
(Uses in a 13-week period)

Use #	Principals	For a Group of 3–5*	6–8*	9 Plus*
1	$ 300.00	$ 219.60	$194.40	$160.80
2	115.95	107.45	92.00	75.30
3	92.00	84.10	76.25	62.35
4–13 each use	92.00	79.40	71.50	58.60
14+	44.10	27.40	23.30	18.90

Should the advertiser wish to guarantee he'll run the commercial 13 times or more during 13 weeks, you'll be paid:

13 guaranteed	1,213.75	1,024.75	916.00	751.80

Then you'll be paid:

14–18, each use	86.94	63.56	55.63	45.43

* Note: Don't confuse being in a group with being an extra. Extras are paid $195.14 for the day's work, with no use-payment fees.

WILD SPOTS

While these commercials may be broadcast on different local stations all over the country (say, Atlanta at 4:30 P.M., Phoenix at 10:00 P.M., etc.), they cannot be broadcast on interconnecting stations (a network). You're paid a flat fee every thirteen weeks. The advertiser has unlimited use of the commercial; he may show it as many times as he likes in those cities he has paid for during those thirteen weeks with no additional payments to you.

The fee is based on the number of cities (and their respective populations) in which the commercial is or will be aired. It must be paid within fifteen working days of each thirteen-week use-cycle date.

Each city across the country is assigned a certain number of "units," based upon its population. The larger the city, the more units it is assigned. (Boston is five units; Cleveland is three units, and so forth.)

The advertiser chooses the cities in which he wants to air his commercial; the units assigned to those cities are added up, and that determines your fee based on the following scale:

Number of Units	What You're Paid Every 13 Weeks
1	$300.00
2–25	12.00 per unit
26–126+	4.45 per unit

As an example, let's say your wild spot airs only in Boston and Cleveland. As mentioned above, Boston equals five units; Cleveland equals three units. Total:

eight units. You're paid $300 for the first unit, leaving seven units at $12 per unit ($84). Total fee every thirteen weeks: $384.

Obviously, since we don't know the cities in which your wild spot will be aired, we can't give you a specific figure as to what you'll be paid. If you can, find out what cities your commercial is running in and call SAG. They'll tell you the number of units assigned to each city. Add those units together, then refer to the scale above. Of course, it is possible for an advertiser to add more markets as the commercial is being run. You'll be compensated accordingly. Below, the rates for three key markets:

New York: $689.45 by itself; add $4.45 per unit for all additional cities.
Los Angeles or Chicago: $600.90 by itself; add $4.45 per unit for all additional
cities.

(Once again, note that these figures are based on the current contract, which expires February 6, 1985. Bear in mind that not only will the dollar amounts change, but due to changing populations, the units assigned to any given city are also subject to change.)

DEALER COMMERCIALS

If a local dealer buys time on the air to show a commercial, that's a dealer commercial. (Often, a local dealer of, say, Honda automobiles, will like that national Honda commercial so much that he'll run it as a promotion not only for the car but for his dealership too. In this case, it's additional revenue for you—you're paid whatever you're supposed to get for the program-usage [national] run of the commercial as well as the fee for the dealer commercial.)

Since dealers don't have the kind of money it takes to be constantly buying air time, and since SAG has no way to check up on them anyway (there's no advertising agency to file a report), you'll be paid a flat fee for the use of the commercial. This fee entitles the dealer to unlimited use of that commercial for *six months.* What that fee will be depends on two things: whether the commercial is a "Type A" or "Type B" and where the commercial is shown.

Type A: If the dealership is *not* owned by the manufacturer of the product.

Type B: If the dealership *is* owned by the manufacturer of the product.

Type A: If the commercial is shown in any or all cities including New York, your fee will be $1,408.70 every six months. If it's shown in any or all cities *not* including New York, your fee will be $1,245.85 every six months.

Note: Your contract must stipulate that the commercial is to be used as a "dealer commercial" (as well as if it's to be used as a "test commercial" or a "seasonal commercial"—see below). When you get your contract, look in the upper-right-hand corner. There you'll see various boxes to be checked off telling you if that's the case. Farther down, there's another box to check if you don't consent.

Type B: Including New York, $2,166.00 every six months; *not* including New York, $1,868.80 every six months.

TEST COMMERCIALS

When an advertiser wishes to see if a given commercial will work, he'll test it in a limited market. Since, by definition, the number of cities in which the commercial will air are limited, the amount of use fees you'll be paid are relatively small. In actual fact, when you do a "test," you're speculating. You're hoping the advertiser will get great reaction to the commercial and go national with it. After all, you'll still be held exclusive to that advertiser for at least 13 weeks and, possibly, for the entire maximum-use period of 21 months.

Since use fees will be small, your agent probably will negotiate an "overscale" session fee. Instead of the usual $300 payment, he'll try to get you more—say, $500—and will also try to negotiate the payment of that $500 every 13 weeks as your "holding fee." In any case, with a test commercial, one of three things will happen:

1. The advertiser tests the commercial during the first thirteen to twenty-six weeks, decides he hates it and drops it. You're released.
2. The advertiser decides he loves the commercial and goes national with it (called a "rollout"). It might then even go to program usage and wild spot.
3. Along with any use fees for running the commercial, the advertiser continues to pay you your holding fee (minimum $300, maximum whatever your agent can get him to agree to) every 13 weeks and keeps you exclusive to him for the maximum-use period of 21 months (during which time he may or may not decide to go national with it). Sometimes, however, your agent will negotiate a deal with the advertiser that gives you a guaranteed cutoff date—a date prior to the end of the 21-month period when you're released by the advertiser.

Usually, however, either the commercial works or it doesn't. Either you're released in the first thirteen to twenty-six weeks or the commercial goes national. In this case, not only must your contract stipulate that you're doing a "test commercial," but you must be told that it is a test *at your audition.*

SEASONAL COMMERCIALS

This kind of commercial can be anything from a national to a local. If, say, you're dressed up as Santa Claus, pitching Christmas trees, that's a "seasonal." This kind of commercial may be used only for a period of thirteen weeks (the advertiser has an option to extend that period for two additional weeks). At the end of that period, the advertiser may opt to pay you an additional holding fee and, the following year, reuse the commercial for one more cycle of thirteen weeks. However, that holding fee may not be applied against use. After that second season, the advertiser may not use the commercial again without your permission.

In any case, with this particular kind of commercial, no matter whether it's used in one season or two, you're *not* held exclusive to the advertiser. You may do a commercial for a competing product provided you inform the second advertiser that you've got a seasonal either running or on hold. If you don't, you could be subject to lawsuit for the second advertiser, as you'll be signing a contract holding you exclusive to *him*.

Once again, your contract must state that the commercial is a "seasonal."

AGENT'S COMMISSION

Your commercial agent gets a 10-percent commission on all session, holding, and use fees for the maximum-use period of twenty-one months. However, as mentioned above, he must notify the advertiser sometime between 120 to 60 days before the end of the maximum period of use that the commercial is coming up for renegotiation. If he fails to do this, the commercial will automatically go into a second twenty-one-month period of maximum use with no change in terms. Should that occur, your agent will no longer have a right to his 10-percent commission.

If he wishes to continue to get his 10 percent, the agent must negotiate the terms of that commercial to above scale—at least "scale plus ten" (percent).

You, of course, have the right to accept or reject any terms he negotiates, or simply to say no to any deal, in which case you'll be released at the end of the twenty-one-month period.

4 "TYPICAL" TAX DEDUCTIONS OF
THE PROFESSIONAL ACTOR

We're not accountants or attorneys, and we don't expect you to use this material in place of a good CPA. Nor do we claim that these deductions are written in concrete. All deductions—in fact, your entire tax return—depend on your circumstances.

Further, while some of these items are totally deductible (your union dues and initiation, for example), others (such as your phone bill) are partially deductible depending on how much of the expense/use is business-related. Once again, what those portions may be depend on your facts and circumstances.

Also, certain items, such as television sets, typewriters, etc., may be wholly deductible in one year, or they may have to be "capitalized" over a period of years—that is, a portion of the expense will be deductible each year, say, for five years. ("Capitalizing" may ultimately prove more beneficial to you anyway.)

Finally, all deductions are applicable only to the extent that the cost *exceeds* any reimbursements you may get.

• *Admissions to plays and movies* (save your ticket stubs).

• *Attorneys/legal fees:* Only if the work pertains to your acting career.

• *Auto expenses:* First, you'll need to estimate how much you use your car for business purposes. An example: Let's say you're going out to make the rounds of the various studios. You'll have many stops along your route. The drive to the first stop is *not* tax-deductible—that's part of your "normal commute." However, each stop after that is business use and therefore deductible, until the last stop. From the last stop to home is *not* deductible—because, again, it's part of your commute.

Here, too, that daily diary we've mentioned throughout the book can come in mighty handy. At the end of the year, look through it and figure out your deduction, based on one of the following two methods:

1. *The mileage method:* If you've got an older car, this is generally the best "tax break" way. Simply estimate the number of business miles you put on the car and multiply that figure times whatever the IRS is allowing for business miles that year. That's your deduction. (The IRS will not ask for receipts.)

2. *The usage method:* Along with your daily diary, you'll need to keep receipts for everything—gas receipts, repair bills, insurance payments, etc. Add all those receipts together, and using your daily diary, estimate the percentage of business use you put on the car. Take that percentage of your bills—that's your deduction. If you have a newer car, this may be more beneficial than using the mileage method.

- *Books:* As long as they pertain to the industry. *War and Peace,* no; *Your Film Acting Career,* yes.

- *Business gifts:* All gifts to agents, personal managers, etc., up to $25 per person per year.

- *Business meals:* This can be a picky area with the IRS. You'll need the receipt for the meal, a record of who was there, how that person or persons relate to your position in the industry, and, basically, what you talked about. Your daily diary can be worth its weight in gold here. If the meal was under $25, you don't have to have a receipt, but the IRS still will want to know why you deducted it. Be sure you can explain *each* and *every* deduction.

- *Classes:* Once you've established yourself as an actor, classes that maintain or improve your skills as a professional actor are generally deductible.

- *Commissions* paid to agents, personal managers, etc.

- *Hairstyling/haircuts:* As long as it's directly related to a role.

- *Industry parties:* This is probably the most difficult area to get the IRS to approve as a deduction. Not only do you need to be able to prove that the party had a direct bearing on your position in the industry, but you will have to keep a guest list and be able to explain how those guests have a direct bearing on your career. A *very* touchy area.

- *Magazine and trade publications: Daily Variety, Hollywood Reporter, Drama-Logue,* etc., and any others as long as at least a portion of the publication pertains to the industry. If you buy these on the newsstands, try to get receipts and attach them to your daily diary. An auditor could disallow these deductions if you don't.

- *Mailing expenses:* Stamps, envelopes, labels, etc.

- *Makeup.*

- *Office supplies:* Typewriter, staples, writing paper, etc.

- *Phonograph records.*

- *Plays.*

- *Publicity materials:* Anything that publicizes you as an actor. Presentation tapes, *Academy Players Directory* listing, postcards, ads in the trades, etc.

- *Résumés:* Typing, printing, and/or photocopying.

- *Résumé shots:* Session and printing costs.

- *Tapes.*

- *Telephone and related:* Your telephone bill, depending on how much you use it for business. Also answering devices and answering services.

- *Television and related:* The cost of the set itself, repairs, cable or pay TV, videotaping machines, *TV Guide,* or other television magazines.

- *Union dues/initiations.*

- *Wardrobe:* See hairstyling.

- *Wardrobe maintenance:* See hairstyling.

. . . And anything else that is directly related to or associated with your profession. You'll need: receipts, a daily diary, and a good CPA (also see "General Financial," Chapter 30).

5 PENSION AND WELFARE

These are certainly among the most important benefits of union membership.

SAG

HEALTH BENEFITS

You, your wife, and your dependent children under the age of nineteen will be covered, provided you meet the eligibility requirement listed below.

It's basically your standard Blue Cross plan. Hospitalization is paid at 100 percent (semiprivate room; phones and TV are not included). Doctor and medicine bills are paid at 80 percent, with a $100 deductible per family member, up to a maximum deductible of $200 ("deductible" simply means you pay the first $100 or $200 yourself).

In order to become eligible the first time, you must earn $1,800 (salaries and/or residuals) cumulatively over a period of four consecutive quarters of three months each. (Obviously, if you earn that $1,800 in one job, it counts.) Once you do earn it, you have a "waiting period" of one additional quarter, then you'll be covered. SAG will mail you notification that your coverage has begun, along with your Blue Cross card.

After the first time you qualify, you'll need to earn slightly less to retain your eligibility: $1,350, under the same rules as above. Should you have a bad year and not make that minimum figure, you may buy your coverage from SAG at reduced rates for one year. After that, you may still buy the coverage, but you'll have to pay the full amount.

SAG DENTAL

The same rules for eligibility apply, but you'll have to earn $2,500. Deductible is $50 for major work; $25 for cleaning, etc. After that, they pay 80 percent; you pay 20 percent.

SAG PENSION

If you earn $2,000 or more in each of a cumulative number of ten years, you're eligible for retirement benefits at age sixty-five. These range (currently) from $150 to $2,000 per month, depending on what you've earned and the number of "years of service" you've put in. (There also are early-retirement benefits available at age fifty-five.)

270

SAG DEATH BENEFITS

If you die (not on the job) while you are insured, your beneficiary will get $10,000. "On the job" has other benefits, too complicated to go into here. For a booklet describing the pension and welfare benefits in detail, call SAG Pension and Welfare offices at 987-9790.

AFTRA

The rules and benefits are fairly close to those of SAG, as follows:

HEALTH BENEFITS

Eligibility: $1,000 in earnings during any one of four 12-month earning periods. The benefits cover you, your spouse, and unmarried children up to age twenty-one (twenty-three, if full-time students). Medical benefits include a $100 deductible for you, $100 deductible for your dependents, after which the policy pays 80 percent and you pay 20 percent. Benefits also include 120 days hospitalization.

AFTRA PENSION

To be eligible, you must earn $2,000 a year or more in each of ten years. If you retire at age sixty-five, you will get $125 a month or more, depending on your length of service and income. Early retirement benefits at age fifty-five are also available.

LIFE INSURANCE

$20,000.

AFTRA also has booklets on all of this. For these, or for answers to any questions you may have, call 462-3244.

APPENDIX B
Lists

LIST ORDER

1. Acting Classes: Colleges/Conservatories
                               Coaches/Workshops
2. Agents
3. Answering Services
4. Bargains: Books on Bargains
                Clothing
                General Merchandise
5. Bookstores/Newsstands
6. Equity Theatres: Equity Dinner Theatres
                        LORT Theatres
7. Extras Casting Offices (Union Only)
8. Industrial Film Houses
9. Photographers
10. Photographic Print Shops
11. Print Shops (Résumés, Etc.)
12. Recommended Reading
13. Résumé Composition & Typing
14. Trade Publications
15. Union Branch Offices: AEA (Equity)
                              AFTRA
                              AGMA
                              AGVA
                              SAG
                              SEG
16. Videotaping Services ("Air Checks," Tape)
17. Miscellaneous: *Academy Players Directory*
                      American Film Institute
                      Breakdown Service
                      Hollywood YMCA
                      Los Angeles Theatre Alliance
                      Performers' Audition Showcase
                      "The Voicecaster" (Bob Lloyd)

ACTING CLASSES

There are scores more good ones than we have room to list.

COLLEGES/CONSERVATORIES

American Conservatory Theatre (ACT)
450 Geary St.
San Francisco 94102
Degrees: MFA, Certificates

American Theatre Arts
6240 Hollywood Blvd.
Hollywood 90028
Certificates

California Institute of the Arts
24700 McBean Pkwy.
Valencia 91355
BFA, MFA, Certificates

Los Angeles City College
855 N. Vermont Ave.
Los Angeles 90029
AA, Certificates

Los Angeles Civic Light Opera
Musical Theatre Workshop
135 N. Grand Ave.
Los Angeles 90012

Loyola Marymount
Loyola Blvd., at W. 80th
Los Angeles 90045
BA (MA in film only)

Pacific Conservatory for the Performing
Arts/Solvang
P.O. Box 1700
Santa Maria 93456
Certificates

South Coast Repertory Theatre
P.O. Box 2197
Costa Mesa 92626
Summer Program

University of California, Los Angeles
(UCLA)
308 Westwood Blvd.
Los Angeles 90024
BA, MA, MFA, Ph.D.

University of Southern California (USC)
University Park
Los Angeles 90007
BA, MA, MFA, Ph.D.

COACHES/WORKSHOPS

A number of coaches and workshops have classes in more categories than are listed here. (The area code for all phone numbers listed below is 213.)

- *Cold readings*

  Charles Conrad
  846-9010

  M. K. Lewis
  826-8118

  Michael Shurtleff
  462-6565

- *Commercials*
  (Casting Director / Coaches Only)

  Pamela Campus
  464-3310

  Dorothy Kelly
  658-6786

  Beverly Long & Assocs.
  652-4144

  Sheila Manning (Children Only)
  852-1046

  Tepper-Gallegos
  469-3577

- *Dance*

  Dupree Dance Academy
  655-0336

  Studio for the Performing Arts
  275-4683

- *Dialects*

  Robert Easton
  463-4811

  George Gilbert
  463-3586

  David Alan Stern (Ph.D.)
  467-7301

- *Film Technique*

  Jackie Benton
  392-4229 / 466-2466

  M. K. Lewis
  826-8118

  Tepper-Gallegos
  469-3577

- *General Acting*

  Jeff Corey
  456-3319

  David LeGrant
  506-0717

  M. K. Lewis
  826-8118

  Lawrence Parke
  466-4297

  Tracy Roberts
  271-2730

  Staircase Studio
  931-4662

  Lurene Tuttle
  464-0101

- *Improvisation*

  The Groundlings
  934-4747

  Rex Knowles / Sherry Landrum
  767-7595

  The L.A. Connection
  467-5399

- *Savvy / Seminars*
  Actor's Symposium
  Presented by the Beverly Hills Bar Ass
  (Annual event—watch the papers)

  Wayne Dvorak (business of the busine
  876-2428

  M. K. Lewis (business of the business)
  826-8118

  Sherwood Oaks College (various)
  462-0669

- *Vocal*

Mark Bucci
763-1593

Dorothy Fries
763-4216

Carlos Noble
828-0077

- *Voice-overs*

Louise Chamis
985-0130

Sandra Gale
273-4025

The Sound Studio
660-5449

Marice Tobias
939-8679

B. J. Ward
653-8322

David Sebastian Williams
(SEB-Net Recording)
469-2953

OTHER ACTING WORKSHOPS

There are many other well known acting coaches and workshops in L.A., including Stella Adler (summertime only—watch the trades), the American Academy of Dramatic Arts, the Film Actors Workshop, the Film Industry Workshop, Estelle Harman Actors Workshop, Lee Strasberg Theatre Institute, Los Angeles Cultural Center, Weist-Barron-Hill, and workshops attached to Equity Waiver theatres, some included in theatre membership, some open to nonmembers.

2. AGENTS

Below is a list of SAG-franchised actors' agents in the Los Angeles metropolitan area. We make no recommendations. Don't assume an agency not listed below is unfranchised until you've checked with SAG, as revisions are frequent. Telephone area code is 213.

Code Key: Theatrical (Film/TV) = T   Young People = Y   Voice-Overs = V
Commercials = C   Modeling = M   Equity-franchised = E

Abrams-Rubaloff & Assoc. Inc., 2106 Live Oak Dr. East, Los Angeles 90068, 469-2299 (CV)

Adams, Bret, 8282 Sunset Blvd. #F, Los Angeles 90046, 656-6420 (TE)

Agency for Performing Arts, 9000 Sunset Blvd. #315, Los Angeles 90069, 273-0744 (TE)

Aimee Entertainment, 13743 Victory Blvd., Van Nuys 91401, 994-9354 (TC)

All Talent Agency, 2437 E. Washington Blvd., Pasadena 91104, 797-2422 (TCYV)

Alvarado, Carlos, 8220 Sunset Blvd., Los Angeles 90069, 652-0272 (TC)

Amaral Agency, 10000 Riverside #11, Toluca Lake 91602, 980-1013 (T)

Amsel & Assoc. Inc., Fred, 291 S. La Cienega Blvd. #307, Beverly Hills 90211, 855-1200 (TCVE)

Arcara, Bauman & Hiller, 9220 Sunset Blvd. #202, Los Angeles 90069, 271-5601 (TE)

Arnold Agency, Maxine, 8350 Santa Monica Blvd. #103, Los Angeles 90069, 650-4999 (T)

Arthur Assoc. Ltd., Irvin, 9200 Sunset Blvd. #621, Los Angeles 90069, 278-5934 (T)

Artists Agency, The, 10000 Santa Monica Blvd. #305, Los Angeles 90067, 277-7779 (TE)

Artists & Junior Artists Unlimited, Talent Agency, 4914 Lankershim Blvd., N. Hollywood 91601, 763-9000 (TCY)

Artists Career Mgmt, 9157 Sunset Blvd., Los Angeles 90069, 278-9157 (T)

Artists First Inc., 8230 Beverly Blvd., Los Angeles 90048, 653-5640 (TE)

Artists Group, The, 10100 Santa Monica Blvd. #310, Los Angeles 90067, 552-1100 (TE)

A Special Talent Agency, 6253 Hollywood Blvd., Los Angeles 90028, 467-7068 (TCYM)

Associated Booking Corp, 292 S. La Cienega Blvd. #136, Beverly Hills 90211, 855-8051 (TE)

Associated Talent International, 8816 Burton Way, Beverly Hills 90211, 271-4662 (TCYMV)

Auer, Miles Bohm, 8344 Melrose Ave. #29, Los Angeles 90069, 462-6416 (TC)

Barr, Rickey Agency, 8833 Sunset Blvd. #308, Los Angeles 90069, 652-7994 (T)

Barskin Agency, 11240 Magnolia Blvd, #202, N. Hollywood 91601, 985-2992 (T)

Beakel & Jennings, 427 N. Canon Dr. #205, Beverly Hills 90210, 274-5418 (T)

Belson & Klass, 211 S. Beverly Dr., Beverly Hills 90212, 274-9169 (TE)

Benson, Lois J., 2221 W. Olive, Burbank 91502, 849-5647 (TY)

Blake Agency Ltd., Merritt, The, 409 N. Camden Dr., Beverly Hills 90210, 278-6885 (TE)

Blanchard, Nina, 1717 N. Highland #901, Los Angeles 90028, 462-7341 (TCM)

Blazing Star Talent Agency, 1489 E. Colorado Blvd. #204, Pasadena 91106, 681-6743 (TCY)

Bloom, J. Michael, 9200 Sunset Blvd. #1210, Los Angeles 90069, 275-6800 (TCE)

Borgnine Agency, Nancee, The, 9100 Sunset Blvd. #210, Los Angeles 90069, 859-0429 (TYM)

Boyd Talent Agency, 4605 Lakershim Blvd. #305, N. Hollywood 91602, 506-7835 (TME)

Brandon & Assoc., Paul, 9046 Sunset Blvd. #201, Los Angeles 90069, 273-6173 (T)

Brandt & Assoc., Werner, 9034 Sunset Blvd. #107, Los Angeles 90069, 273-8554 (T)

Brewis Agency, Alex, 8721 Sunset Blvd. #104, Los Angeles 90069, 274-9874 (TE)

Bridges Talent Agency, Jim, 933 N. La Brea Ave., Los Angeles 90038, 874-3274 (TCY)

Brooke Assoc., James, 9165 Sunset Blvd. #202, Los Angeles 90069, 859-1405 (TC)

Burton, Iris, 2450 Belfast Dr., Los Angeles 90069, 652-0954 (TCYM)

Calder Agency, 4116 Riverside Dr., Burbank 91505, 845-7434 (TV)
Career Artists International, 11030 Ventura Blvd. #3, Studio City 91604, 980-1315
or 980-1316 (TYV)
Career Mgmt., 8833 Sunset Blvd. #307, Los Angeles 90069, 657-1020 (T)
Carey-Phelps-Colvin, 1407 N. La Brea Ave., Los Angeles 90028, 874-7780 (CV)
Carroll Agency, William 448 N. Golden Mall, Burbank 91502, 848-9948 (TC)
Cassell & Levy, Inc., 843 N. Sycamore Ave., Los Angeles 90038, 461-3971 (CV)
Cavaleri & Assoc., 6605 Hollywood Blvd. #220, Los Angeles 90028, 461-2940
(TCYMV)
Cedar Agency, Paula, 9090 Burton Way, Beverly Hills 90211, 273-7700 (T)
Century Artists Ltd., 9744 Wilshire Blvd. #206, Beverly Hills 90212, 273-4366 (TE)
Chandler, Inc., 8833 Sunset Blvd. #311, Los Angeles 90069, 659-2600 (T)
Charter Mgmt., 9000 Sunset Blvd. #1112, Los Angeles 90069, 278-1690 (TE)
Chasin-Park-Citron, 9255 Sunset Blvd. #910, Los Angeles 90069, 273-7190
(TCVE)
Chutuk & Assoc., Jack, 9908 Santa Monica Blvd., Beverly Hills, 90212, 552-1773
(C)
C.L.O.U.T. Talent Agency, 2029 Century Park East #2760, Los Angeles 90067,
463-8191 (T)
Colton & Assoc., Kingsley, 321 S. Beverly Dr., Beverly Hills 90212, 277-5491 (TV)
Commercials Unlimited Inc., Sonjia W. Brandon's, 7461 Beverly Blvd. #400, Los
Angeles 90036, 937-2220 (CYV)
Compass Mgmt. Inc. 211 S. Beverly Dr., Beverly Hills 90212, 271-5122 (T)
Contemporary-Korman, 132 Lasky Dr., Beverly Hills 90212, 278-8250 (TCE)
Coralie, Jr., 4789 Vineland Ave. #100, N. Hollywood 91602, 766-9501 (TCYME)
Cosden, Robert, 15233 Ventura, Sherman Oaks 91403, 788-1881 (TE)
Cosmopolitan Talent & Model Agency, 8142 W. 3rd St., Los Angeles 90048, 655-
9952 (TCM)
Coughlin Agency, Kerwin, 10850 Riverside Dr., N. Hollywood 91602, 980-7200 (T)
Creative Artists Agency, 1888 Century Park East #1400, Los Angeles 90067, 277-
4545 (TCE)
Crickett Company, The, 13455 Ventura Blvd. #215, Sherman Oaks 91423, 501-
5586 (T)
Cronin Agency, Bernyce, 439 S. La Cienega Blvd., Los Angeles 90048, 273-8144
(TCY)
Cumber, Lil, 6515 Sunset Blvd. #300A, Los Angeles 90028, 469-1919 (TCYMVE)
Cunningham & Assoc., William, 261 S. Robertson Blvd., Beverly Hills 90211, 855-
1700 (CV)

Dade/Rosen Assoc., 9172 Sunset Blvd. #2, Los Angeles 90069, 278-7077 (TE)
David, Hunter, Kimbale, Parseghian & Rifkin, 7319 Beverly Blvd., Los Angeles
90036, 857-1234 (TVE)

Davies Agency, Dona Lee, 3518 Cahuenga Blvd. West #318, Los Angeles 90068, 850-0143 (TCYV)

DeMille, Diana Talent Agency, 12457 Ventura Blvd. #104, Studio City 91604, 761-7171 (TC)

Deuser Agency, Lew, 449 S. Beverly Dr., Beverly Hills 90212, 553-8611 (TE)

Devroe Agency, 3365 Cahuenga Blvd. West, Los Angeles 90068, 666-2666, résumés to Box 8370, Universal City 91608 (TC)

Diamond Artists, Ltd., 9200 Sunset Blvd. #909, Los Angeles, 90069, 278-8146 (TCYMVE)

Dickens & Co., Richard, 5550 Wilshire Blvd. #306, Los Angeles 90036, 937-3080 (TE)

Dietrich Agency, 10850 Riverside Dr. #501, N. Hollywood 91602, 985-4824 (T)

Elias & Assoc., Thomas C., 1801 Ave. of the Stars #535, Los Angeles 90067, 557-1220 (TCM)

Elite Model Mgmt./John Casablancas, Inc., 9255 Sunset Blvd. #1125, Los Angeles 90069, 274-9395 (TCM)

Entertainment Ent., 1680 Vine St., Los Angeles 90028, 462-6001 (T)

Exclusive Artists Agency, 4040 Vineland Ave., Studio City 91604, 761-1154 (TCVE)

Faber, Sharron, 6331 Hollywood Blvd. #401, Los Angeles 90028, 462-3299 (TC)

Felber, Wm., 2126 Cahuenga Blvd., Los Angeles 90068, 466-7629 (TCE)

Ferrell, Carol, 9034 Sunset Blvd. #214, Los Angeles 90069, 273-7511 (TCY)

Fields, Assoc., Jack, 9255 Sunset Blvd., Los Angeles 90069, 278-1333 (TVE)

Film Artists Assoc., 9200 Sunset Blvd. #431, Los Angeles 90069, 275-6193 (T)

Film Artists Mgmt. Enterprises, 8278 Sunset Blvd., Los Angeles 90046, 656-7590 (T)

Flaire Agency, 8693 Wilshire Blvd. #204, Beverly Hills 90211, 659-6721 (CM)

Fontaine Agency, Judith, 6525 Sunset Blvd. #406, Los Angeles 90028, 467-6288 (CYM)

Freeman Agency, Mark, 6331 Hollywood Blvd. #1122, Los Angeles 90028, 464-4866 (TC)

Frings Agency, Kurt, 9440 Santa Monica Blvd. #400, Beverly Hills 90210, 274-8881 (TE)

Gage Group, The, 8732 Sunset Blvd. #750, Los Angeles 90069, 652-8833 (TE)

Garrick, Dale, 8831 Sunset Blvd. #402, Los Angeles 90069, 657-2661 (TCY)

Gerritsen International, 8721 Sunset Blvd. #203, Los Angeles 90069, 659-8414 (TCY)

Gersh Agency, Phil, 222 N. Canon Dr., Beverly Hills 90210, 274-6611 (TCVE)

Gibson, J. Carter, 9000 Sunset Blvd., Los Angeles 90069, 274-8813 (TV)

Gilly/Levee, 8721 Sunset Blvd. #103, Los Angeles 90069, 657-5660 (TE)

G.M.A., 1741 N. Ivar #119, Los Angeles 90028, 466-7161 (TCYM)

Goldin-Dennis-Karg & Assoc., 470 San Vicente Blvd., Los Angeles 90048, 651-1700 (TCYE)

Goldman & Novell Agency, 6363 Wilshire Blvd. #114, Los Angeles 90048, 651-4578 (T)

Goldstein & Assoc., Allen, 9000 Sunset Blvd. #910, Los Angeles 90069, 278-5005 (T)

Gordean Agency, Inc., Jack, 9570 Wilshire Blvd. #400, Beverly Hills 90212, 273-4195 (TE)

Granite Agency, 1920 S. La Cienega Blvd. #205, Los Angeles 90034, 934-8383 (TCYV)

Greene's Creative Expressions, Gloria, 439 S. La Cienega Blvd. #104, Los Angeles 90048, 278-9902 (TCY)

Greenvine Agency, 9021 Melrose Ave., #304, Los Angeles 90069, 278-5800 (TV)

Grossman-Stalmaster Agency, 8833 Sunset Blvd. #100, Los Angeles 90069, 657-3040 (T)

Harris Mgmt., Mark, 12019 Guerin St. #4, Studio City 91604, 760-8870 (TC)

Hecht Agency, Beverly, 8949 Sunset Blvd. #203, Los Angeles 90069, 278-3544 (TCYM)

Henderson/Hogan, 247 S. Beverly Dr., Beverly Hills 90212, 274-7815 (TE)

Hughes Agency, The, 8721 Sunset Blvd. #103, Los Angeles 90069, 659-8956 (C)

Hunt & Assoc., George B., 8350 Santa Monica Blvd., Los Angeles 90069, 654-6600 (TE)

Hunter & Assoc., Ray, 132 Lasky Dr., Beverly Hills 90212, 276-1137 (CV)

Hussong Agency, Inc., Robert O., 701 N. La Brea Ave., Los Angeles 90038, 655-2534 (TE)

Hyman Talent Agency, Ansley Q., 3123 Cahuenga Blvd. West, Los Angeles 90068, 760-1336 (T)

Ingersoll, George 6513 Hollywood Blvd. #217, Los Angeles 90028, 874-6434 (TVE)

International Associates Agency, 7743 Coldwater Canyon, N. Hollywood 91605, 982-4648 (TCYMV)

International Creative Mgmt., 8899 Beverly Bld., Los Angeles 90048, 550-4000 (TCVE)

Kaplan-Stahler Agency, The, 119 N. San Vicente Blvd., Beverly Hills 90211, 653-4483 (T)

Kassell Agency, Carolyn, 2401 W. Magnolia, Burbank 91506, 761-1525 (CYM)

Kelman & Assoc., Toni, 7813 Sunset Blvd., Los Angeles 90046, 851-8822 (Y)

Kemp Agency, Sharon, 9701 Wilshire Blvd. #700, Beverly Hills 90212, 553-9486 (T)

Kerwin Agency, William, 1605 N. Cahuenga Blvd. #202, Los Angeles 90028, 469-5155 (T)

Kjar Agency, Tyler, 8961 Sunset Blvd. #B, Los Angeles 90069, 278-0912 (TCYMVE)
Kohner Inc., Paul, 9169 Sunset Blvd., Los Angeles 90069, 550-1060 (T)

Lane, Stacey Talent Agency, 13455 Ventura Blvd. #223, Sherman Oaks 91423, 501-2668 (Y)
Lantz Office, Inc., The 9255 Sunset Blvd. #505, Los Angeles 90069, 858-1144 (TE)
La Rocca & Assoc., John, 3907 W. Alameda, Burbank 91505, 841-8000 (T)
Lazar, Irving Paul, 211 S. Beverly Dr., Beverly Hills 90212, 275-6153 (T)
Leonetti, Ltd., Caroline, 6526 Sunset Blvd., Los Angeles 90028, 463-5610 (TCYMV)
Lesser Assoc., Gene, 8230 Beverly Blvd. #29, Los Angeles 90048, 658-8321 (T)
Levin Assoc., Mark, 328 S. Beverly Dr., Beverly Hills 90212, 277-8881 (TE)
Lichtman Co., Terry, 12345 Ventura Blvd. #X, Studio City 91604, 761-0640 (TCE)
Light Agency, Robert, 8281 Melrose Ave., 305, Los Angeles 90046 (T)
Light Co., The, 113 N. Robertson Blvd., Los Angeles 90048, 273-9602 (TCYMVE)
Littman Co., Robert, 409 N. Camden Dr., Beverly Hills 90210, 278-1572 (T)
Lloyd Talent Agency, Johnny, 6381 Hollywood Blvd. #412 & 414, Los Angeles 90028, 464-2738 (TCYM)
Longnecker Agency, Robert, 11704 Wilshire Blvd. #200, Los Angeles 90025, 477-0039 (TCV)
Loo Agency, Bessie, 8235 Santa Monica Blvd. #202, Los Angeles 90046, 650-1300 (TCYVE)
Lovell & Assoc., 1350 N. Highland, Los Angeles 90028, 462-1672 (TCYV)
Lund Agency, Starmakers Unlimited, 7985 Santa Monica Blvd. #201, Los Angeles 90046, 656-1067 (TCYMVE)
Lynn & Reilly Artists Mgr., 6290 Sunset Blvd. #1002, Los Angeles 90028, 461-2828 (TCYM)

MacArthur & Assoc., 1633 Vista Del Mar, Los Angeles 90028, 461-2727 (TE)
Marie's Talent Agency, Tina, 1823 N. Western Ave., Los Angeles 90027, 469-9270 (TCYMV)
McCartt, Oreck & Barrett, 9200 Sunset Blvd. #531, Los Angeles 90069, 278-6243 (TE)
McHugh Agency, James, 8150 Beverly Blvd. #303, Los Angeles 90048, 651-2770 (TE)
McMillan, Hazel, 126 N. Doheny, Beverly Hills 90211, 276-9823 (TCYM)
Marshall, Alese Model & Commercial Agcy., 24050 Vista Montana, Torrance 90505, 378-1223 (CM)
Merit Agency, The, 12926 Riverside Dr. #C, Sherman Oaks 91423, 986-3017 (T)
Messenger, Fred, 8235 Santa Monica Blvd., Los Angeles 90046, 654-3800 (TV)
M.E.W., Inc. 151 N. San Vicente, Beverly Hills 90211, 653-4731 (T)
MGA/Mary Grady, 10850 Riverside Dr., N. Hollywood 91602, 985-9800 (TCYMVE)

Michaud Agency, George, 4950 Densmore, Encino 91436, 981-6680 (TV)

Mishkin Agency, 9255 Sunset Blvd. #62, Los Angeles 90069, 274-5261 (TE)

M.M.C. Agency, 3518 Cahuenga Blvd. West #109, Los Angeles 90068, 846-9863 (TCYV)

Morris Agency, William, 151 El Camino Dr., Beverly Hills 90212, 274-7451 (TCYVE)

Moss Agency, Burton, 113 San Vicente Blvd. #202, Beverly Hills 90211, 655-1156 (T)

Moss & Assoc., H. David, 113 San Vicente Blvd. #302, Beverly Hills 90211, 653-2900 (TE)

Moss, Marvin, 9200 Sunset Blvd. #601, Los Angeles 90069, 274-8483 (T)

Murphy, Mary, 10701 Riverside Dr., N. Hollywood 91602, 985-4241 (TCYV)

Oliver & Assoc. Maurine, 9165 Sunset Blvd. #202, Los Angeles 90069, 859 1405 (TCE)

Pacific Artists, 515 N. La Cienega Blvd., Los Angeles 90048, 657-5990 (TCYM)

Pearson Agency, Ben, 606 Wilshire Blvd. #614, Santa Monica 90401, 451-8414 (TE)

Performing Artists, Talent Agency, 8214 Sunset Blvd., Hollywood 90046, 656-7744 (TCYM)

Perillo Talent Agency, Victor, 9229 Sunset Blvd. #611, Los Angeles 90069, 278-0251 (TE)

Pickman Co., Inc. 9025 Wilshire Blvd. #303, Beverly Hills 90211, 273-0273 (T)

Prescott, Guy, 8920 Wonderland Ave., Los Angeles 90046, 656-1963 (T)

Preston & Preston Agency, 3371 Cahuenga Blvd./W. Kilberg Suite, Los Angeles 90068, 469-6189 (T)

Progressive Artists, 400 S. Beverly Dr., Beverly Hills 90212, 553-8561 (TE)

Raison Assoc., Inc. Robert, 1930 Century Park West #403, Los Angeles 90067, 277-2460 (T)

Raper Enterprises Agency, 9441 Wilshire Blvd. #620D, Beverly Hills 90212, 273-7704 (T)

Rappa Agency, Ray, 7471 Melrose Ave. #11, Los Angeles 90046, 653-7000 (T)

Regency Artists, Ltd., 9200 Sunset Blvd., Los Angeles 90069, 273-7103 (T)

Robinson, Luttrell & Assoc., Inc., 132 S. Rodeo Dr., Beverly Hills 90212, 275-6114 (T)

Robinson Co., The, 9220 Sunset Blvd. #230, Los Angeles 90069, 275-4970 (T)

Robinson-Weintraub & Assoc., 554 S. San Vicente Blvd., Los Angeles 90048, 653-5802

Romaine Artists Mgr., Dick, 211 S. Beverly Dr. #204, Beverly Hills 90212, 277-2987 (CV)

Rose Agency, Jack/Dorothy Day Otis, 6430 Sunset Blvd., Los Angeles 90028, 463-7300 (TCYMVE)

Sackheim Agency, 9301 Wilshire Blvd. #606, Beverly Hills 90210, 858-0606 (T)

Sanders Agency, Honey, 721 N. La Brea #200, Los Angeles 90038, 938-9113 (TE)

Sanders Agency, Norah, 1100 Glendon Ave. Penthouse, Los Angeles 90024, 824-2264 (TCVE)

Savage Agency, The, 6212 Banner Ave., Los Angeles 90038, 461-8361 (TCYE)

Scagnetti Talent Agency, Jack, 5330 Lankershim Blvd. #210, N. Hollywood 91601, 762-3871 (TMV)

Schaefer, Peggy, 10850 Riverside Dr., N. Hollywood 91602, 985-5547 (CYV)

Schechter Co., Irv, 404 N. Roxbury Dr., Beverly Hills 90210, 278-8070 (TE)

Schut Agency, Booh, 10200 Riverside Dr. #205, Toluca Lake 91602, 760-6669 (Y)

Schwartz & Assoc., Don, 8721 Sunset Blvd. #200, Los Angeles 90069, 657-8910 (TCYVE)

Screen Children's Agency, 12444 Ventura Blvd., Studio City 91604, 985-6131 (TCY)

Selected Artists Agency, 12711 Ventura Blvd. #460, Studio City 91604, 763-9731 (T)

S.G.A. Representation, Inc. 12750 Ventura Blvd. #102, Studio City 91604, 506-6622 (T)

Shapira & Assoc., Inc., David, 15301 Ventura Blvd. #345, Sherman Oaks 91403, 906-0322 (TE)

Shaw Agency, Glenn, 3330 Barham Blvd., Los Angeles 90068, 851-6262 (TE)

Sherrell Agency, Ltd., Lew, 7060 Hollywood Blvd., Los Angeles 90028, 461-9955 (TCYE)

Shiffrin Artists, Inc. 7466 Beverly Blvd. #205, Los Angeles 90036, 937-3937 (TE)

Shiloh Agency, The, 12444 Victory Blvd. #407, N. Hollywood 91606, 508-0300 (TE)

Shipley-Ishimoto, 8721 Sunset Blvd., Los Angeles 90069, 652-7067 (T)

Sho-U-Right Talent Agency, 5617 Hollywood Blvd. #115, Los Angeles 90028, 469-0705 (TCYM)

Smith-Freedman & Assocs., 9869 Santa Monica Blvd. #207, Beverly Hills 90212, 277-8464 (TE)

Special Artists Agency, 9155 Sunset Blvd. #7, Los Angeles 90069, 278-7806 (CY)

STE Rep. Ltd., 211 S. Beverly Dr. #201, Beverly Hills 90212, 550-3982 (TE)

Stern Agency, Charles H., 9220 Sunset Blvd. #218, Los Angeles 90069, 273-6890 (CYV)

Stevens-Gray Agency, 4932 Lankershim Blvd. #201, N. Hollywood 91601, 508-6173 (T)

Stewart Co., Carole, 8230 Beverly Blvd. #25, Los Angeles 90048, 655-4330 (TYE)

Stone/Master Agency, 1052 Carol Dr., Los Angeles 90069, 275-9599 (TC)

Sturdivant & Assoc., Bill, 3050 W. 7th St. #200, Los Angeles 90005, 382-8483 (TCYM)

Sugho's Agency, Larry, 1017 N. La Cienega #305, Los Angeles 90069, 657-1450 (TY)

Sutton Barth & Vennari, Inc., 8322 Beverly Blvd., Los Angeles 90048, 653-8322 (CYMVE)

Talent Enterprises, 1607 N. El Centro #2, Los Angeles 90028, 462-0913 (TCY)

Talent Group, Inc., 8831 Sunset Blvd. Penthouse E., Suite A, Los Angeles 90069, 659-8072 (CYV)

Talent Mgmt. International, 6380 Wilshire Blvd. #910, Los Angeles 90048, 273-4000 (TYE)

Talent Search Artist Agency, 6253 Hollywood Blvd. #800, Los Angeles 90028, 462-2237 (TCYM)

Tannen & Assoc., Herb, 6640 Sunset Blvd. #203, Los Angeles 90028, 466-6191 (TCV)

Thompson Talent Agency, Willie R., 3902 6th St. #213, Los Angeles 90020, 380-0676 (TCYM)

T.K. Talent Group, 119 N. San Vicente Blvd. #203, Beverly Hills 90211, 657-5031 (T)

TKO Talent Agency, Inc., 13455 Ventura Blvd. #225, Sherman Oaks 91423, 906-0344 (T)

Tobias & Assoc., 1901 Ave. of the Stars #840, Los Angeles 90067, 277-6211 (TE)

Topps Enterprise Agency, 1610 N. Argyle Ave., Los Angeles 90028, 469-2591 (T)

Turco Talent Agency, Terri, 7469 Melrose Ave. #30, Los Angeles 90046, 653-2520 (TCYM)

Twentieth Century Artists, 13273 Ventura Blvd., Studio City 91604, 990-8580 (TCE)

Tyiama Artists Talent Agency, 10648 Balboa Ave., Granada Hills 91344, 366-1761 (TY)

Ufland Agency, 190 N. Canon, Beverly Hills 90212, 273-9441 (TE)

Universal Artists Agency, Inc., 9465 Wilshire Blvd. #616, Beverly Hills 90212, 278-2425 (T)

Vannerson Talent Agency, Ione, 10810 Bloomfield, N. Hollywood 91602, 985-8725 (TCYV)

Variety Artists Int'l., Inc., 9073 Nemo St. 3rd Fl., Los Angeles 90069, 858-7800 (TCY)

Wain Agency, Erika, 1418 N. Highland Ave. #102, Los Angeles 90028, 460-4224 (T)

Wasserman Co., Hillel Avery, 704 N. Gardner Ave. #3, Los Angeles 90046, 653-3616 (TE)

Waugh Talent Agency, Ann, 4731 Laurel Cyn. Blvd. #5, N. Hollywood 91607, 980-0141 (TCY)

Webb Ent. Inc., Ruth, 7500 Devista Dr., Los Angeles 90046, 874-1700 (TE)

Wever, Warren, 1104 S. Robertson Blvd., Los Angeles 90035, 276-7065 (T)

Whitehill Talent Agency, Marcia, 9229 Sunset Blvd. #515, Los Angeles 90069, 858-7751 (T)

Wilder Agency, The, 8721 Sunset Blvd. #101, Los Angeles 90069, 854-3521 (T)

Wilhelmina Artists' Representatives, Inc., 6430 Sunset Blvd. #701, Los Angeles 90028, 464-8577 (TE)

Williamson & Assoc., 932 N. La Brea, Los Angeles 90038, 851-1881 (TCYE)

Witkin, Francine, 3518 Cahuenga Blvd. West #209, Los Angeles 90068, 874-0901 (TE)

Witzer Agency, Ted, 1900 Ave. of the Stars #2850, Los Angeles 90067, 552-9521 (TE)

Wood & Assoc., Billy, 4219 Lankershim Blvd. #5, N. Hollywood 91602, 769-1226 (TCYM)

World Class Talent Agency, 8530 Wilshire Blvd. #203A, Beverly Hills 90211, 655-9326 (C)

Wormser-Heldfond & Joseph, 1717 N. Highland, Los Angeles 90028, 466-9111 (CYMV)

Wosk Agency, Sylvia, 435 S. La Cienega, Los Angeles 90048, 274-8063 (TY)

Wright Assoc., Ann, 8422 Melrose Pl., Los Angeles 90069, 655-5040 (TCYMVE)

Writers & Artists Agency, 450 N. Roxbury Dr., Beverly Hills 90210, 550-8030 (TE)

Zimmerman Agency, Herman, 6736 Laurel Cyn. Blvd. #302 N. Hollywood 91606, 982-0303 (T)

In addition, here are some out-of-town SAG-franchised agencies in Southern California:

Altoni, Esq. Inc., Buddy, 3901 MacArthur Blvd. #211, Newport Bch. 92660 (213) 467-4939 or (714) 851-1711 (TCYME)

Berzon, Marian, 336 E. 17th, Costa Mesa 92627 (714) 631-5936 (TCYM)

Conejo Agency, 247 Green Heath Pl., Thousand Oaks 91361 (805) 497-2214 (TC)

DeSpain Talent Agency, June, 3481 Old Canejo Rd. #A5-3, Newbury Park 91360 (805) 495-7800 (TCYM)

Gerard Talent Agency, Paul, 2918 Alta Vista Dr., Newport Bch. 92660 (714) 644-7950 (T)

Good Company Talent Agency, 5400 Orange Ave. #126, Cypress 90630 (213) 598-2741 or (714) 827-0889 (TCYM)

Labelle Agency, El Paso Studio 110, Santa Barbara 93102 (805) 965-4575 (TCYM)

Marie's Modeling & Talent Agency, Linda, 626 W. Commonwealth #H, Fullerton 92632 (714) 870-7640 (TCYM)

Shreve Artists Manager, Dorothy, 729 W. 16th, Costa Mesa 92627 (714) 642-3050 (TCYM)

Star Quality Mgmt. Talent Agency, 895 Park Ln., Santa Barbara 93108 (805) 969-9250 (TCYM)

3. ANSWERING SERVICES

Actorfone West
462-6565

Sunset Dial
876-5500

Seven Lively Arts
855-1033

4. BARGAINS

• *Guidebooks*

Bargain Hunting in L.A. (Various)
Barbara Partridge
J. P. Tarcher Inc., 1980

Glad Rags II (Women's clothing)
Leigh Charlton and Annette Swanberg
Chronicle Books, 1982

LAbyrinth (A Student Guide to L.A.) (Various)
Edited by Hae K. Yoon
USC Press, 1982

• *Clothing*

Garment District, downtown, roughly bordered by 7th St. on the north, the
Santa Monica Freeway on the south, Broadway on the west, Maple St. on the
east. S. Los Angeles is its "main street."

The Cooper Building
860 S. Los Angeles St.
Seven floors of discount shops.

Dorman-Winthrop
3030 S. La Cienega Bl./Other locations
870-8585
Men's wear.

Ladies Apparel
840 S. Los Angeles St.
627-6861

Leon's Sportswear
7215 Whitsett Ave., N. Hwd.
765-9561
Men's wear.

Loehmann's
6220 W. Third St./Other locations
933-5675
Women's wear.

The Re-Take Room
3953 Laurel Grove Ave.
Studio City
508-7762
Men's and women's wear from
studio wardrobe departments.

• *General merchandise*

Adray's
5575 Wilshire Blvd.
935-8191

Pic 'N' Save
2430 E. Del Amo Blvd.
Carson/Other locations
537-9220

5. BOOKSTORES/NEWSSTANDS

● *Books*

Larry Edmunds Cinema and Theatre Book Shop
6658 Hollywood Blvd.
463-3273

Samuel French, Inc.
7623 Sunset Blvd.
876-0570

● *Newsstands*

Art's News
1150 Westwood Blvd.
(Westwood)

Universal News
1655 N. Las Palmas
(Hollywood)

Studio City News
12133 Ventura Blvd.
(Studio City)

World Book and News
1652 Cahuenga Blvd.
(Hollywood)

6. EQUITY THEATRES

EQUITY DINNER THEATRES

Petite house—$225.25
Small house—$257.25

Medium house—$316.25
Large house—$328.50

Fiesta Dinner Theatre
9665 Campo Rd., Box 247
Spring Valley 92077
(714) 697-8977
Medium house

Lawrence Welk Village Theatre
8845 Lawrence Welk Dr.
Escondido 92026
(714) 749-3448
Small house

The Grand Dinner Theatre *
Grand Hotel—One Hotel Way
Anaheim 92802
(714) 772-7710
Medium house

Lyric Dinner Theatre*
7578 El Cajon Blvd.
La Mesa 92041
(714) 465-9997
Petite house

Harlequin Dinner Playhouse
3503 S. Harbor Blvd.
Santa Ana 92704
(714) 979-7550
Medium house

Sebastian's West Dinner Playhouse *
140 Avenida Pico
San Clemente 92672
(714) 492-9950
Small house

* Member, American Dinner Theatre Institute

LEAGUE OF RESIDENT THEATRES (LORT CONTRACT)

"A" size house—$352
"B" size house—$320
"C" size house—$309
"D" size house—$282

Intern, "B" house—$246
Intern, "C" house—$238
Intern, "D" house—$221
Journeyman—$215

American Conservatory Theatre (ACT)
450 Geary St.
San Francisco 94102
(415) 771-3880
"A" size house

Berkeley Repertory Theatre
2025 Addison St.
Berkeley 94704
(415) 841-6108
"C" size house

Long Beach Civic Light Opera
518 East 4th St.
Long Beach 90801
(213) 435-7605
"A" size house
with a "D" pro/nonpro ratio

Los Angeles Public Theatre
6253 Hollywood Blvd., Suite 222
Los Angeles 90028
(213) 469-3974
"C" size house

Los Angeles Stage Company
Los Angeles Stage Company Theatre
1642 N. Las Palmas Ave.
Hollywood 90028
(213) 461-2755
"B" size house

Mark Taper Forum
Center Theatre Group
135 N. Grand Ave.
Los Angeles 90012
(213) 972-7353
"A" size house

Old Globe Theatre
P.O. Box 2171
San Diego 92112
(714) 231-1941
Three houses, two "B" and one "D"

South Coast Repertory Theatre
P.O. Box 2197
Costa Mesa 92626
(714) 957-2602
Two houses, one "B" and one "D"

7. EXTRA CASTING OFFICES (UNION)

Central Casting
9200 Sunset Blvd.
Los Angeles 90069
550-0166

Hollywood Casting Agency
1717 N. Highland, Suite 805
Los Angeles 90028
461-9281

Producer's Casting (Commercials only)
6331 Hollywood Blvd., Suite 1103
Hollywood 90028
464-8233

Richmar Casting
6115 Selma Ave.
Hollywood 90028
464-6501

National Casting (Commercials only)
7469 Melrose Ave.
Los Angeles 90046
650-7044

Universal City Casting
Universal Studios
3875 Lankershim Blvd.
Universal City 91608
877-1056

8. INDUSTRIAL FILMS

Association of Multi-Image/Southern California (AMI)
2210 Wilshire Blvd. #241
Santa Monica 90403
427-7120 (Meeting announcements)

Informational Film Producers Association (IFPA)
750 E. Colorado Blvd.
Pasadena 91101
795-7866

By joining these two organizations, you'll get a fairly complete list of industrial filmmakers (see Chapter 25). Also see the *Producers Guide* (mentioned in Chapter 8).

Some industrial film producers that hire actors:

Cally Curtis Co.
1111 N. Las Palmas Ave.
Hollywood 90038
467-1101

Stacy Keach Prods.
5216 Laurel Canyon Blvd.
N. Hollywood 91607
877-0472

Churchill Films
662 N. Robertson Blvd.
Los Angeles 90069
657-5110

Wexler Film Prods.
801 N. Seward St.
Los Angeles 90038
462-6671

9. PHOTOGRAPHERS

Charles Fretzin
760-0464

Tama Rothschild
658-7862

John Sanchez
462-8938

Herb Weil
874-8492

John Gibson
666-6238

Buddy Rosenberg
464-9475

Dale Tarter
857-1957

10. PHOTOGRAPHIC PRINT SHOPS

Anderson Graphics
6037-45 Woodman
Ave.
Van Nuys
786-5235; 876-4235

Custom Print Shop
1759 N. Las Palmas
Hollywood
461-3001

Libbea and Watkins
Lithographers
152 N. La Brea
Hollywood
936-4156

The Print Shop
1161 N. Las Palmas
Hollywood
464-0747

Quantity Photos Inc.
5432 Hollywood Blvd.
Hollywood
467-6178

11. PRINT SHOPS (RÉSUMÉS, ETC.)

The Copy Spot
712 Wilshire Blvd. or
3330 Ocean Park Blvd.
Santa Monica
393-0693/450-9002

PIP
(Various locations)
6613 Sunset Blvd.
Hollywood
465-4144

Sir Speedy
(Various locations)

West Hollywood Printing & Copy Center
8134 Santa Monica Blvd.
W. Hollywood
650-0107

12. RECOMMENDED READING

- *About L.A.*

  500 Free Things to Do in L.A.
  Carol MacConaugha
  New Century Publishing Co., 1981

  LA/Access
  Richard Saul Wurman
  L.A. Access Press, 1982

- *Acting*

  Acting Is Believing
  Charles McGaw
  Holt, Rinehart & Winston, 4th Edition, 1980

  Respect for Acting
  Uta Hagen
  Macmillan, 1973

  An Actor Prepares and *Building a Character*
  Constantin Stanislavski
  Theatre Art Books, 1948 and 1949

- *Auditioning*

  Audition   *How to Audition*
  Michael Shurtleff   Gordon Hunt
  Walker & Co., 1978   Harper & Row, 1977

- *Business of acting*

  Acting Professionally   *Your Acting Career*
  Robert Cohen   Rebecca Nahas
  Mayfield Publishing Co., 1975 Crown Publishing Co., 1976

- *Commercials*

  Acting in Television Commercials   *How to Get Work and Make Money*
  Squire Fridell   *in Commercials and Modeling*
  Harmony Books, 1980   Cecily Hunt
                                       Van Nostrand Reinhold Co., 1982

- *General insight*

  Actors on Acting   *The Cool Fire*
  Edited by Toby Cole, Helen Krich Chinoy   Bob Shanks
  Crown Publishers, Inc., 1970   Vintage Books, 1976

- *Others*

  Body Language by Julius Fast; *How to Attract Good Luck*, A.H.Z. Carr;
  How to Read a Person Like a Book, Gerard I. Nierenberg; *Power of Positive
  Thinking*, Norman Vincent Peale; *Think and Grow Rich*, Napoleon Hill;
  and any book on salesmanship.

13. RÉSUMÉ COMPOSITION & TYPING

Cindy Randall   Résumé Writers   Studio Typing Pool
650-8165   453-4900   Hollywood: 652-0325
                                          W. Los Angeles: 474-5311

14. STUDIOS

See Studio Map, Chapter 3.

15. THEATRES

See Theatre Maps, Chapter 26.

16. TRADE PUBLICATIONS

Key: (N) = Newsstand sales

(S) = Subscription

Daily Variety (N/S)
1400 N. Cahuenga Blvd.
Los Angeles 90028
469-1141

Drama-Logue (N/S)
1456 N. Gordon St.
Los Angeles 90028
Mailing: P.O. Box 38771
          Los Angeles 90038
464-5079

Entertainment Monthly (N/S)
(Formerly Commercials Monthly)
470 S. San Vicente Blvd. #103
Los Angeles 90048
852-0322

Hollywood Reporter (N/S)
6715 Sunset Blvd.
Hollywood 90028
464-7411

OTHER TRADES OF INTEREST

American Film (N/S)
Broadcast (N/S)
Casting Call (N/S)
Dialog (S) (Official publication of AFTRA)
Performer (N/S)
Screen Actor (S) (Official publication of SAG)
SAG Newsletter (S) (Official publication of SAG)
State of the Arts (S):   California Arts Council
                        1901 Broadway, Suite A, Sacramento 95818
Talent (N/S)

NEW YORK PUBLICATIONS

Backstage

Show Business

Weekly Variety

17. UNION BRANCH OFFICES

ACTORS' EQUITY ASSOCIATION

6430 Sunset Blvd. #616
Hollywood, CA 90028
(213) 462-2334

CANADA:

64 Shuter St.
Toronto, Ontario, Canada M5B 2G7

CHICAGO:

360 N. Michigan Ave. #1401
Chicago, IL 60601

NEW YORK: 165 W. 46th St.
(Main ofc.)   New York, NY 10036
                  (212) 869-8530

SAN FRANCISCO: 182 Second St.
                  San Francisco, CA 94105

THE AMERICAN FEDERATION OF TELEVISION AND RADIO ARTISTS

1717 N. Highland Ave.
Los Angeles, CA 90028
(213) 461-8111

ALBANY:	341 Northern Blvd. Albany, NY 12204	**DENVER:**	6825 E. Tennessee #639 Denver, CO 80224
ATLANTA:	3110 Maple Dr. N.E. #210 Atlanta, GA 30305	**DETROIT:**	24901 N. Western Hwy. #406 Southfield, MI 48075
BINGHAMTON:	50 Front St. Binghamton, NY 13905	**FRESNO:**	P.O. Box 11961 Fresno, CA 93776
BOSTON:	11 Beacon St. #1000 Boston, MA 02018	**HAWAII:**	P.O. Box 1350 Honolulu, HI 96807
BUFFALO:	635 Brisbane Building Buffalo, NY 14203	**HOUSTON:**	2620 Fountainview #215 Houston, TX 77057
CHICAGO:	307 N. Michigan Ave. Chicago, IL. 60601	**INDIANAPOLIS:**	20 N. Meridian St. 7th Floor Indianapolis, IN 46204
CINCINNATI/ COLUMBUS/ DAYTON:	1814-16 Carew Tower Cincinnati, OH 45202	**KANSAS CITY/ OMAHA:** *	406 W. 34th St. #310 Kansas City, MO 46111
CLEVELAND: *	1367 E. Sixth St. #229 Cleveland, OH 44114	**LOUISVILLE:**	730 W. Main St. #250 Louisville, KY 40202
DALLAS/ FT. WORTH:	3220 Lemmon Ave. #102 Dallas, TX 75204	**MIAMI:**	70 N.E. 167th St. N. Miami Beach, FL 33162

NASHVILLE:	P.O. Box 121087 Acklen Station Nashville, TN 37212	**SACRAMENTO/ STOCKTON:**	1216 Arden Way Sacramento, CA 95815
NEW ORLEANS:	808 St. Ann St. New Orleans, LA 70116	**SAN DIEGO:**	3045 Rosecrans St. #308 San Diego, CA 92110
NEW YORK: (Main ofc.)	1350 Ave. of the Americas, 2nd Fl., New York, NY 10019 (212) 265-7700	**SAN FRANCISCO:**	100 Bush St. San Francisco, CA 94104
PEORIA:	2907 Springfield Rd. E. Peoria, IL 61611	**SCHENECTADY:**	1400 Balltown Rd. Albany, NY 12309
PHILADELPHIA:	1405 Locust St. #811 Philadelphia, PA 19102	**SEATTLE** *	158 Thomas St. Seattle, WA 98104
PHOENIX:	3030 N. Central #919 Phoenix, AZ 85012	**ST. LOUIS** *	818 Olive St. #1237 St. Louis, MO 63101
		STAMFORD:	117 Prospect St. Stamford, CT 06901
PITTSBURGH:	One Thousand, The Bank Tower Pittsburgh, PA 15222	**TWIN CITIES** *	2500 Park Ave.. South #A Minneapolis, MN 55404
PORTLAND:	915 N.E. Davis St. Portland, OR 97232	**WASHINGTON/ BALTIMORE:**	35 Wisconsin Circle #210 Washington, D.C. 20015
RACINE/ KENOSHA:	929 52nd St. Kenosha, WI 53140		
ROCHESTER:	1 Exchange St. #900 Rochester, NY 14614	**SOUTH BEND:**	826 S. 25th St. S. Bend, IN 46615

AMERICAN GUILD OF MUSICAL ARTISTS

Silverton, Miller, Norvid & Moss
12650 Riverside Dr.
N. Hollywood, CA 91607
(213) 877-0683

CANADA:	64 Shuter St. Toronto, Ontario, Canada M5B 2G7	**CHICAGO:**	107 N. Michigan Ave. Chicago, IL 60601

* AFTRA offices which handle SAG for their area

NEW ENGLAND:	11 Beacon St. Boston, MA 02108	**PHILADELPHIA:**	Lafayette Bldg., 8th Fl. 5th and Chestnut Philadelphia, PA 19106
NEW ORLEANS:	34 San Jose Ave. Jefferson, LA 70121	**SAN FRANCISCO:**	100 Bush St. #1500 San Francisco, CA
NEW YORK: **(Main ofc.)**	1841 Broadway New York, NY 10023 (212) 265-3687-8-9	**TEXAS:**	94104 4745 Shands Dr. Mesquite, TX 75149
NORTHWEST:	704 Bellevue East Seattle, WA 98102	**WASHINGTON, D.C.:**	Chevy Chase Center Bldg. #210 Washington, D.C. 20015

AMERICAN GUILD OF VARIETY ARTISTS

4741 Laurel Canyon Blvd. #208
N. Hollywood, CA 91607
(213) 508-9984

1540 Broadway
New York, NY 10036
(212) 675-1003

For regional branches, write AGVA in New York City.

THE SCREEN ACTORS GUILD

7750 Sunset Blvd.
Los Angeles, CA 90046
(213) 876-3030

ARIZONA:	3030 N. Central #919 Phoenix, AZ 85012	**CLEVELAND:** *	1367 East 6th St. #229 Cleveland, OH 44114
ATLANTA:	3110 Maple Dr. NE, Suite 210 Atlanta, GA 30305	**DALLAS:**	3220 Lemmon Ave. #102 Dallas, TX 75204
BOSTON:	11 Beacon St., Room 1000 Boston, MA 02108	**DENVER:**	6825 E. Tennessee Ave. #639 Denver, CO 80222
CHICAGO:	307 N. Michigan Ave. Chicago, IL 60601		

DETROIT:	28690 Southfield Rd. Lathrup Village, MI 48076	**NEW YORK:**	1700 Broadway, 18th Floor New York, NY 10019 (212) 957-5370
FLORIDA:	145 Madeira Ave. #317		
	Coral Gables, FL 33134	**PHILADELPHIA:**	1405 Locust St., #811
HOUSTON:	2620 Fountainview, Suite 215		Philadelphia, PA 19102
	Houston, TX 77057	**ST. LOUIS:** *	818 Olive St. #617
KANSAS CITY: *	406 W. 34th, Suite 310		St. Louis, MO 63101
	Kansas City, MO 64111	**SAN DIEGO:**	3045 Rosecrans #308 San Diego, CA 92110
MINNEAPOLIS / **ST. PAUL:**	2500 Park Ave., Suite A Minneapolis, MN 55402	**SAN** **FRANCISCO:**	100 Bush St. San Francisco, CA 94104
NASHVILLE:	P.O. Box 121087 Nashville, TN 37212	**SEATTLE:** *	158 Thomas St. Seattle, WA 98109
NEVADA & **NEW MEXICO:**	7750 Sunset Blvd. Hollywood, CA 90046	**WASHINGTON,** **D.C.**	35 Wisconsin Circle #210 Chevy Chase, MD 20015

SCREEN EXTRAS GUILD
3629 Cahuenga Blvd. West
Los Angeles 90068
(213) 851-4301

HONOLULU:	1127 Eleventh St. #205 Honolulu, HI 96816
NEW YORK: †	551 Fifth Ave. New York, NY 10017 ° (212) 957-5370

* AFTRA offices which handle SAG for their area
† SAG affiliate

SAN DIEGO: 3045 Rosecrans St. #308
                                 San Diego, CA 92110

SAN FRANCISCO: 100 Bush St.
                                 San Francisco, CA 94104

18.   VIDEOTAPING SERVICES—"AIR CHECKS," ETC.

Actors Budget Video   Jan Naterno
843-4876   462-5511

USED BLANK TAPE:

Studio Film & Tape, Inc.
6670 Santa Monica Blvd.
Hollywood 90038
466-8101

19.   MISCELLANEOUS

Academy Players Directory
Academy of Motion Picture Arts & Sciences
8949 Wilshire Blvd.
Beverly Hills 90211
278-8990

The American Film Institute
2021 N. Western Ave.
Los Angeles 90027
856-7600

Breakdown Services, Ltd.
658-5684

Hollywood YMCA
1553 Hudson Ave.
Hollywood 90028
467-4161

Los Angeles Theatre Alliance (LATA)
6253 Hollywood Blvd. #312
Hollywood 90028
467-6690

Performers Audition Showcase
P.O. Box 9818
N. Hollywood 91609-1818
980-2740

"The Voicecaster"
(Bob Lloyd)
3413 Cahuenga Blvd. West
Los Angeles 90068
874-1933

INDEX

Academy of Motion Picture Arts and Sciences, 70, 232
Academy Players Directory, 93, 223, 232, 296
  choosing agents and, 97–98, 111
  listing of actors in, 70–71, 103, 106, 170
Accents, 165
  affecting of, 129, 136
  getting rid of, 13
Acting classes and training, 32–33, 85, 208–212
  auditing of, 32–33, 211
  changing of, 209, 212
  choosing of, 209–211
  for cold readings, 82, 138, 143, 209, 229
  for commercials, 166, 170, 178, 181, 209
  contacts made with agents through, 95, 210
  evaluating of, 211–212
  before going to L.A., 9–10
  importance of, 208
  included on résumés, 59
  "industry nights" in, 209
  lists of, 74, 273–275
  videotape used in, 211, 229
Acting Coaches and Teachers Association (ACTA), 210
Actors
  appearance as concern of, 13
  attitudes beneficial to, 79–85
  billing of, 112, 149, 151
  careers assessed by, 234–237
  confidence exuded by, 9
  courage needed by, 80–81
  craft learned by, 81
  daily goals set by, 82
  earnings of, 1, 7, 66, 111, 110, 149, 150, 161, 166, 190, 201
  emotional involvements of, 7–8
  ethnic-looking, 8–9, 15, 165
  idealistic, 6
  job skills needed by, 13–14
  long view taken by, 122
  male vs. female, roles available to, 8
  negative behavior avoided by, 84–85
  nonworking, as bad company, 83
  other interests pursued by, 80
  personality traits beneficial to, 5–6, 9
  as products, 81
  recommended reading for, 289–290
  rejections handled by, 81
  roles turned down by, 79–80
  "screw you" money needed by, 79–80
  selling abilities needed by, 3
  "starving," 79–80
  stress-filled lives of, 5–6, 9
  successful demeanor presented by, 83
  talent assessed by, 9–10
  as too hard on themselves, 82–83
  typecasting of, 41
  uprooted lives of, 6
Actors Equity Association (AEA; Equity), 12, 15, 28, 59, 92, 233. See also Equity Waiver theatre
  branch offices of, 291
  entering SAG from, 65, 69
  entries into, 62–63, 69

importance of, 69
  jurisdiction of, 61
  L.A. theatres and, 201–203, 286–287
Actors for Themselves, 233
Actors Helping Actors (AHA), 233
Adler, Stella, 59
Ads, placed in trades, 106, 217–218
Age
  discussed in interviews, 128
  omitted from résumés, 55–56
  role availability and, 8
Agencies
  clout of, 111
  commercial, best-known, 169
  size of, 100, 169
Agents, 24, 83, 215, 218, 230
  Academy Players Directory and, 70, 71. See also Commercial agents; Theatrical agents
  actors' anger at, 84, 85
  categories of, 89–90, 101–103
  discussed in interviews, 127–128
  franchised, 73, 92, 93, 99
  importance of, 89
  labels preaddressed to, 72
  legitimate, 89, 91, 92
  lists and directories of, 73–74, 275–284
  modeling, 89, 195
  personal managers and, 221, 222, 223
  résumés and, 55, 56, 58, 106
  résumé shots and, 39, 42, 48, 52, 106
  sub-, 92
  variety, 89, 197
  voice-over, 89, 193
Air checks, 74, 106
Air Quality Management District (AQMD), 17
American Federation of Television and Radio Artists (AFTRA), 15, 28, 91, 104, 177
  branch offices of, 291–293
  contracts with agents and, 104, 113
  credit union of, 230
  entering SAG from, 65, 68
  entry into Equity and, 63, 69
  joining of, 62
  jurisdiction of, 61
  pension and welfare benefits of, 271
American Film Institute (AFI), 29, 191–192, 296
American Guild of Musical Artists (AGMA), 67–68, 293–294
American Guild of Variety Artists (AGVA), 66–67, 195, 293
Answering machines and services, 27, 58, 71, 106, 285
Apartments, 20–23
  "career areas" of, 76
  finding of, 21–23
  furnished vs. unfurnished, 20
  furnishing of, 25
  locations recommended for, 21–22
  standard rental agreements for, 20
  tenants rights and, 23
  types of, 20
Appointment books, 76, 226
Are You Now or Have You Ever Been, 233
Arnold, Maxine, 131

Assistant directors, 66
  first, 156
  second, 153, 157, 161
Association of Multi-Image/Southern California, 190
Attorneys, 220
Auditions, 85, 90, 106, 118, 123, 191. *See also* Cold readings; Commercial auditions; Office scenes
  missing work for, 24
  for theatre work, 200, 201

Bandlow, Vikki, 12, 71, 94–95, 106
Bank accounts, opening of, 14, 28
Bankers, 220–221
Barefoot in the Park (Simon), 146
Becker, Mel, 106
Best, Barbara, 3, 97, 216, 224
Billing, 112, 149, 151
  hierarchy in, 149
Black, Noel, 58, 117, 123, 127, 140, 157
Blake, Merritt, 82
Blank, Mel, 226
Booking slips, 150, 153
Books
  for casting, 168, 170, 172, 192
  modeling shots in, 125, 195
Breakdown Service, 72, 73, 90, 118, 134, 218, 221, 296
Breakthru Service, 168
Bregman, Buddy, 37, 124, 203, 208, 236
Budget, basic, 37–38
Burger, Richard, 73
Buses
  RTD, 19
  to and from LAX, 19
Business expenses, 12, 37–38
Business managers, 74, 223–224

Cable television, 199–200
Cabs, 19
Calendar datebooks, 76, 226
California Driver's Handbook, 18
California Registration Handbook, 18
California Theatre Annual, 202
Callbacks, 142–143, 180–181
Call forwarding, 27, 106
Call sheets, 161
Call waiting, 27
Campus, Michael, 92
Campus, Pamela, 127, 140, 165, 166, 180
Card files, 72
Cars, 18–19
  Angelinos' love affair with, 18
  costs of, 19
  as necessities in L.A., 12, 19
  tips on driving of, 18–19
Casting breakdowns, 72
Casting Call, 146
Casting directors, 83, 96, 134, 144, 190, 218. *See also* Commercial casting directors
  agents' dealings with, 90, 107–108, 112, 142
  deals negotiated with, 90, 149–151
  functions of, 117
  information gathered on, 72
  interviews with, 117–118, 123–133
  keeping in touch with, 118–120
  labels preaddressed to, 72
  lists and directories of, 73–74
  for networks, 121–122

  for voice-overs, 194
Certificates of Compliance (Smog Certification), 18
Certified public accountants (CPAs), 220, 223, 226, 227
Cheating toward camera, 156
Ciminelli, Don, 119, 189, 190
Classics, office scenes taken from, 145–146
Clothing, 13, 109, 125
  for cold readings, 135
  for commercial auditions, 176
  for extra work, 65
  for résumé shots, 46
  shooting wardrobe and, 152–153, 181
  shopping for, 27–28, 285
Cohn, Jerry, 99, 223
Cold readings, 98, 123, 134–143
  acting partners in, 141
  arriving early for, 135
  asking questions before, 139–140
  being stopped during, 141–142
  callbacks and screen tests after, 142–143
  classes for, 82, 138, 143, 209, 229
  clothing for, 135
  of completely cold scenes, 142
  expecting the unexpected in, 139
  flubbing or changing lines in, 141
  information gathered for, 134
  listening and reacting in, 136, 137
  looking at script in, 136, 137
  memorizing lines for, 136, 137, 138
  negativism avoided in, 139, 140, 141
  nervousness in, 139
  picking a direction in, 136–137
  preparing scenes for, 135–138
  reading a second time in, 141
  rehearsal time for, 138
  rehearsing out loud for, 138
  scripts or sides for, 134–135
  stage directions ignored in, 138
  starting over in, 141
  starting to read in, 140
Colleges. *See also* student films
  seminars and continuing education courses at, 232
  theatre credits from, 56
Commercial agents, 89, 99, 100, 165, 168–175, 176, 185, 218
  clients' expectations of, 171
  clients' responsibilities to, 170
  composites and, 72, 170, 171, 172, 173
  conflicts and, 171, 182–183
  contracts with, 104, 247
  functions of, 168–169, 171
  newcomers signed by, 166, 167
  payment of, 170, 184–185
  seeking and choosing of, 169–170
  theatrical agents separate from, 102–103, 169
Commercial auditions, 166–167, 168, 171, 176–181
  callbacks after, 180–181
  clothing for, 176
  enthusiasm at, 84, 176
  fees for, 177, 180
  general auditions as, 177
  "idiot cards" in, 180
  improvisations in, 177
  listening in, 180
  negativism avoided in, 180
  portable equipment for, 176
  scenes in, 177–178

signing in and out of, 176–177, 180
"slates" in, 179–180
for spokesmen, 178–179
Commercial casting directors, 168
at auditions, 177, 179–180
workshops taught by, 170, 181
Commercial headshots, 40, 175
in *Academy Players Directory*, 70, 71, 170
basic qualities of, 41, 46
submitted to commercial agents, 42, 169, 172
Commercial riders, 104
Commercials, 165–167
actors discovered through, 166
contracts for, 261–266
credits for, listed on résumés, 58, 59, 60
dealer, 184
deals for, 168, 181
dental care and, 13, 41
directory of actors for, 71
as entrée for newcomers, 91, 166–167
exclusivity and conflicts in, 170, 171, 182–183, 184
modeling roles in, 195
network (Program Usage), 183
pay for actors in, 166, 181
pay for extras in, 66
records on running of, 185
residuals for, 66, 166, 168, 170, 171, 182, 183–185, 193
seasonal, 184
shooting of, 181–182
spokesman, 178–179, 181, 229
test, 184
videotapes of performances in, 77
voice-overs in, 192–193
"white bread" as look in, 9, 165, 167, 171
wild spots as, 183
Commercial workshops, 170, 181, 209
Community theatre
credits for, listed on résumés, 56
industry professionals at, 96
union membership and, 61–62, 96
Composites, 78, 171, 172–175, 195, 197. *See also*Résumé shots
finish recommended for, 49, 172
planning pictures for, 173–175
playing to type in, 175
printing of, 173
sessions for, 172
shots suggested for, 174–175
specifications for, 172
when to invest in, 42, 72, 165, 170
Continuity persons, 155
Contracts, 153. *See also* Deals
with commercial agents, 104, 247
for commercials, 261–266
daily, three-day, or weekly basis for, 149–150
for films and TV, 149–150, 248–260
phone calls as, 150
signing of, 154
with theatrical agents, 103–104, 113, 243–246
Corporate-image films, 189
"Co-Star" billing, 149
Costumers, 152–153, 181
Credit, establishing of, 14, 28, 221
Credits
discussing of, in interviews, 126, 127–128, 130
listed on résumés, 58–60
Credit unions, 230
Critics, notices and thank-you notes sent to, 219

Daily Variety, 33, 74, 75, 106, 121, 215, 216, 217, 219
Dancing abilities, 56
Davis, Bette, 80
Day players, 79–80, 160
agencies limited to, 111
contracts for, 64
pay for, 150
Dealer commercials, 184
Deals, 90, 149–151, 191. *See also* Contracts
billing in, 112, 149, 151
for commercials, 168, 181
conflicting start dates and, 150–151
duration of employment and, 149–150, 151
firming up of, 150
money in, 111–112, 149–150, 151
Dennison, Sally, 124
Desks, for "career areas" for apartments, 76
Dialect coaches, 13
DiCenzo, Karen, 165, 189, 195, 196, 198
Dickinson, Angie, 82
Directories
of agents and casting directors, 73–74
of directors, 121
of film producers, 73, 121
of theatres and workshops, 74
Directors, 83. *See also* Assistant directors; Casting directors
in casting process, 90, 117, 123
at cold readings, 140, 141, 142, 143
developing relationship with, 120–121
directory of, 121
interviews with, 118, 123–133
on sets, 153, 157, 158, 159, 160, 161
Directors Guild of America (DGA), 121
Documentaries, 189
Douglas, Georg, 12, 80, 85
Drake, Sylvia, 219
Drama-Logue, 33, 70, 74, 95, 146, 100, 101, 202
Drama-Logue Guide to Southern California Theatre, 74, 202, 210
Dressing rooms, 153, 154, 160
Dubbing, 156

Education, inclusion on résumés of, 59
Educational films, 189
Edwards, Bill, 219
Edwards, John, 11, 176
Employment, 13–14, 23–24
day vs. night jobs as, 14, 23
temporary, 23
"End Title" billing, 149
Entertainment Monthly, 33, 74–75, 218
Equity. *See* Actors Equity Association
Equity Waiver theatre, 62, 96, 118, 199, 201–203, 233
benefits of working in, 201–202
choosing plays and theatres for, 202–203
getting into, 202
Ethnic-looking actors, 165
name changes for, 15
roles for, 8–9
Extra work, 65–66, 96, 160, 196
assistant directors and, 66
casting offices for, 287
pay for, 66
registering for, 65
unscripted lines and, 64, 66

"Featured" billing, 149

Feature films, 58, 66, 96, 157–158
Feinberg, Jane, 143
Fenton, Mike, 197, 212
Files, on casting directors and contacts, 72
FILMEX, 232
Films. See also Commercials; Television shows
  character development in, 136
  contracts for, 149–150, 248–260
  credits in, listed on résumés, 58, 59–60
  feature, 58, 66, 96, 158
  industrial, 58, 60, 77, 166, 189–191
  low-budget, 166, 190–191
  performances in, seen by agents, 96
  pornographic, 196
  in production, lists of, 75
  student, 77, 191–192
  videotapes of performances in, 77
"First team," 156
Fisher, John, 168
Foley effects, 193, 194
Fonseca, Larry, 47, 91, 119, 140, 199, 236
Franks, Jerry, 40, 125
"Freelance" contracts, 150
Furniture
  buying of, 25
  renting of, 25

General interviews. See Look-sees and general
  interviews
General Telephone, 26–27
Geographical Casting Guide, 73, 118
Gibson, Jim, 9, 89, 111
Gilbert, Edmund, 83
Glicksman, Susan, 78, 121, 138, 203
Gloss-tone finish, 49, 50
Glossy finish, 49
"Go-Between" service, 218
Goldwyn, Samuel, 103
"Guest Star" billing, 149
Guthrie, Tani, 233

Hairstyles, for résumé shots, 40, 46, 173
Hamilton, Dran, 233
Hamilton School of Photography, 231
Headshots, 40–42. See also Résumé sessions;
  Résumé shots
  basic qualities of, 40
  commercial, 40, 41, 42, 46, 70, 71, 169, 170,
    172, 175
  theatrical, 40, 41–42, 46, 70
Hitchcock, Alfred, 82
Hoffman, Bobby, 139
Holding fees, 183
Hollywood Actor's Newsletter, 192
Hollywood Reporter, 33, 74, 75, 106, 121, 215,
    216, 217
Hollywood YMCA, 20, 296
Holstra, Judith, 39, 133, 136, 137
Holstra, Tawn, 94
Hot sets, 157
Housing. See also Apartments
  temporary, 19–20

ICM, 93, 102, 111
Improvisation auditions, 177
Industrial films, 77, 166, 189–191, 288
  credits for, listed on résumés, 58, 60
  nonunion, 190–191
  seeking work in, 190
  types of, 189

Informational Film Producers Association (IFPA),
    190
Insurance, 227
Insurance agents, 221
Interviews. See also Auditions; Look-sees and gen-
    eral interviews
  appearance as concern in, 13, 125
  arranged by agents, 106, 109, 110
  in seeking of agents, 97–98, 101–102, 113
  types of, 117–118
Investments, 227

Jacobs, Tracey, 172
Jaymes, Cathryn, 108, 221
Jeffer, Marsha, 190
Joan Magnum Agency, 195

Kayden, William, 71, 127, 136, 140, 150
Key light, 156

Labels
  blank, for manila envelopes, 72
  preaddressed to casting directors and agents, 10,
    218
Laidman, Harvey, 137, 152
Larry Edmunds Bookstore, 29, 73
League of Resident Theatres (LORT), 200–201,
    286
Legitimate agents, 89, 91, 92
LeLouch, Claude, 132
Lichtman, Terry, 123
Light, key, 156
Liroff, Marci, 110, 131
Lloyd, Bob, 194, 229
Locher, Mark, 80
Look-sees and general interviews, 121, 123–133,
    177, 229
  as conversations vs. monologues, 124–125, 130
  defined, 118
  discussing credits in, 126, 127–128, 130
  evaluating of, 132–133
  five general precepts for, 124–125
  humor and jokes in, 124, 130
  importance of, 123
  listening in, 132
  lying in, 128
  negativism and hostility avoided in, 129–130
  nervousness in, 131
  personality vs. business approach to, 123, 127
  practicing for, 132
  preparing for, 125–126, 127, 129
  questions asked in, 126–129
Looping (sync), 156, 193, 194
Los Angeles, Calif. (L.A.)
  architecture in, 17
  bargain hunting in, 285–286
  bookstores and newsstands in, 286
  clothing stores in, 27–28, 285
  deciding to go to, 3–11, 128
  divisions of, 16–17, 18
  downtown, 17–18
  food and entertainment in, 17, 24–25
  furniture sources in, 25
  housing in, 19–23
  making rounds in, 118–120, 168–169
  people in, 17
  phone services in, 26–27
  preparing to go to, 12–15
  signing with agents in, 89–90
  sizing up of, 28–33

theatre in, 91, 95, 199–203, 286–287
transportation in, 12, 18–19
weather in, 18
Los Angeles Actors Guide (Sims), 74, 202, 210
Los Angeles County Popular Street Atlas, 18
Los Angeles Herald Examiner, 21
Los Angeles International Airport (LAX), bus service to, 19
Los Angeles International Film Exposition, 232
Los Angeles Theatre Alliance (LATA), 29, 32, 199, 202, 203, 210, 231, 296
Los Angeles Times, 18, 21
Low-budget films, 166, 190–191
Lowry, Judy, 197
Luck, 9

McGowan, Mickie, 194
Mahoney, John, xi, 10, 17, 215
Mailing services, 219
Makeup
    for camera, 153
    for résumé shots, 40, 46
Management team, 220–224. *See also* Personal managers
    business managers in, 74, 223–224
    immediate needs for, 220–221
    publicists in, 224
Mandelker, Philip, 141
Manila envelopes, 70, 72
Maree, A. Morgan, 220, 223, 227
Marks, hitting of, 154
Mark Taper Forum/Center Theatre Group (Los Angeles), 200
Master shots, 155
Matching of movements, 155
Matte finish, 49, 172
Maximum-use period, 183
Mekrul, John, 40
Memorizing of lines
    for cold readings, 136, 137, 138
    for commercial auditions, 178, 179
Miller, Arlin, 193
Modeling, 125, 189, 194–196
    types of, 194–195
Modeling agents, 89, 195
Money
    in deal negotiations, 111–112, 149–150, 151
    saved for move to L.A., 12
    "screw you," 79–80
Moss, Dennis, 68
Motels, 20
Motion pictures. *See* Films

Name, changing of, 14–15
Negative behavior, avoiding of, 84–85, 139, 140, 141, 180
Nelson, Gary, 136
Nervousness, 131, 139
Network commercials, 183
Networking, 232–233
Networks, casting directors for, 121–122
New York City, N.Y., 12, 235
    Equity card important in, 69
    as fashion and communications center, 195
    making rounds in, 118, 119, 168–169
    roles for ethnic-looking actors in, 8
    signing with agents in, 89
    stage auditions in, 142
    theatre credits from, 58, 59–60
Nightclub work, 196–197

O'Bryan, Fran, 83
Office scenes, 98, 144–146
    acting partners for, 145, 146
    choosing scenes for, 144–146
    length of, 144
    reactions to, 146
    rehearsing of, 146
Open calls, 63
Optional Residence Telephone Service (ORTS), 26
Organization of Professional Acting Coaches and Theatres (OPACT), 210
Out to Lunch, 233
Overlapping of dialogue, 157

Pacific Coast Studio Directory, 74
Pacific Telephone, 26, 27
"P & G Housewives with Perk," 165
Pedestrians, stopping for, 18
Per diems, 226
Performers Audition Showcase, 96–97, 144, 296
Perren, David, 225
Personal expenses, 12, 37
Personal managers, 71, 74, 90, 197, 218, 221–223
    choosing of, 223
    functions of, 221–222
    payment of, 221, 222, 223
Photographers, 42–48, 288
    for composites, 172–173, 175
    finding of, 42–43, 74
    jargon of, 43
    judging work of, 44–46
    questions for, 44
Physical exams, preferred rates on, 233
Pilots, 121
Pitts, Don, 168–169, 179, 183, 193
Polo Lounge, Beverly Hills, 35
Pornography, 198
Postage, 70
Postcards, with actors' photos, 75, 78, 106
Presentation tapes, 77, 108
Printing of takes, 155
Producers, 83, 218
    in casting process, 90, 108, 117, 142, 143
    developing relationships with, 120–121
    directories of, 73, 121
    interviews with, 118, 123–133
    nonunion actors cast by, 63, 64
    on sets, 153, 155, 156, 157, 161
    unscripted lines assigned by, 64
Producers, The (Burger), 73, 121, 190
Program Usage Commercials, 183
Proof sheets, 43, 44
    examining of, 47–48
Publicists, 224
Publicity, 215–219
    critics and, 219
    special services for, 218
    trade ads as, 217–218
    in trade columns, 215–216

Ralphe, David, 29, 199
Randall, Cindy, 235
Rapid Transit District (RTD), 19
Rather, Dan, 61, 158
Recycler, The, 25
Rehearsals
    for filmed TV shows, 157–158
    for three-camera shows, 159

Remsen, Barbara, 137
Residuals (use fees), 66, 166, 168, 170, 171, 182, 193, 228
  records on running of commercials and, 185
  usages of commercials and, 183–184
Résumés, 39, 54–60, 91, 197
  color of, 55
  discussed in interviews, 129
  example of, 56–57
  graphic touches for, 56
  information included on, 56–59, 127
  items omitted from, 55–56
  name printed on, 55, 56
  padding of, 59–60
  paper for, 54, 55
  printing of, 54, 55, 289
  submitting of, 65, 70, 72, 93–94, 106, 119–120, 122, 169
  typing of, 54, 75, 290
Résumé (headshot) sessions, 43, 44, 47. See also Photographers
  outdoor, 46
  practicing for, 42
  preparing for, 46–47
Résumé shots, 14, 39–53, 76, 91. See also Composites; Headshots
  in Academy Players Directory, 70–71, 99–100
  borders and bleeds on, 49, 51, 52
  checking copies of, 52
  choosing pictures for, 47–48
  choosing printers for, 50–51
  clothing for, 44, 46
  criteria for judging of, 44–46, 48, 52
  finding and selecting photographers for, 42–46
  finishes for, 48, 50, 51, 172
  "free," 231
  hair and makeup for, 40, 46, 173
  looking like oneself in, 39–40
  name printed on, 48–50, 51, 52, 55
  negatives of, 43, 44, 52
  printing of, 48–53, 288
  proofs of, 43, 44, 47–48
  submitting of, 55, 65, 70, 72, 93–94, 106, 112, 119–120, 122, 169, 170, 195
  test prints of, 52
  updating of, 53
Re-Take Room, Studio City, 28
Reviews, 33, 84
Rhodes, Michael, 141, 160, 208
Robinson, Ruth, 83, 215, 217, 224, 234
Roommates, 22
Rose, Jack, 83, 149, 151
Ross, Doris, 106, 211

Sabbagh, Doris, 136
St. Johns, Mac, 81
Samuel French, Inc., 29, 73
Sanchez, John, 48
Scale, 7, 150, 181
  "over-," commercials, 181
  "plus ten," 111, 150
Scene auditions, 177–178. See also Cold readings; Office scenes
Schell, Maximilian, 10
Screen Actors Guild (SAG), 4, 13, 15, 29, 37, 91, 166, 185, 233, 234
  agents and casting directors listed by, 73, 92, 100, 169
  being "Taft-Hartleyed" into, 64, 167
  branch offices of, 294–295

commercial auditions and, 177, 180
conservatory program of, 29, 191–192, 229–230
contracts or agreements with agents and, 102–103, 113
credit union of, 230
datebooks published by, 76
entry from other unions into, 64–68, 69
film society of, 230–231
firm engagements as defined by, 150
grievance and advice sessions of, 231
industrial or low-budget films and, 190
initiation and dues of, 63, 68
jurisdiction of, 61
merger of AFTRA and, 62
pension and welfare benefits of, 270–271
scale for, 7
stunt work and, 197, 198
unscripted lines as entry into, 64, 66
Screen Extras Guild (SEG), 65, 66, 233, 295
Screen tests, 143
Script supervisors, 155
Seasonal commercials, 184
"Second team," 156
Secretaries, dealing with, 94
Senensky, Ralph, 81, 140
Separate card billing, 149
Session fees, 181
Sets, shooting on. See Shoots
Shear, Barry, 79
Sheen, Martin, 230
Shepherd, Tony, 141
Shoots, 152–161
  arriving at, 153
  calls for, 153, 161
  caste system in, 160–161
  costumes and scripts for, 152–153
  direction provided during, 157, 160
  hitting marks in, 154
  lingo for, 154–157
  matching movement in, 155
  preparing for, 153
  rehearsing during, 157–158, 159, 160
  signing out of, 161
  spouses brought to, 160–161
  training needed for, 158–160
  waiting around during, 154
Shots, types of, 155–156
Showcases, 96–97, 144, 145
Sides, 135
Siegal, Sandra, 46, 105
"Silent Bits," 66
Simon, Neil, 230
Sims, Noreen, 74
Singing abilities, 56
Skills, job, needed by actors, 13–14
Skills, special, 129
  extra work and, 65, 66
  listed on résumés, 56, 59
Smith, Kathy, 53, 176, 181
Soap operas, 159–160
  office scenes taken from, 145, 146
Somers, Suzanne, 166
Speed calling, 27
Spencer, Mary, 9, 54, 106, 139–140, 167, 208
Spielberg, Steven, 191
Spokesman commercials, 181, 229
  auditioning for, 178–179
Stage managers, in Equity, 63
Stallone, Sylvester, 109

Stalmaster, Lea, 16
"Star" billing, 149
Stars, 160
    earnings of, 7
    glamorous lives of, 6–7
Stationery, 72
Stephenson, Ron, 75, 121, 124, 134, 150, 217
Stimpson, Viola Kate, 201, 238
Strasberg, Lee, 59
Student films, 58, 77, 191–192
Studio Blu-Book, The, 74, 121, 190, 223
Studios
    commissaries at, 120
    visits to, 32, 119
Stunt work, 197–198
Sukman, Susan, 130
Sultan, Arne, 70
Sync (looping), 156, 193, 194

Taft-Hartley Reports, 64, 167
Tarter, Dale, 46–47
Taxes, 75, 220, 224, 225–228
    auditing of, 220, 226–227
    records kept for, 226
    typical deductions on, 267–269
    withholding of, 225
Tayback, Vic, 166
Teeth, for commercial work, 13, 41
Telephone calls
    answering machines and services for, 27, 58, 71, 106, 285
    to casting directors, 120
    considered as contracts, 150
    tips for, 94–95
Telephone services
    for long-distance calls, 27
    rate structures for, 26–27
    special, 27, 106
Television, cable, 199–200
Television shows
    contracts for, 149–150, 248–260
    credits for, listed in résumés, 58, 60
    filmed, rehearsing and shooting of, 157–160
    lists of, 75
    live, taping of, 29, 32
    office scenes taken from, 144–145, 146
    pay for extras in, 66
    performances in, seen by agents, 96
    performances in, taped for videocassettes, 76
    three-camera, 157, 159
Temporary employment, 23
Temporary housing, 20
Test commercials, 184
Thank you notes, 72, 109, 219
Theatre, 91, 106, 199–203, 208
    actors' attendance at, 29, 30–33
    agents' attendance at, 95–96
    character development in, 136
    Equity Waiver, 62, 96, 118, 199, 201–203
    publicity for, 218, 219
    seeking work in, 199–200, 202
    union membership and, 61–62
Theatre credits, 58, 59–60
    college- or community-, 56
    from New York, 58, 59–60
Theatres
    directories of, 74
    Equity, list of, 286–287
    sizing up of, 32

Theatrical agents, 89–113, 144, 153. See also
    Agencies; Agents
    assessing performance of, 110–112
    casting directors and, 90, 107–108, 111, 142
    changing of, 110–113
    choosing of, 99–104
    clients' contacting of, 101–102, 106, 108
    clients' expectations of, 107–108, 118
    clients' responsibilities to, 105–107
    clout of, 111
    cold readings and, 98, 134, 142
    commercial agents separate from, 102–103, 169
    conflicts among clients of, 99–100
    contacted through acting classes, 97, 210
    contracts with, 103–104, 113, 243–246
    deals negotiated by, 90, 111–112, 149–151
    dropping in on, 94
    enthusiasm of, 103
    firing of, 111–113
    functions of, 90–91, 105
    independent seeking of work and, 102, 105–106
    interviews with, 97–98, 101–103, 113, 123–133
    letters to, 93–94, 96
    motivating of, 108–109
    number of clients handled by, 100
    offices and employees of, 94, 100–101, 108
    payment of, 90, 93, 106, 111, 150
    performances seen by, 95–97, 108
    phone calls to, 94–95
    referrals to, 93, 97
    seeking of, 92–97
    submissions made by, 90, 112
    time spent on clients by, 105, 109
    typecasting of, 100
    unusual approaches to, 97
    verbal agreements with, 103
    warnings about, 92–93
    when to look for, 91
Theatrical headshots, 40, 41–42, 46, 70
Thomas Bros. Maps, 18
Three-camera shows, 157, 159–160
Three-way calling, 27
Tony Awards, 8
Trades, 33, 42, 74–75, 84, 146, 210, 290–291.
    See also specific trades
    publicizing oneself in, 106, 215–218
Twofer L.A. Company, 231
Typewriters, buying of, 75

Unemployment compensation, 227–228, 230
Unions, 12–13, 61–69, 70. See also Actors Equity
    Association; American Federation of Televi-
    sion and Radio Artists; Screen Actors Guild
    agents franchised by, 73, 92, 93, 99
    branch offices of, 291–294
    choosing of, 69
    discounts on dues and initiation fees of, 68–69
    entries into, 62–69
    jurisdictions of, 61, 65, 66, 67
    listed on résumés, 57
    non-union theatre and, 61–62, 96
    "parent," 64, 68–69
    visiting of, 28–29
University of California, Los Angeles (UCLA), 30, 191, 231
University of Southern California (USC), 30, 191, 231

Unscripted lines, 64, 66
Use fees. *See* Residuals

Vacations, after arriving in L.A., 15
Van services, 19
Variety agents, 89, 197
Videocassettes of actors' work, 76–78, 128
  importance of, 76
  prepared scenes on, 76–78
  presentation tapes as, 77, 108
  quality of, 77
  services for, 295
  taping of performances for, 76–77
Viedelle, Colee, 90, 208
Vital statistics, 58
"Voice-caster, The," 194, 296
Voice-over agents, 89, 193
Voice-overs, 192–194
  demo tapes for, 192–193

pay for, 193, 194

Walla, 193–194
Wallack, Roy, 196
Weight, losing of, 13
Westberg, David, 202–203
Westwood Clinic Preventative Medicine, 233
Wexler, Howard, 155
"White bread," 9, 165, 167, 171
Wild spots, 183
Wild tracks, 156
William Morris Agency, Inc., 93, 102, 111
Wollin, Bob, 142, 154, 180, 182
Women in Film (WIF), 232–233
Women in Theatre, 232
Workshops. *See* Acting classes and training

Yellow Pages, 121
YMCA, Hollywood, 19–20, 296